IMPOSSIBLE PHOTOGRAPHY

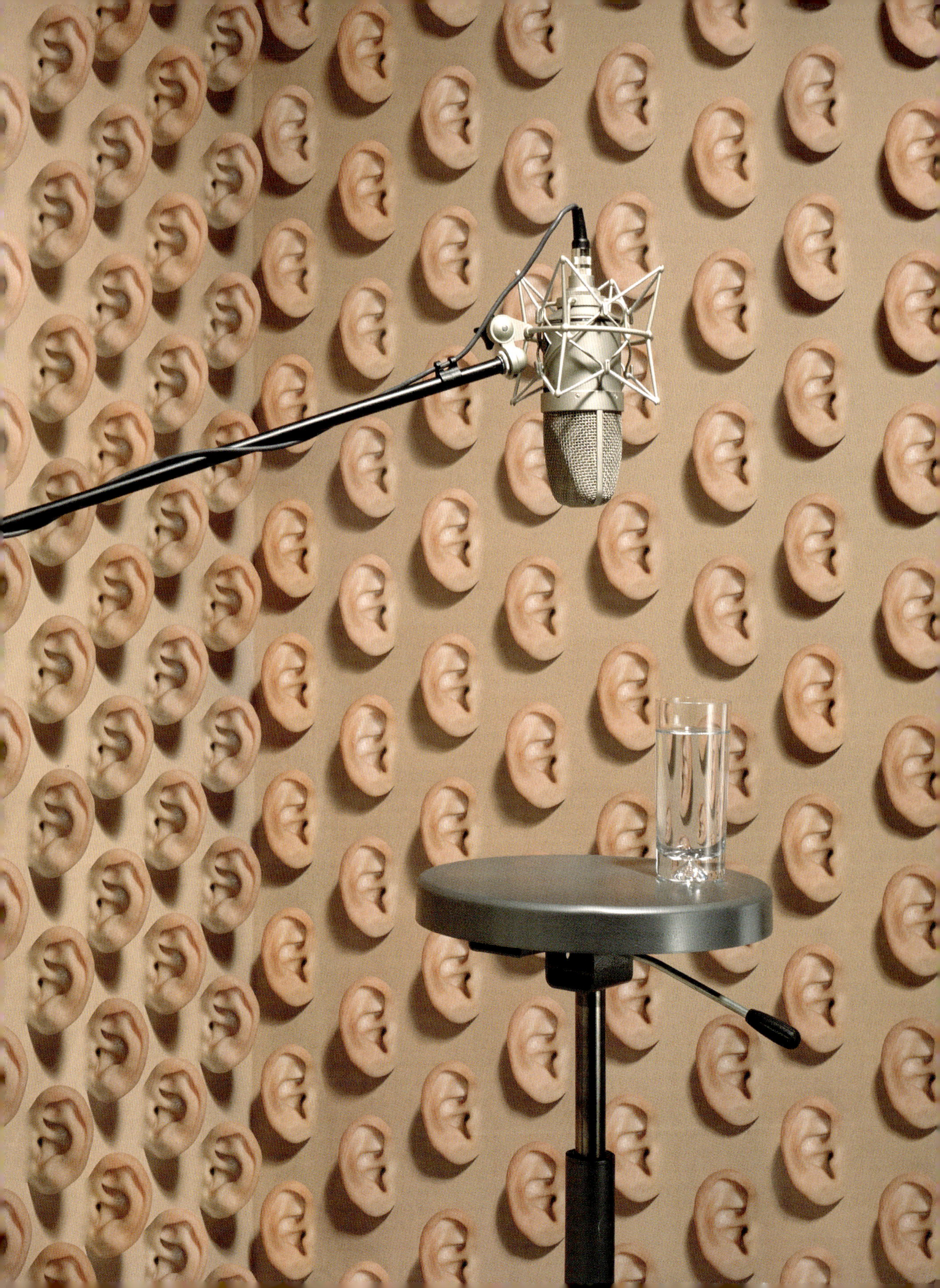

IMPOSSIBLE PHOTOGRAPHY

SURREAL PICTURES THAT CHALLENGE OUR PERCEPTION

AGATA TOROMANOFF

EKEN
PRESS

TABLE OF CONTENTS

INTRODUCTION

In the age of digital manipulation photography displays a new exciting face. The technology of today allows the manipulation of images in ways we could not have previously imagined. 'Impossible Photography' makes everything possible. Photographers do not simply capture moments anymore, they capture ideas. Their innovative methods offer a twist on traditional approaches to the medium bringing amazing effects. Unconventional, mind-bending, freaky, fanciful, mischievous, ironic, shocking and playful—you name it.

Our selection of images shows how addictive this way of thinking can be. Erik Johansson, one of the most famous surreal photographers, calls his own work photo-realistic surrealism. 'Surreal ideas realized in a realistic way with a touch of humor', he explains. This is a perfect description for many other photographers whose works trick the eye. While a lot of the photographers featured in this book make clear references to surrealism—the first artistic movement to use photography to distort reality—the new generation takes the idea one step further creating parallel worlds, which mirror ours in an ironic, critical way.

In the pursuit of originality and with the desire to elicit a special kind of response, photographers tend to avoid the obvious. They pursue all possible avenues for interpreting the world around them in an attempt to challenge conventions, forms, functions and meanings. Their photos result in pointed expressions, which due to their often odd, yet whimsical character, initiate interesting dialogues with the viewer.

Whatever blueprint the artists decide to follow, the goal

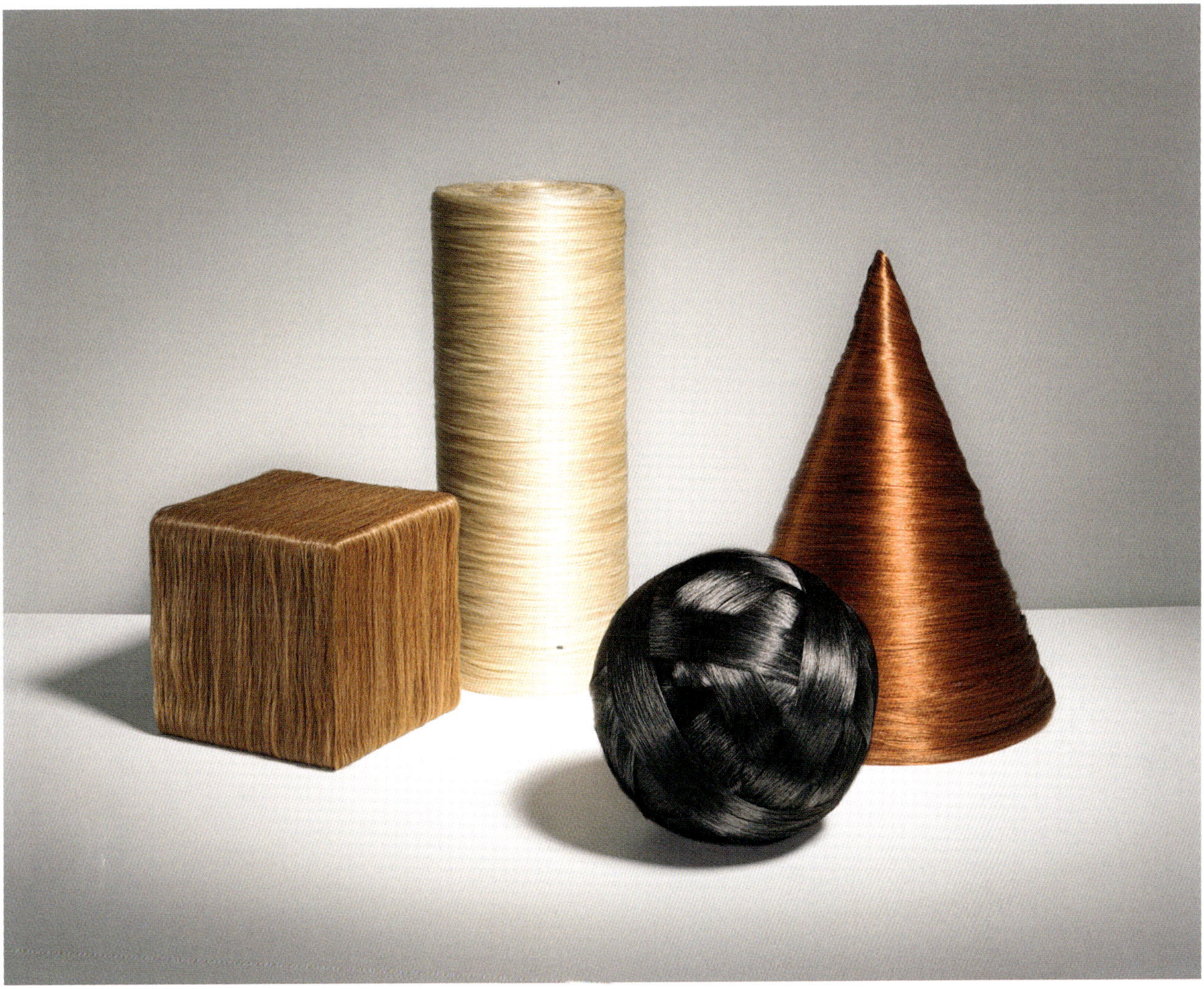

© HUGH KRETSCHMER, COLOR & SHAPE

is to create a surprising outcome. Shocking contradictions, often humorous or ironic, offer the unexpected. As much as these juxtapositions play with our perception, they also challenge the mind and turn everyday life into an entertaining experience.

We have gathered here a selection of remarkable photographs from established and emerging artists across the globe, whose work plays with us and flirts with our senses. This fascinating collection will tease your eyes and stimulate unconventional ways of thinking. These photographs provoke and challenge us, pushing the boundaries and making us see things in a different way.

MANUEL ARCHAIN

#LITTLE PEOPLE

Argentinian artist Manuel Archain (b. 1983) started his artistic education early. At the age of 5, in the studio of his artist-mother, he was already exploring his first steps in sculpting, drawing, and painting. Photography caught Manuel's attention when he was 13 and he began working as assistant photographer to numerous artists where he evolved his personal style. He has been working as a professional photographer since 2004 and been commissioned by international clients in advertising and cinema. He also continues creating his personal work.

In the 'Small World' series Manuel plays with the scale to change our perception of the hustle and bustle of ordinary routines. The photographer populated the world of objects we use in our everyday life with tiny inhabitants. This new perspective on a perfectly common environment seems challenging. His 'Thinking about...' series looks into the ways we co-exist in the public space. Whimsical reflections on how what's individual and what's collective intertwine.

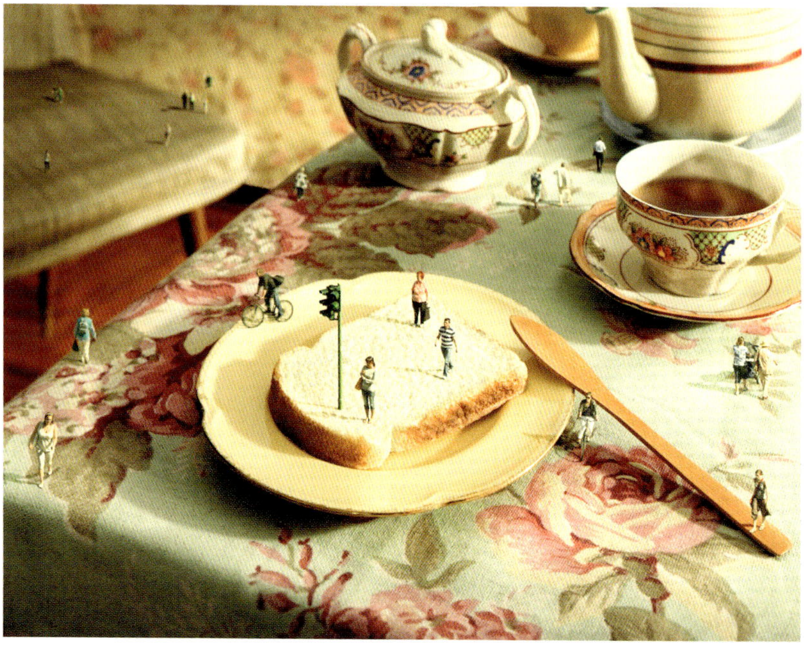

© MANUEL ARCHAIN, BREAKFAST (SERIES: SMALL WORLD), 2010

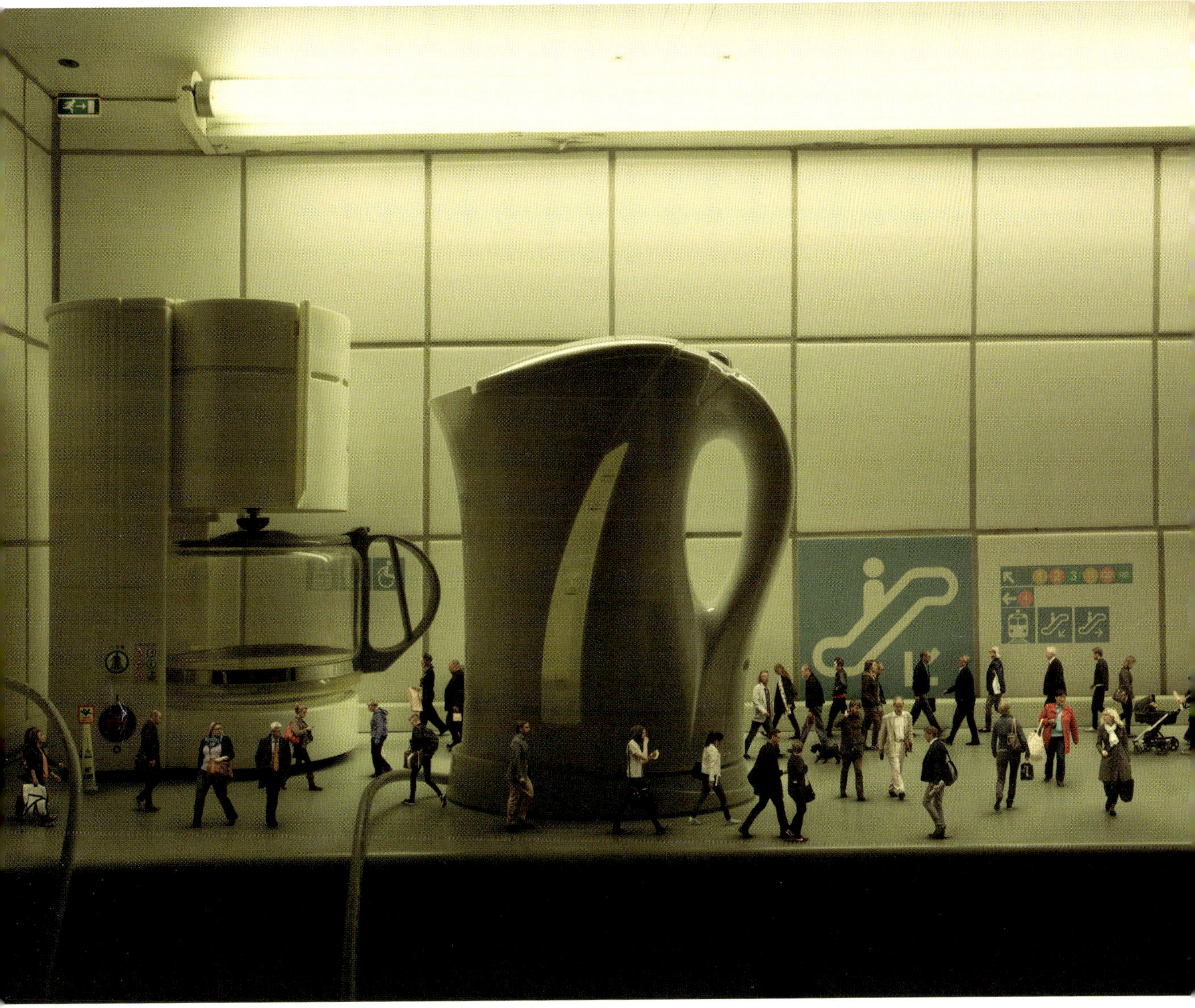

© MANUEL ARCHAIN, CENTRAL STATION (SERIES: SMALL WORLD), 2013

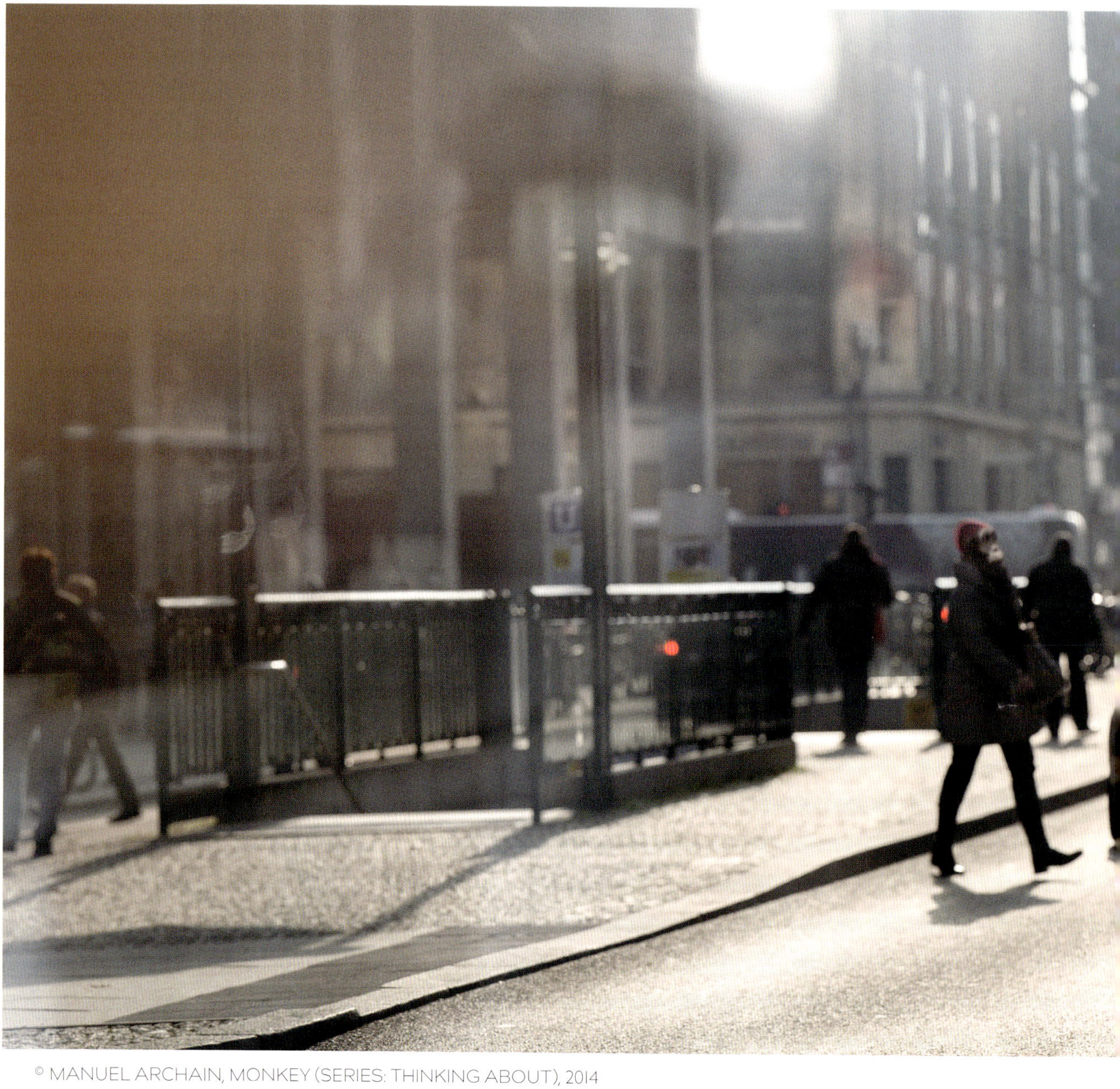

© MANUEL ARCHAIN, MONKEY (SERIES: THINKING ABOUT), 2014

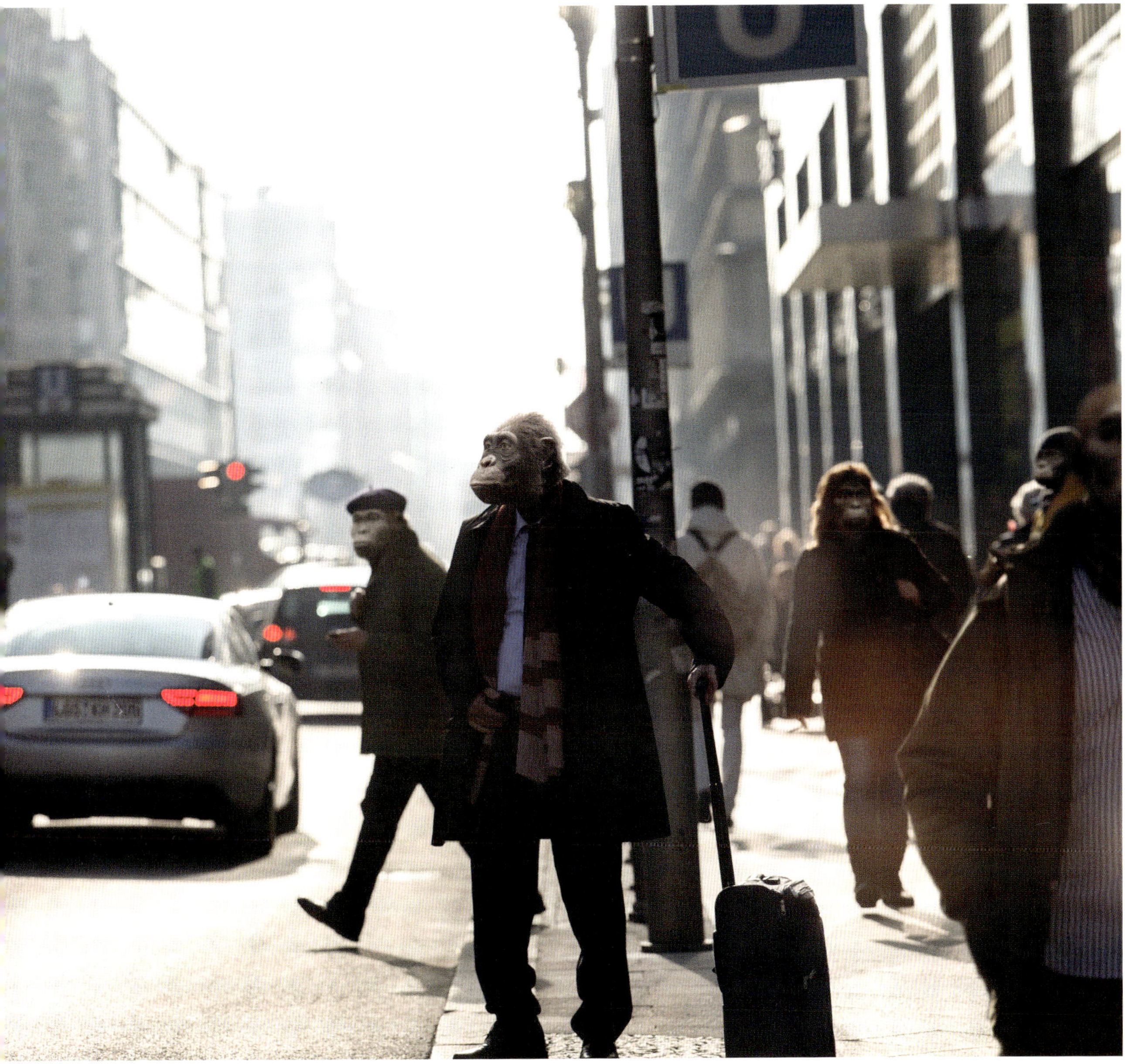

ASILE

In French Asile means asylum, protection typically referring to those seeking safety when forced to leave their own countries. Paris-based Asile has coined their own definition: 'a creative lab – a shelter that preserves and protects creativity while respecting the essence of being human.' Christophe Huet, the founder of the studio explains the choice of the name by offering Claude Monet's words about the Water Lilies installation in Musée de l'Orangerie, that was supposed to soothe the stress of Parisians.

The world of Asile's realizations, whether these are commissioned or personal works, takes the viewer to a place where everything is possible. Reality is featured but with an original approach that teases the eye with unexpected contexts. Full of sophisticated humour along with a great sense of form and color, the images relax and soothe our senses, and in this sense offer an asylum for our overwhelmed and overloaded eyes. No wonder the studio received more than 300 awards for their creative works!

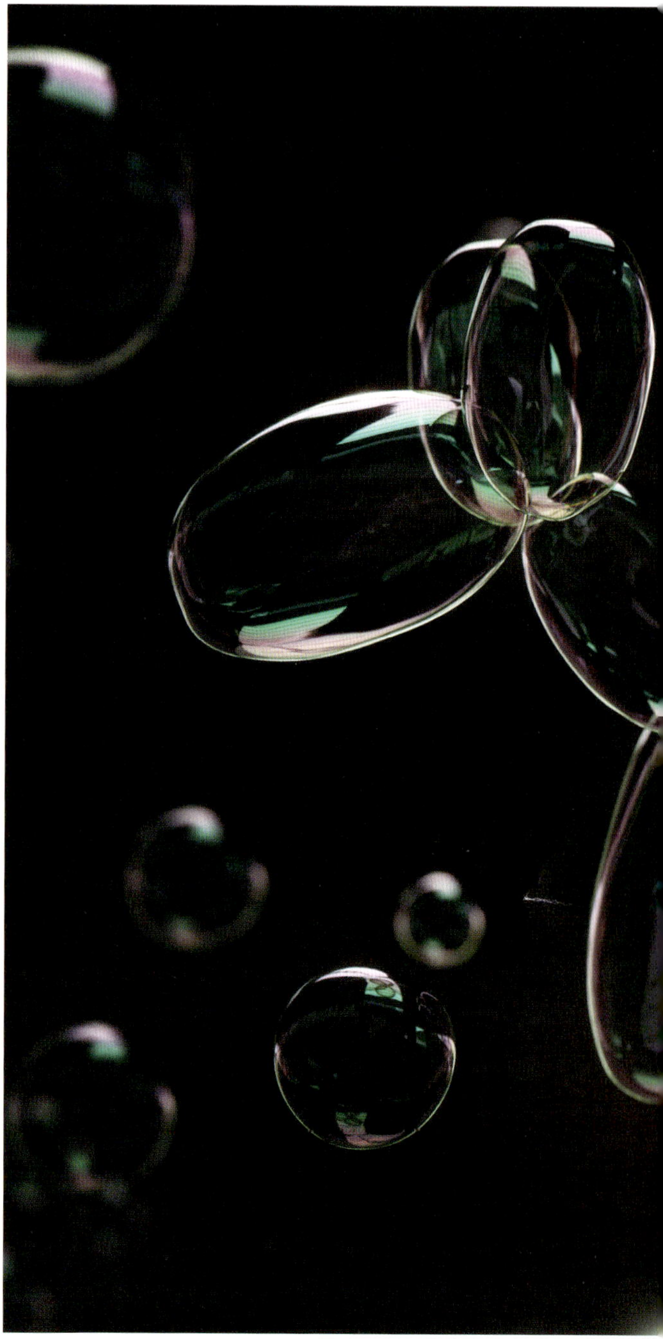

© BULLE-DOG BY ASILE-PARIS.COM

#ANIMALS

#LAND-SCAPE

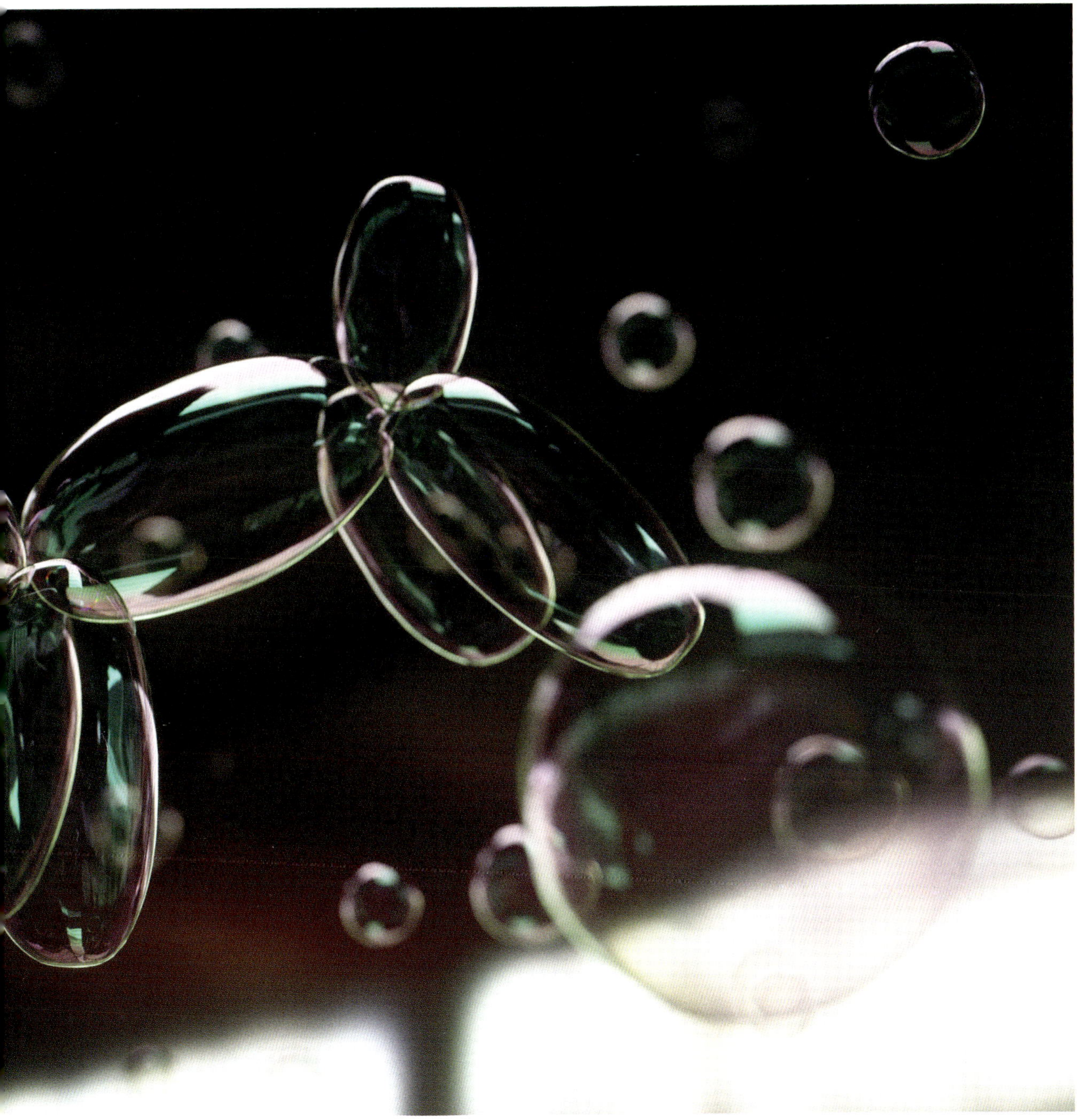

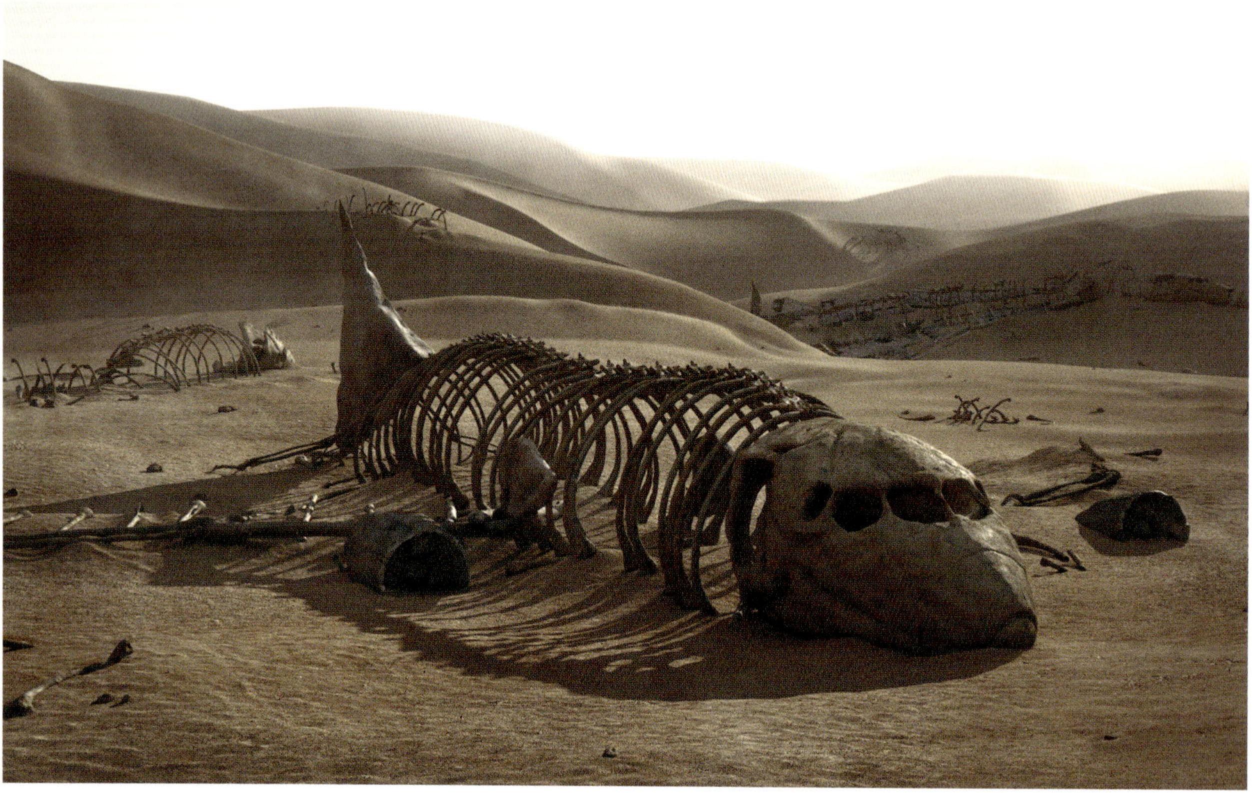

© PLANE GRAVEYARD BY ASILE-PARIS.COM

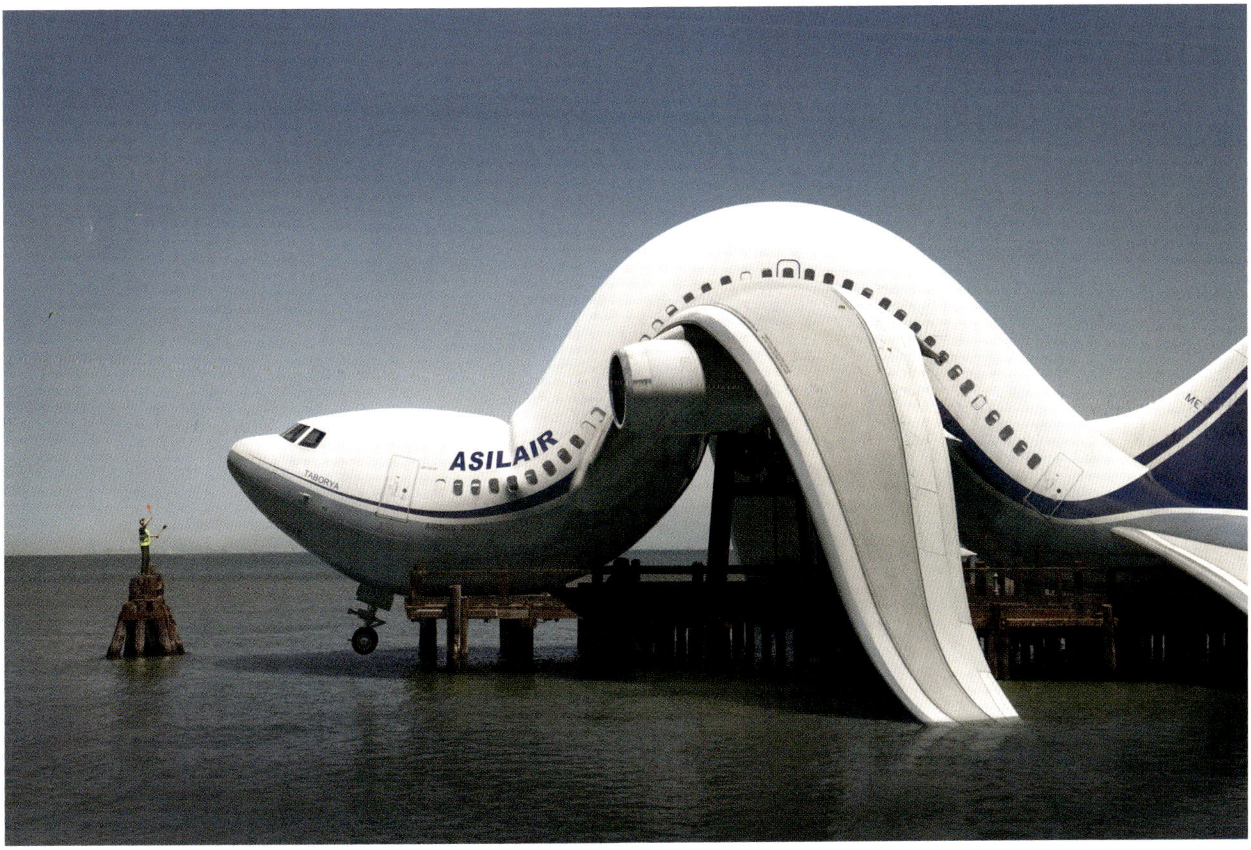

© PLANE TRAINER BY ASILE-PARIS.COM

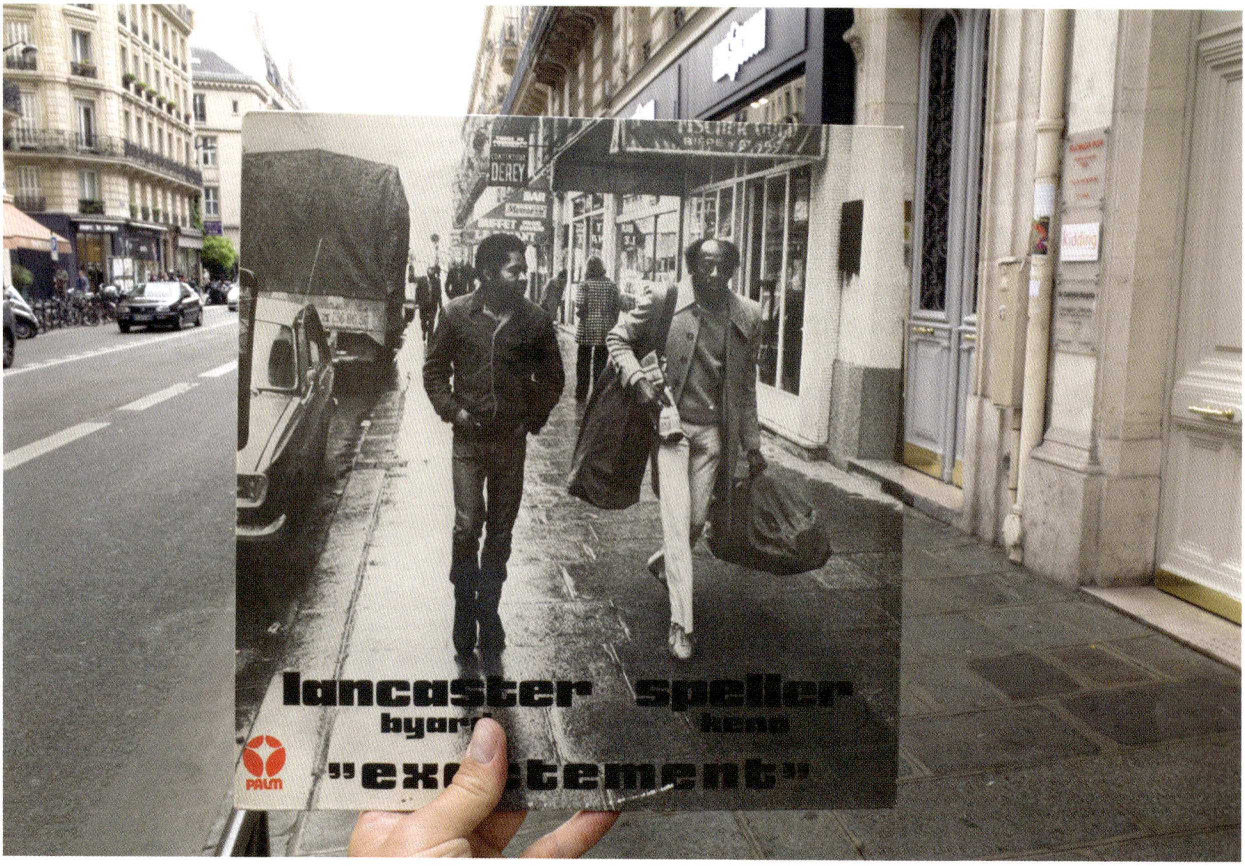

© ALEX BARTSCH, BYARD LANCASTER / KENO SPELLER, EXACTEMENT (PALM 1974), REPHOTOGRAPHED ON RUE ÉTIENNE MARCEL, PARIS I, 42 YEARS LATER

ALEX BARTSCH

#NOW &THEN

London-based photographer Alex Bartsch decided in 2014 to start a series of photos that would capture album covers in the places where they were originally photographed (some of them were released more than 40 years ago!). Initially the project was realized only in London, but it soon expanded to include other cities such as Paris. As the photographer recalls, finding some of the locations was very easy, but others took months of detective work.

Celebrating both the music and the places, Alex successfully recreates the atmosphere of the past. In the photos we can see the original vinyl cover, which is held at arms-length in front of the camera, perfectly adjusted within the bigger picture of a particular spot. Bartsch's aim was to bring the viewers closer to the time as well as the location of the original photo shoots. Indeed, as we look at the collages of historical context and contemporary urbanscapes, we're travelling in time.

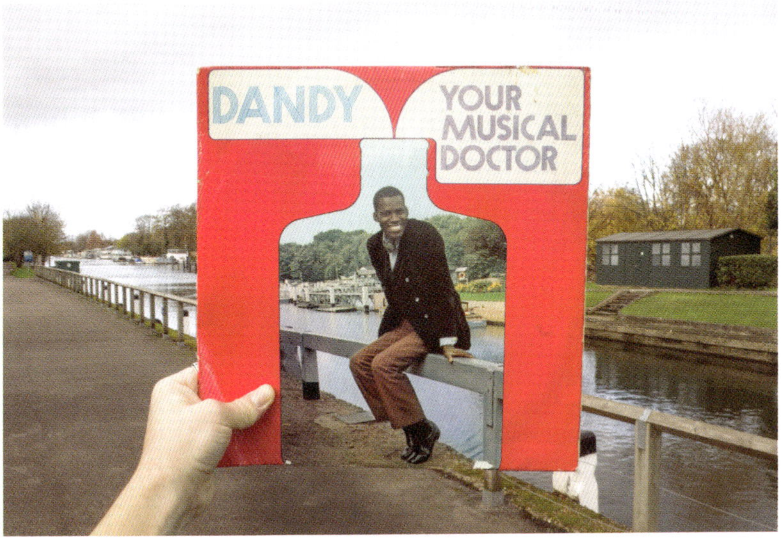

© ALEX BARTSCH, DANDY LIVINGSTONE, YOUR MUSICAL DOCTOR (DOWNTOWN, 1969), REPHOTOGRAPHED AT MOLESEY LOCK, LONDON KT8, 46 YEARS LATER

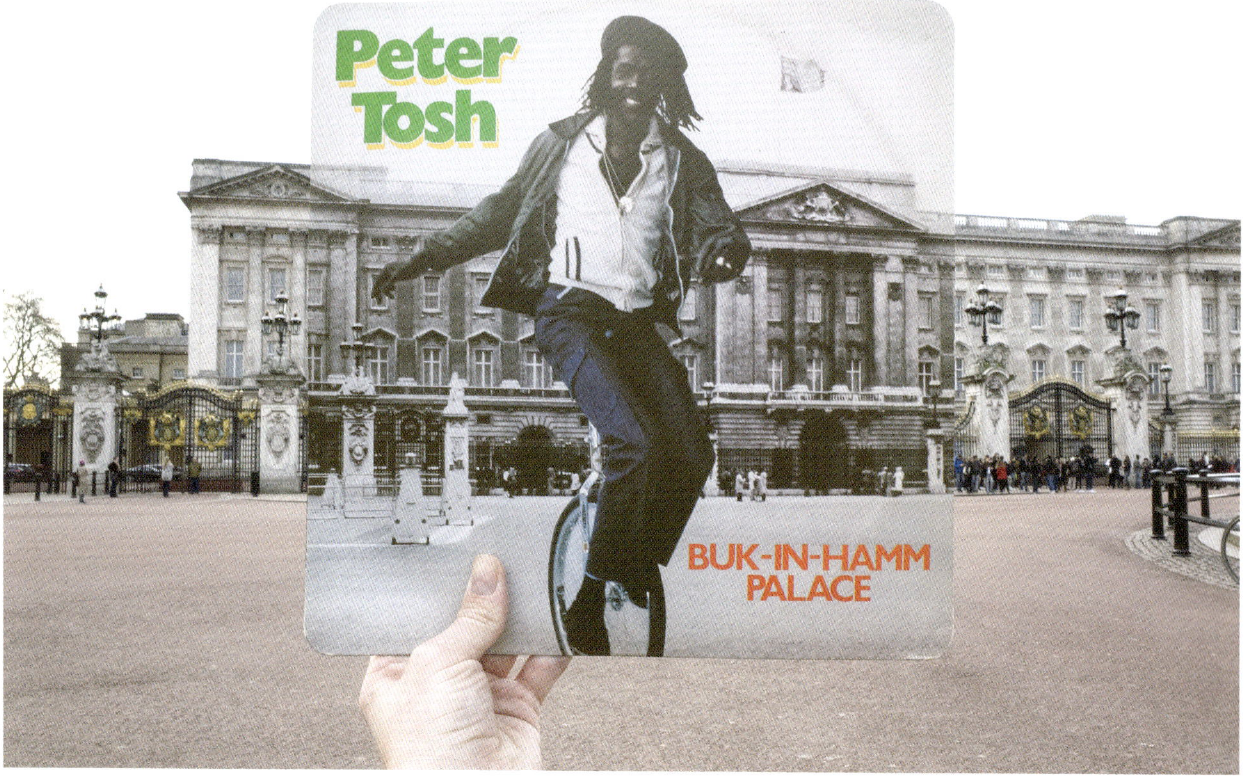

© ALEX BARTSCH, PETER TOSH, BUK-IN-HAMM-PALACE (ROLLING STONES, 1979), REPHOTOGRAPHED AT BUCKINGHAM PALACE, LONDON SW1, 36 YEARS LATER

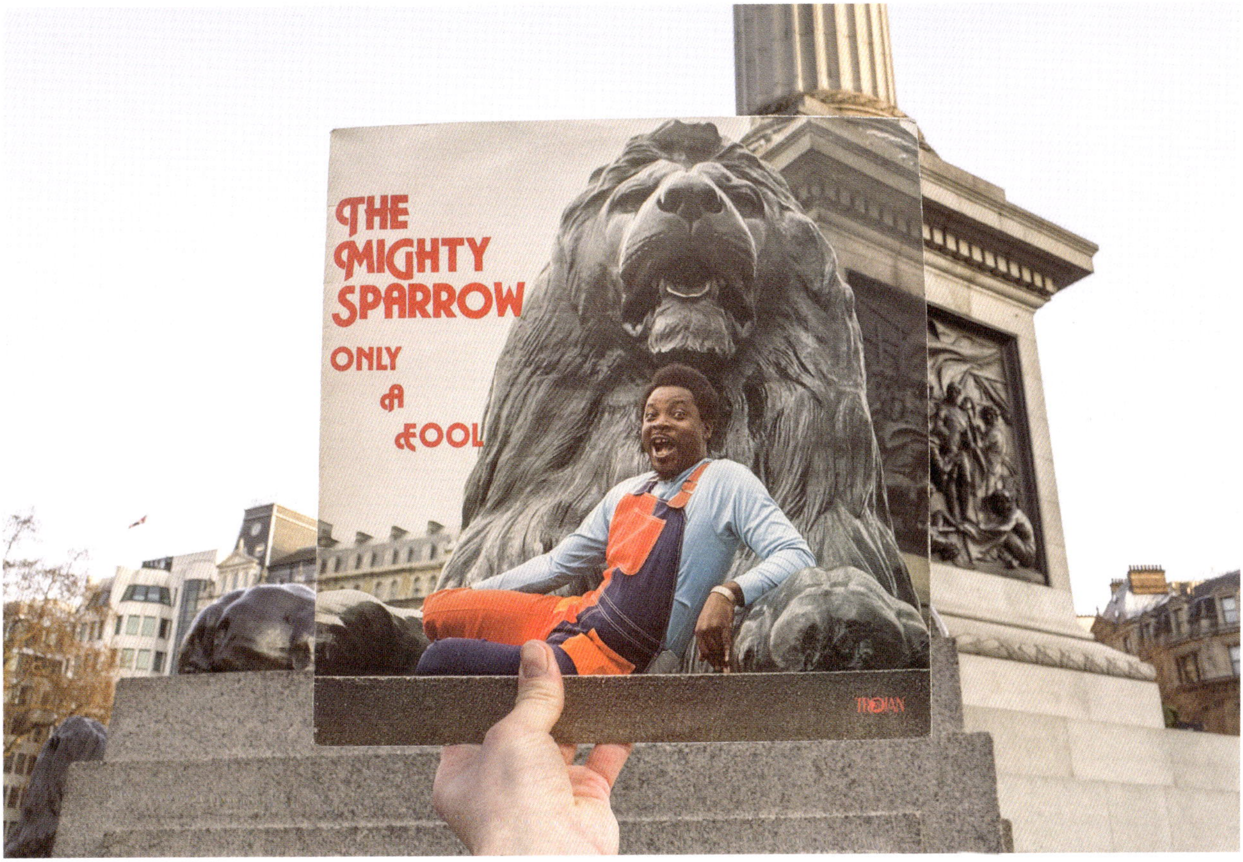

© ALEX BARTSCH, THE MIGHTY SPARROW, ONLY A FOOL (TROJAN, 1978), REPHOTOGRAPHED AT TRAFALGAR SQUARE, LONDON WC2, 37 YEARS LATER

BOBBY BECKER

#BODY

Formally trained in photography and sculpture at the School of the Art Institute of Chicago and Belmont University, Bobby Becker is a multidisciplinary artist creating work through the use of set design, post manipulation, and prop creation. He states that through his surreal images, he examines the legacy of abuse in a familial context, whether it be psychological, sexual or emotional.

In his first large body of work, 'History', Bobby offers an imaginative retelling of past events surrounding his life. The artist often becomes a part of the minimalist yet striking compositions. The visual simplicity of the scenes contrasts intriguingly with the powerful substance. The photographer employs not only surreal means to deal with the past, but also uses a very specific light that adds a melodramatic tone. Bobby's photographs are a theatrical play, providing visual evidence of an intangible yet enduring moral distress. The artist lives and works in Nashville, Tennessee, USA.

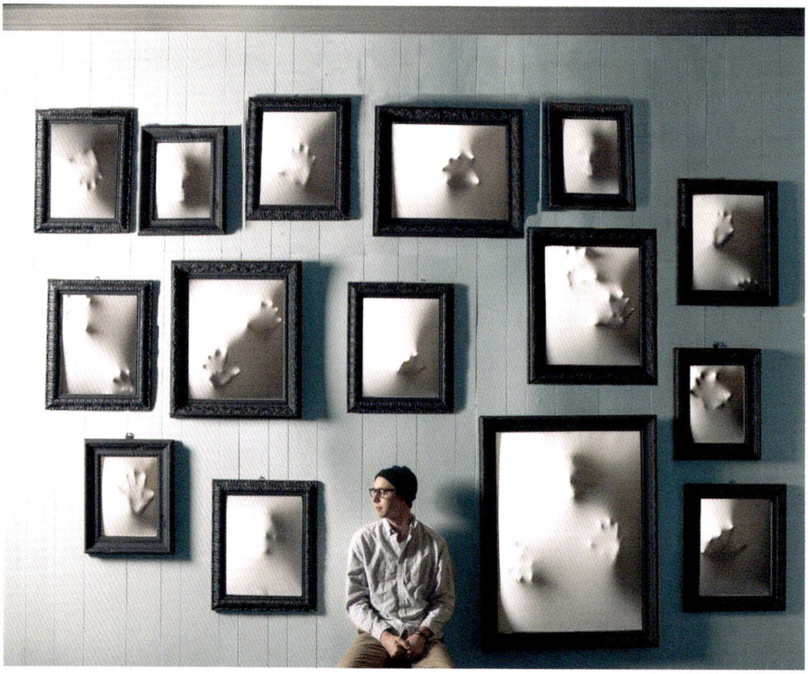

© BOBBY BECKER, WANDERING HAUNT 16/52, 2013

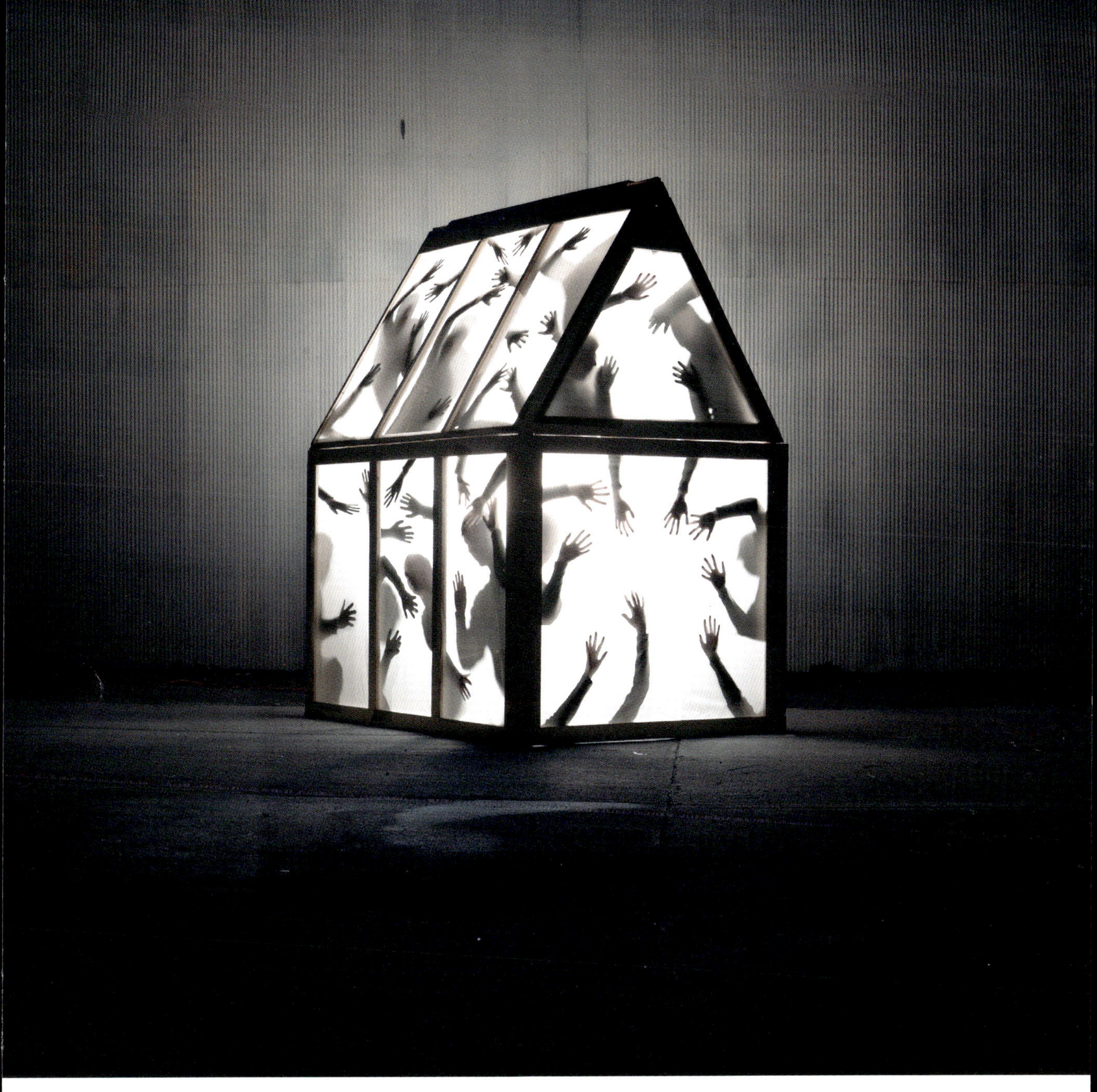

© BOBBY BECKER, HAUNT 23/52, 2013

LIU BOLIN

Liu Bolin (b. 1973) studied sculpture at the Central Academy of Fine Arts in Beijing, where he currently lives and works. Liu gained recognition thanks to 'The Invisible Man' series. In the photos, be it in the forest, tube station, a shop or in front of a building, human bodies (sometimes only the photographer's likeness) disappear into the environments they are photographed against. As if covered with a camouflage that allows them to become more or less invisible. Careful examination of each photo reveals its visual layers. Liu's artistic practice is an important comment on social issues in China.

In 2015, the United Nations commissioned Liu to create a work for The Global Goals campaign. It was supposed to raise awareness of 17 goals such as ending poverty, fighting inequality and injustice and encouraging sustainable development. In the work, the artist camouflages himself against the 193 flags of the world. His works have been exhibited internationally in numerous solo and group shows.

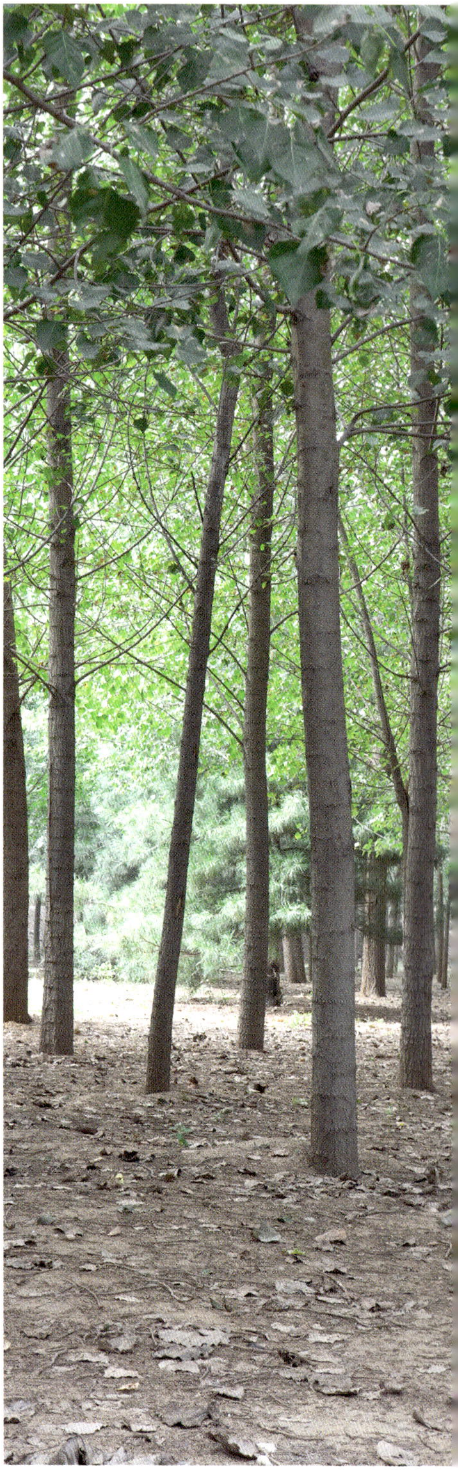

© LIU BOLIN, IN THE WOODS

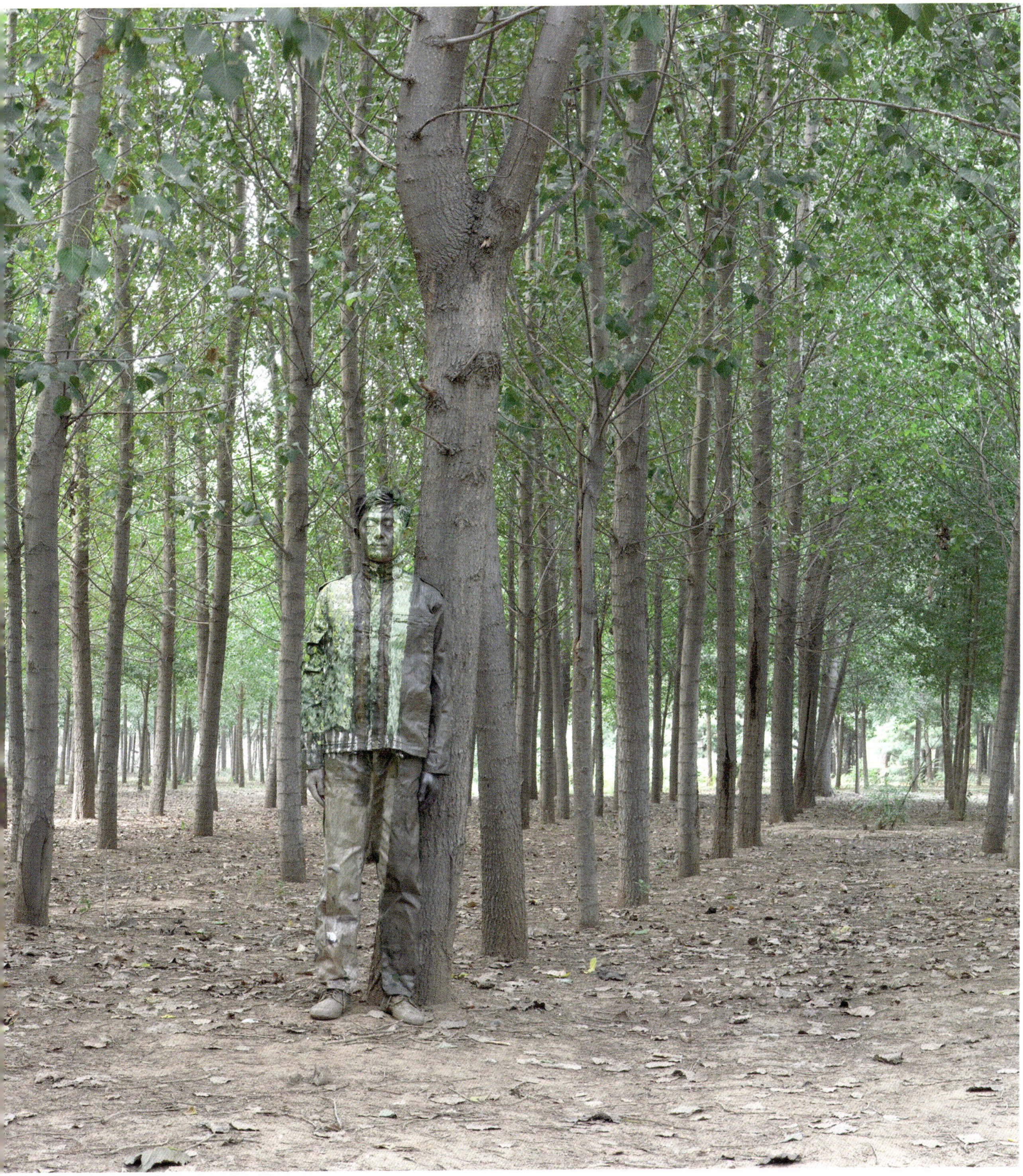

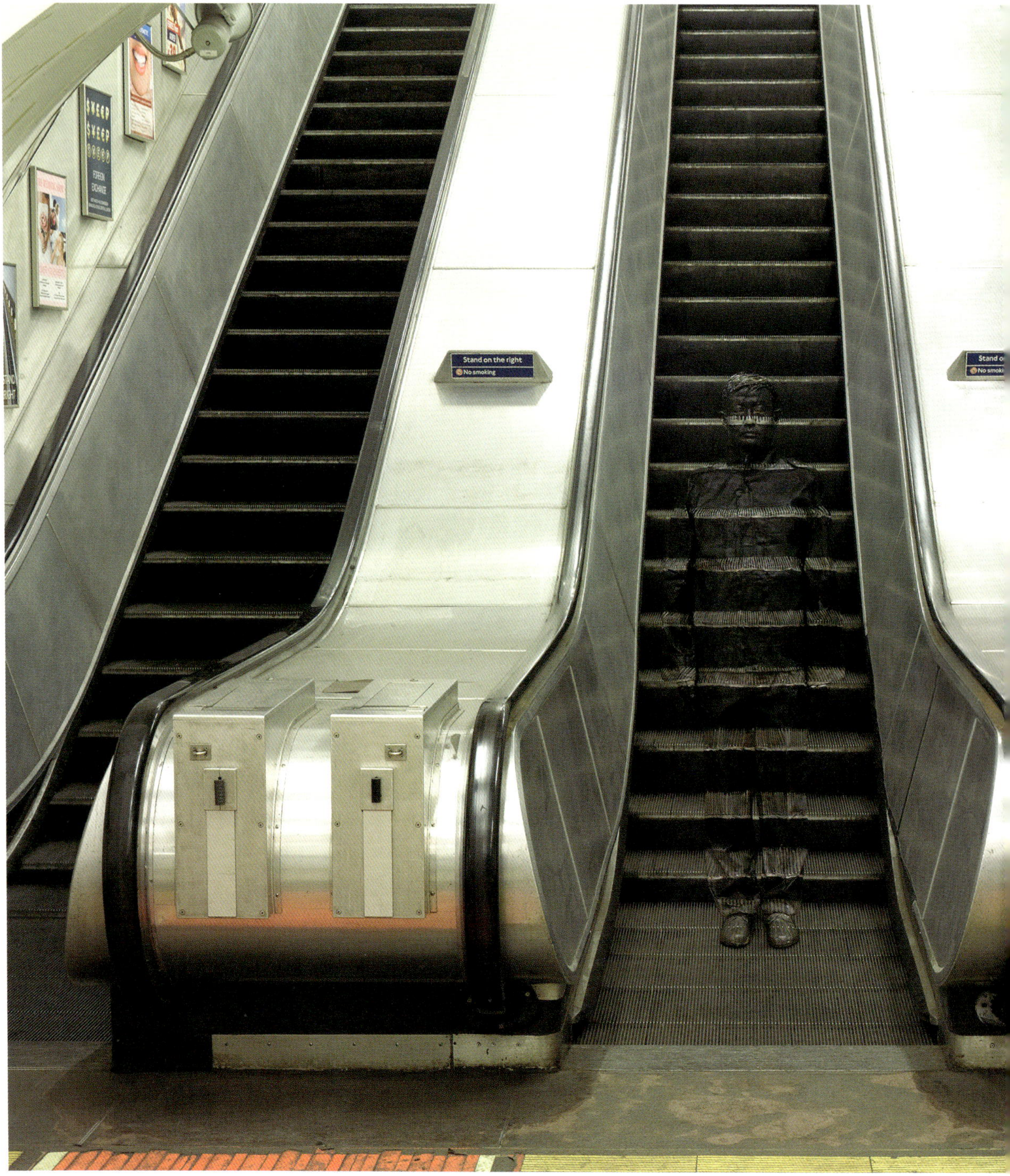

© LIU BOLIN, UNDERGROUND ESCALATORS

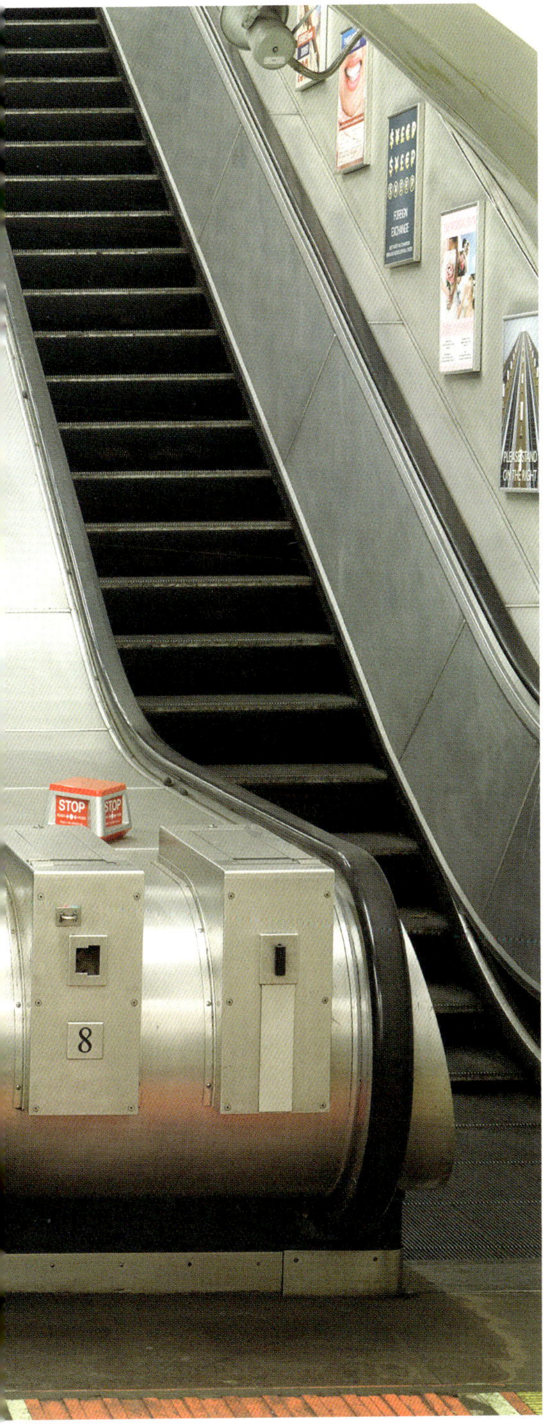

#BODY

#PORTRAIT

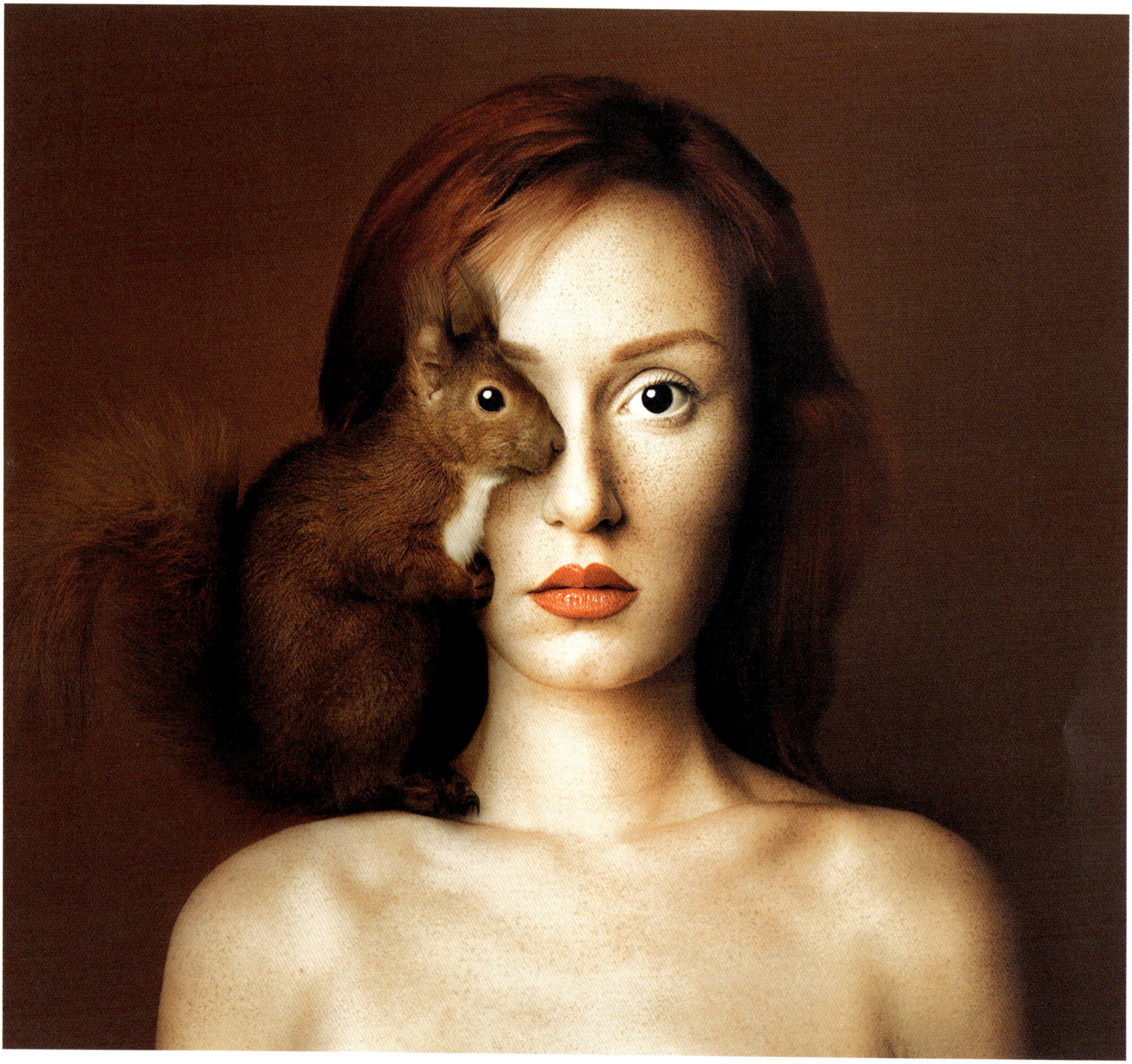

© FLÓRA BORSI, ANIMEYED (SELF-PORTRAITS), 2016

FLÓRA BORSI

#ANIMALS

#PORTRAIT

Flóra Borsi comes from Hungary and is a talented young photographer creating amazing digital manipulations (her artwork was the face of Adobe Photoshop in 2014). Identity, relationships, emotions and fantasies are among the subjects she addresses in her work. As she states, Flóra aims to capture the complex strength and fragility of the human psyche as well as to question female representation.

Her 'Animeyed' series was created in 2016 and features the artist's surreal self-portraits. In each image Flóra's face (each time looking completely different!) is complemented by a profile of another animal. Whether it is a squirrel, a snake or a flamingo, the photographer dons a matching skin – dyes her hair accordingly and selects a corresponding background. The stunning effect is achieved through formal interventions that trick the eye and the skillful use of colour. This very atmospheric collection of animated portraits is powerful and mysteriously attractive. Simply alluring!

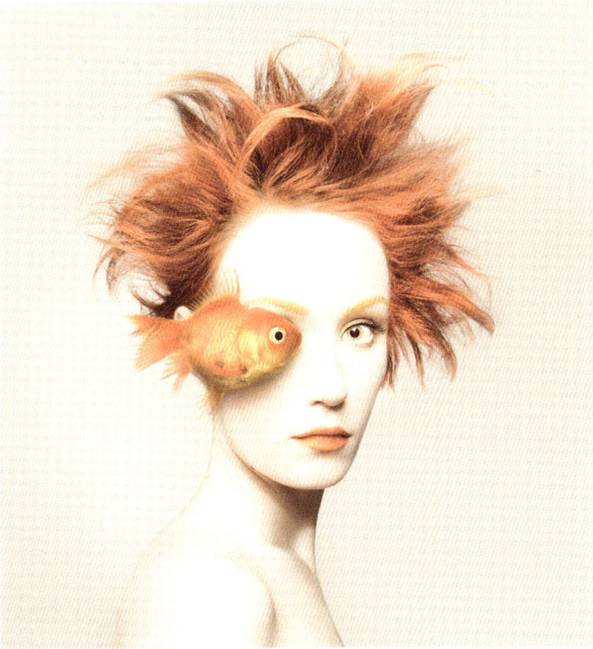

© FLÓRA BORSI, ANIMEYED (SELF-PORTRAITS), 2016

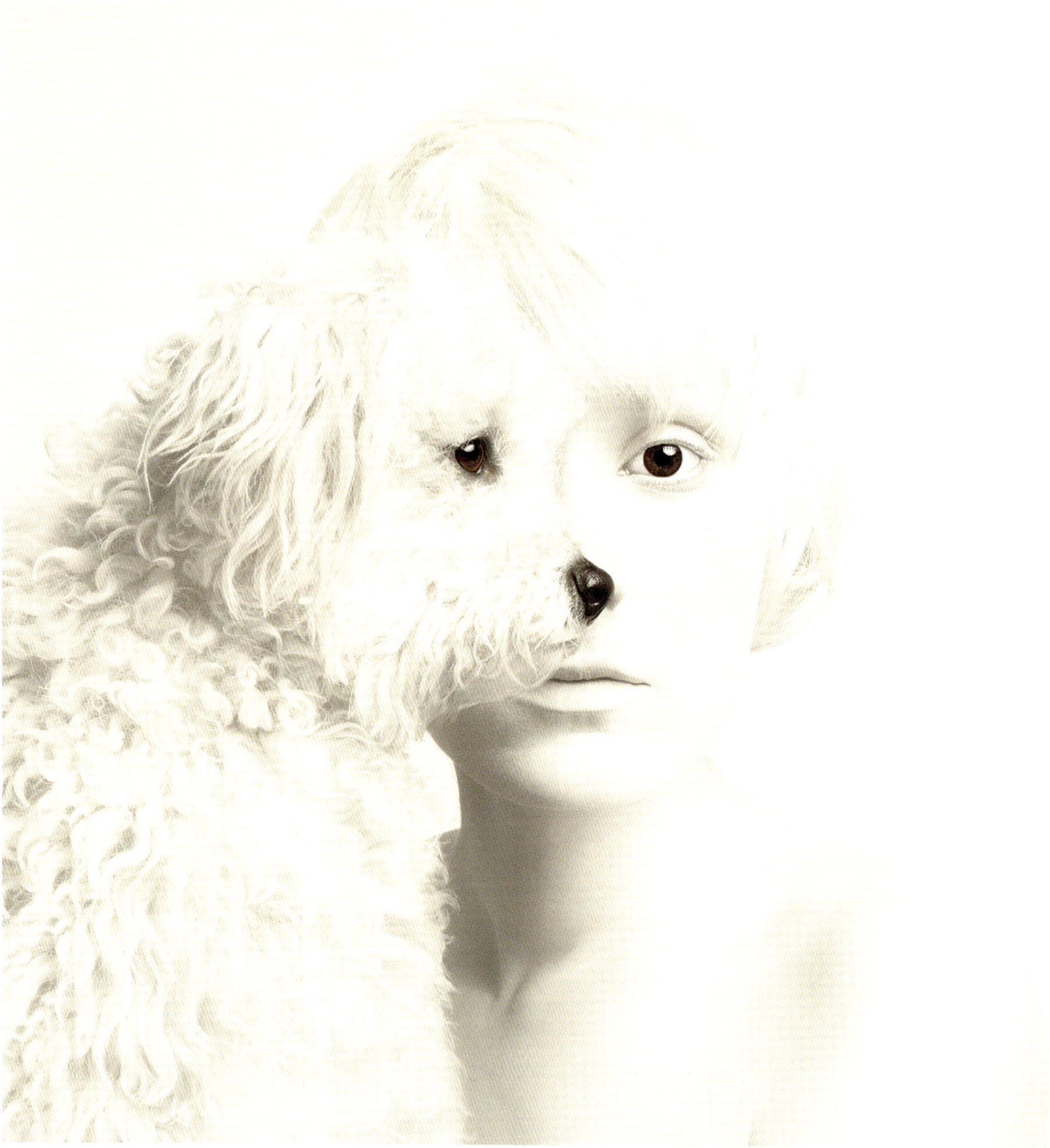

© FLÓRA BORSI, ANIMEYED (SELF-PORTRAITS), 2016

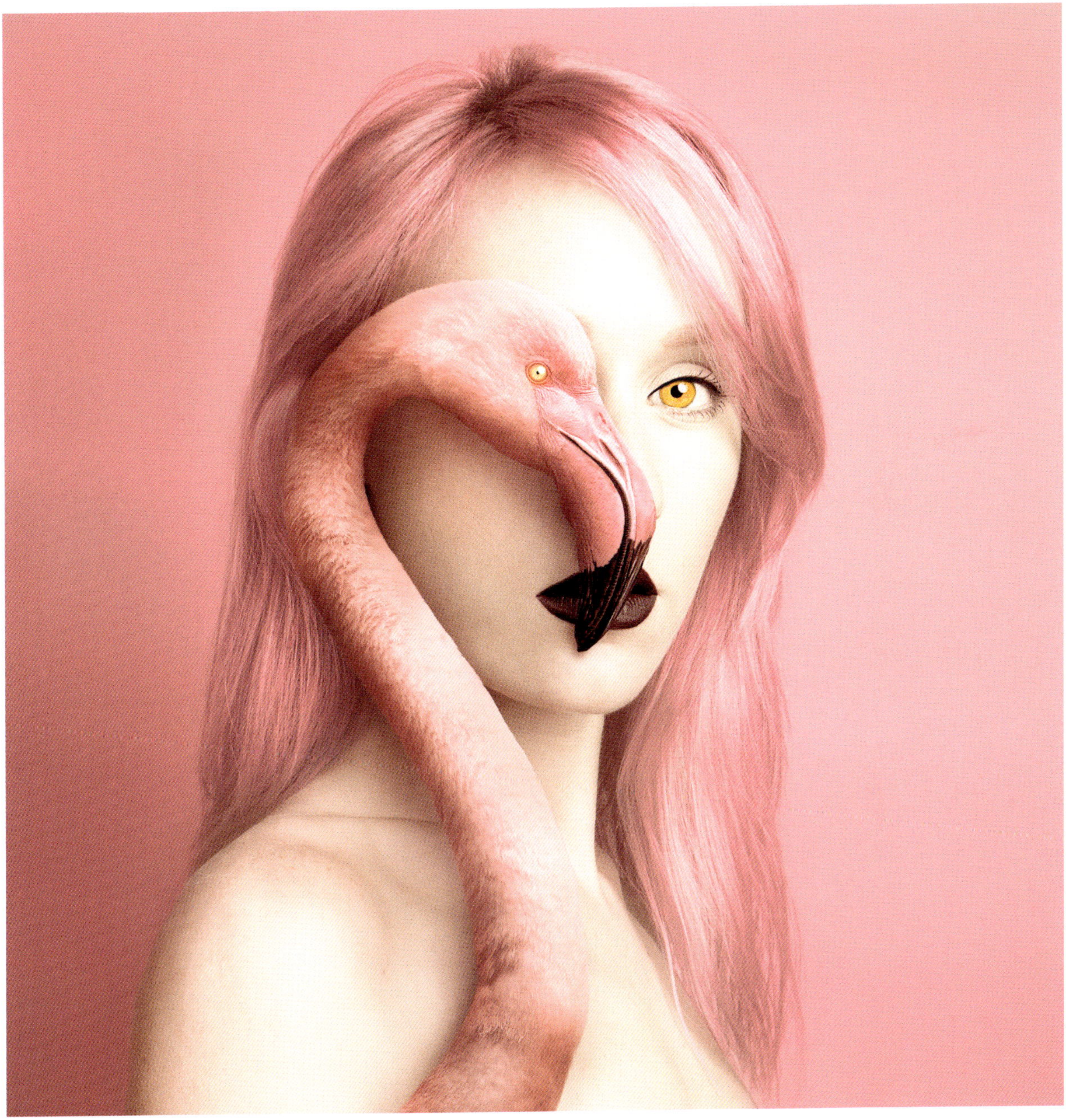

© FLÓRA BORSI, ANIMEYED (SELF-PORTRAITS), 2016

MARCK BOTHA

#LAND-SCAPE

Marck Botha is an indomitable water photographer. Making the most of the natural beauty of Durban in South Africa, where he is based, Marck shares his passion for water through breathtaking photography . He grew up along the coast of Natal and from his early years he loved wave riding. With his over 20 years of experience practicing this exciting sport, Marck realized that what he sees while surfing deserved to be shared. So, as he says, he captures the unique and often dangerous perspective of the coast line, for all to enjoy and experience from the safety of their own homes.

How he can surf and take astonishing pictures at the same time remains a mystery, but the shots are truly amazing. The viewers join Marck in his adventures in the ocean. Images are often taken seconds before the waves break over the photographer's head. We feel the powerful energy of the water and admire the ingenious shapes it constantly forms.

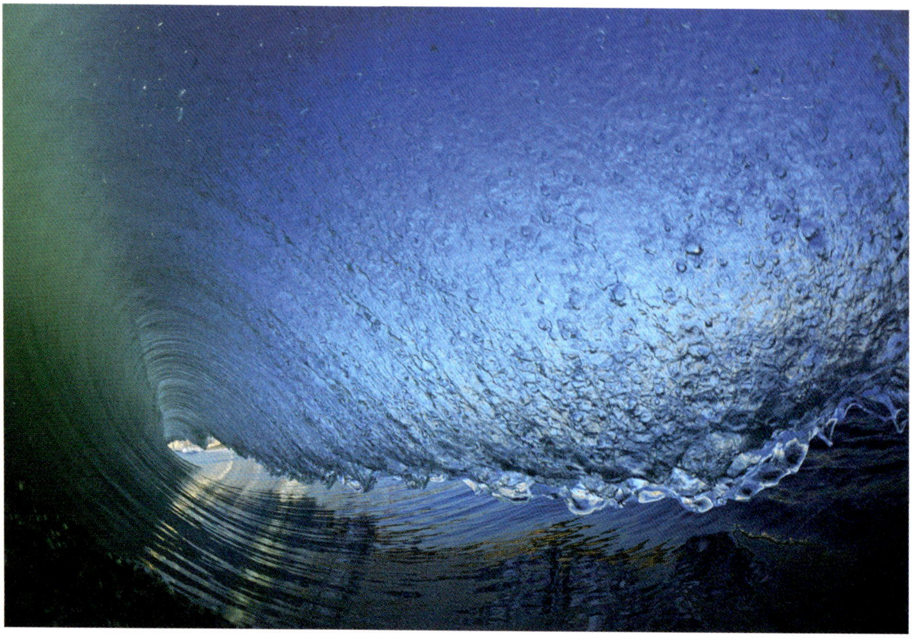

© MARCK BOTHA, FISH EYE

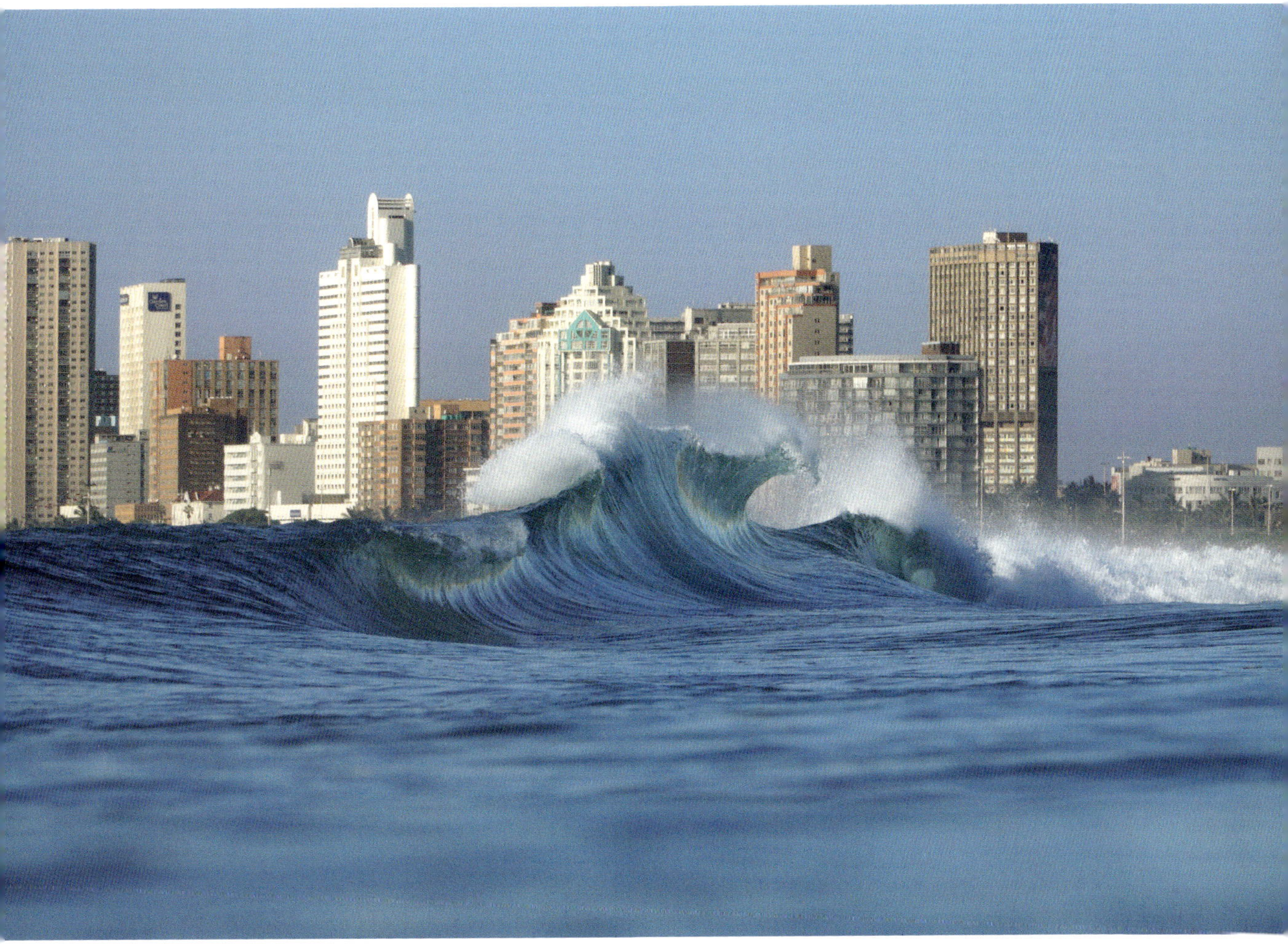

© MARCK BOTHA, CELEBRATE

next page © MARCK BOTHA, PAUSE

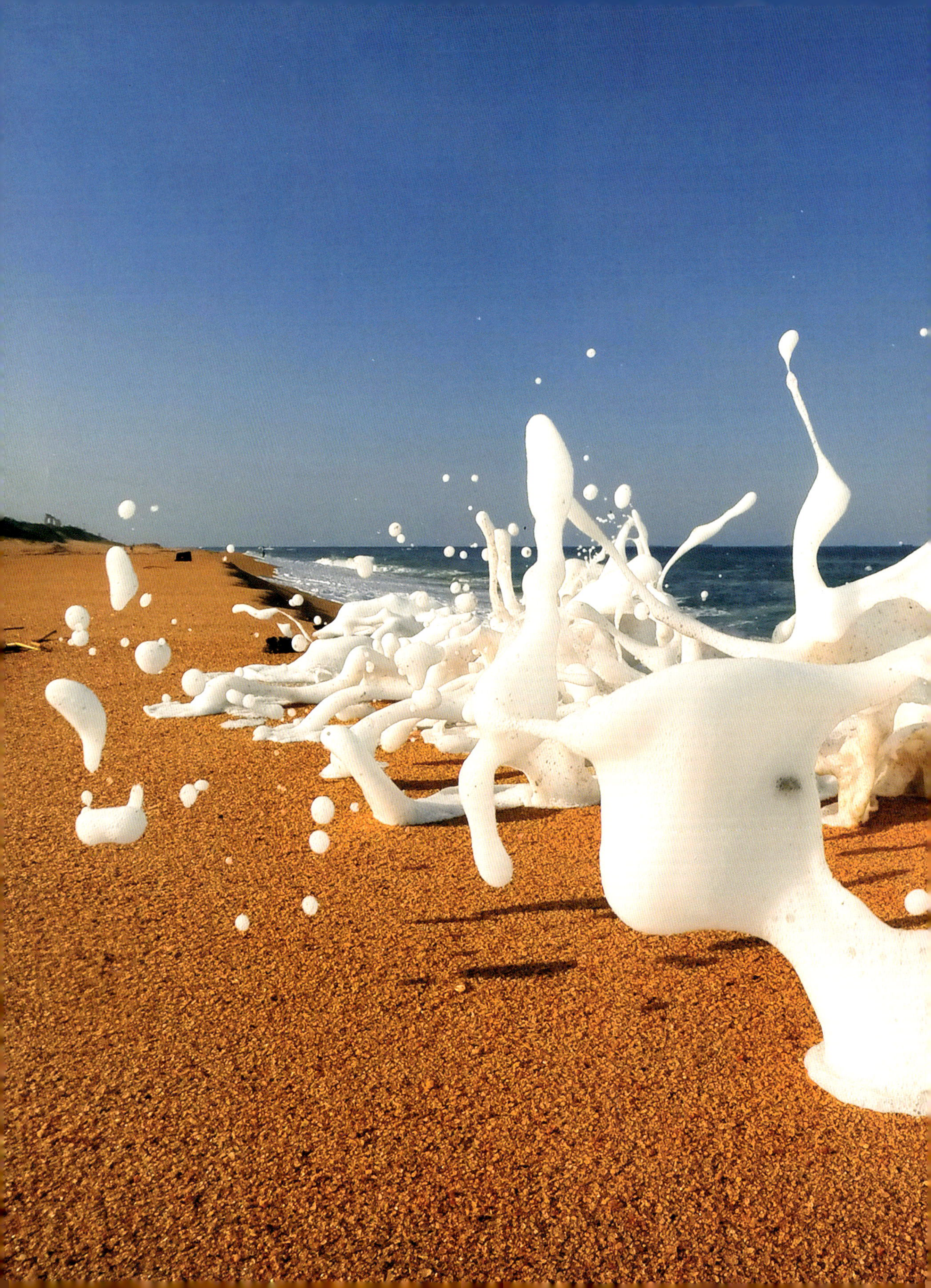

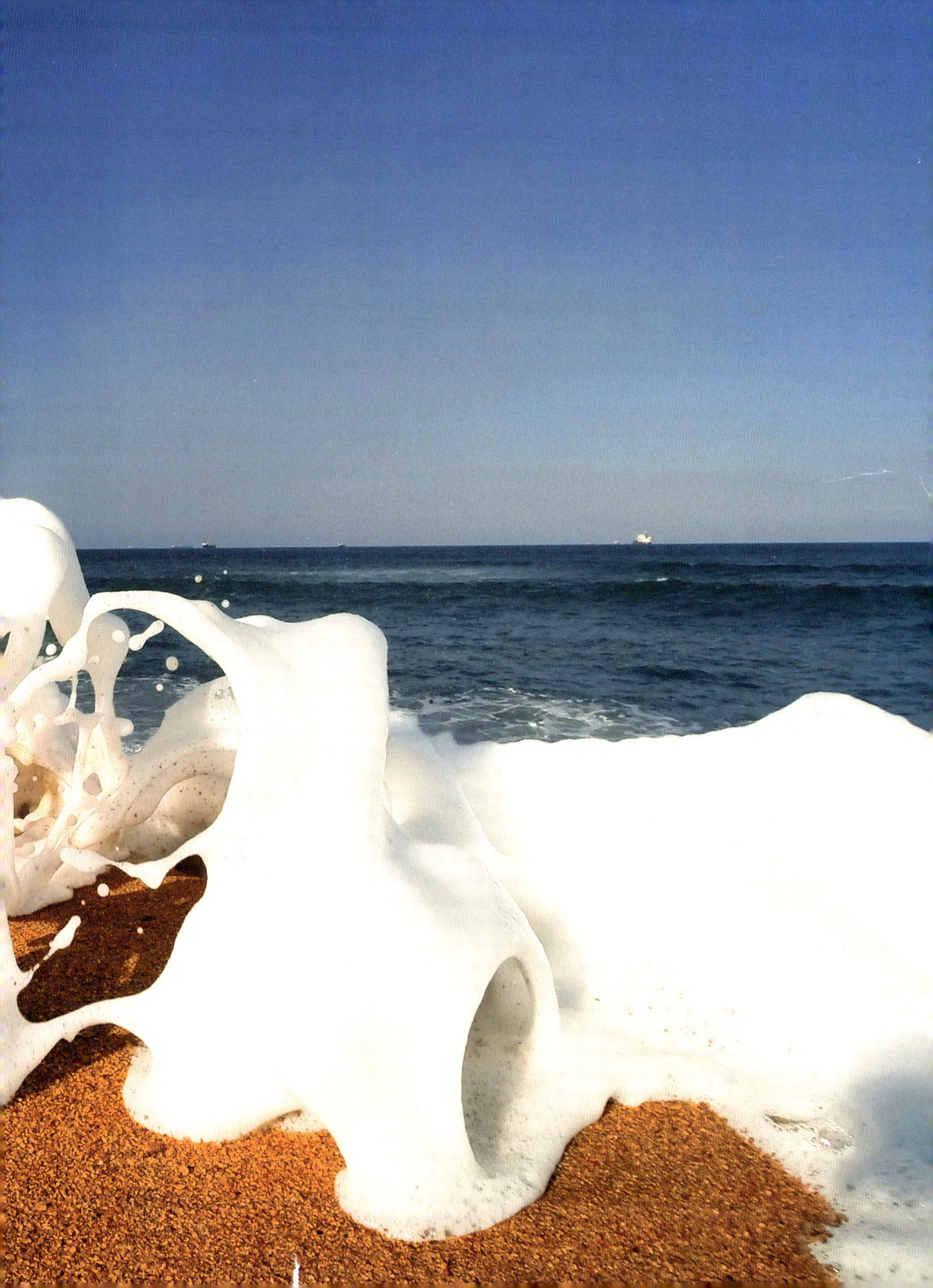

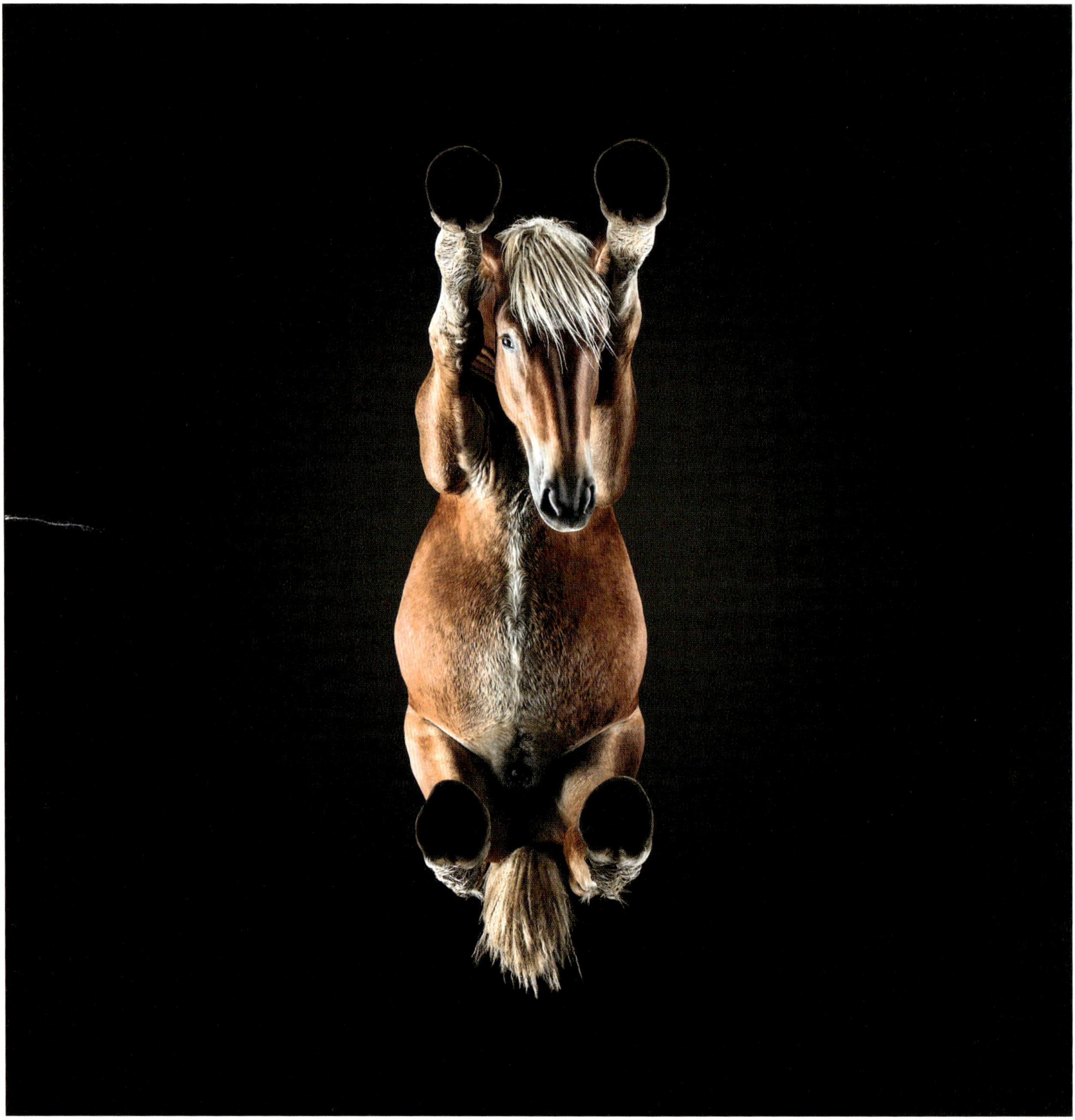

© ANDRIUS BURBA, UNDER-HORSE SERIES

ANDRIUS BURBA

#ANIMALS

Photos of animals, particularly pets, are very common, but looking at them from underneath is quite an original perspective. This is the approach of the Lithuanian photographer Andrius Burba. It all started at the International Cat Show in Vilnius, where Andrius organized the first photoshoot of the Underlook project. Published online, his crazy images of cats went viral and were quickly publicized in press and publications.

The photographer works in series, each of which is devoted to a different species. After cats, Andrius photographed dogs and rabbits. 'The most difficult part of shooting a rabbit', says the artist, 'is that they hardly moved on the glass at all. Anyway, I have got some fluffy pictures and even got a rabbit for myself since they are so adorable.' The fourth series is called 'Under-Horse' and was the biggest and most challenging one so far. Not only did it require beautiful horses, but also serious equipment and strong and resistant glass. The effects are impressive and fun!

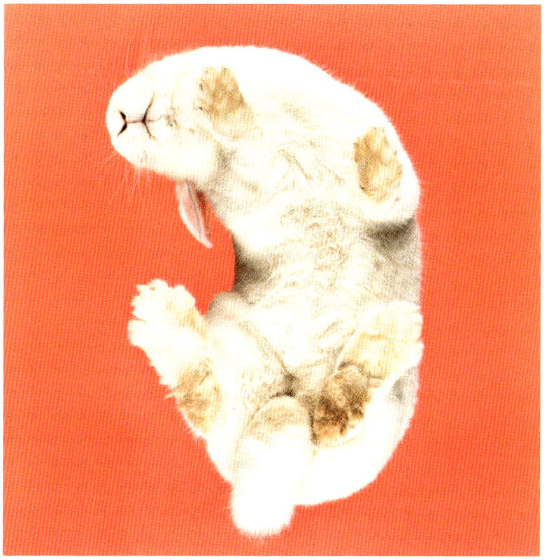

© ANDRIUS BURBA, UNDER-RABBIT SERIES

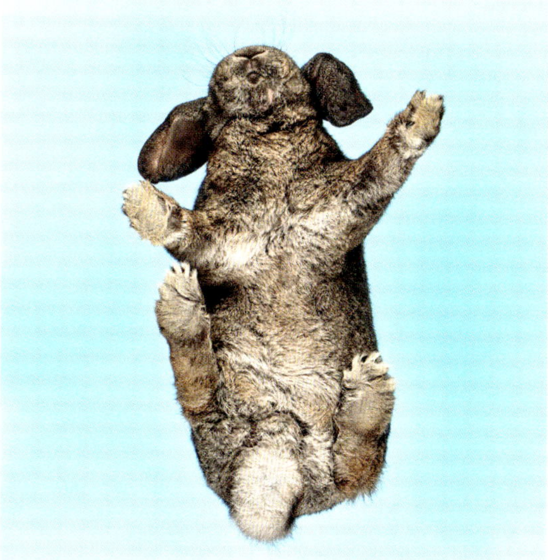

LÉO CAILLARD

#PORTRAIT

If you happen to see images of classical figures from the collection of the Parisian Louvre dressed up in contemporary clothes, that's the signature work of French photographer Léo Caillard (b. 1985) realized in his playful 'Hipster in Stone' series between 2012 and 2016. After photographing sculptures in the museum, he took images of models in selected street fashion items and then merged them, creating a meeting of the past with today. In effect, the icons of antiquity look as if they are posing for a fashion shoot.

The photographer's aim was to surprise: 'The viewer is drawn to the familiar within the image', he remarks, 'but closer inspection reveals many layers of incongruous information. This collision of elements forces the observer to question his assumptions and question the roles of the subjects presented.' Léo Caillard (b. 1985) is based in Paris. He graduated from Les Gobelins, University of Photography, in 2008. In his creative practice questioning our social environment, Léo's ingenious ideas are supported with the newest technologies.

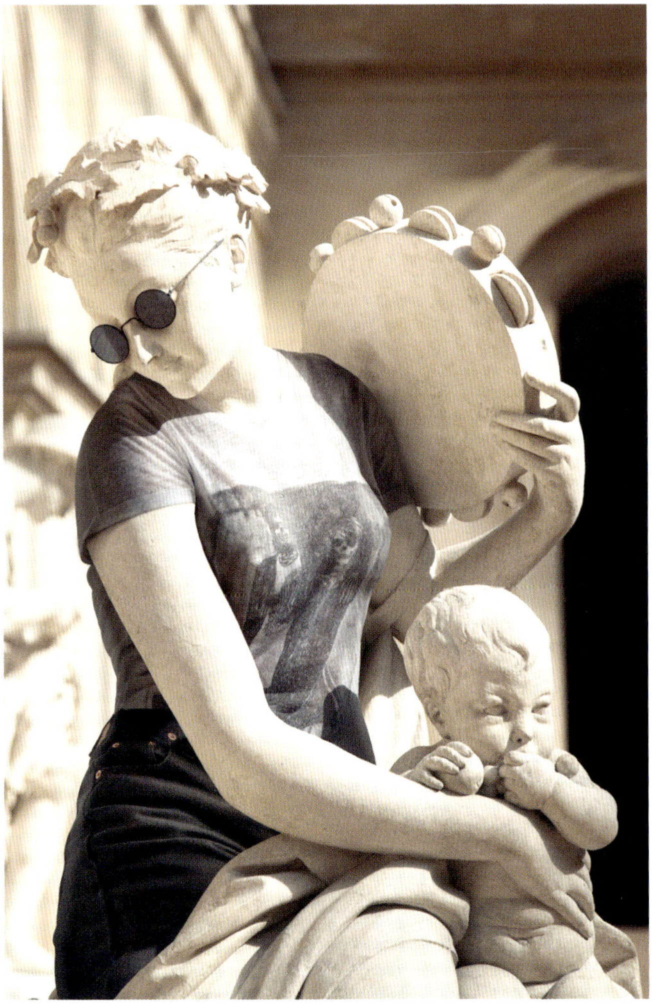

© LÉO CAILLARD, HIPSTER IN STONE 26, 2012-2016

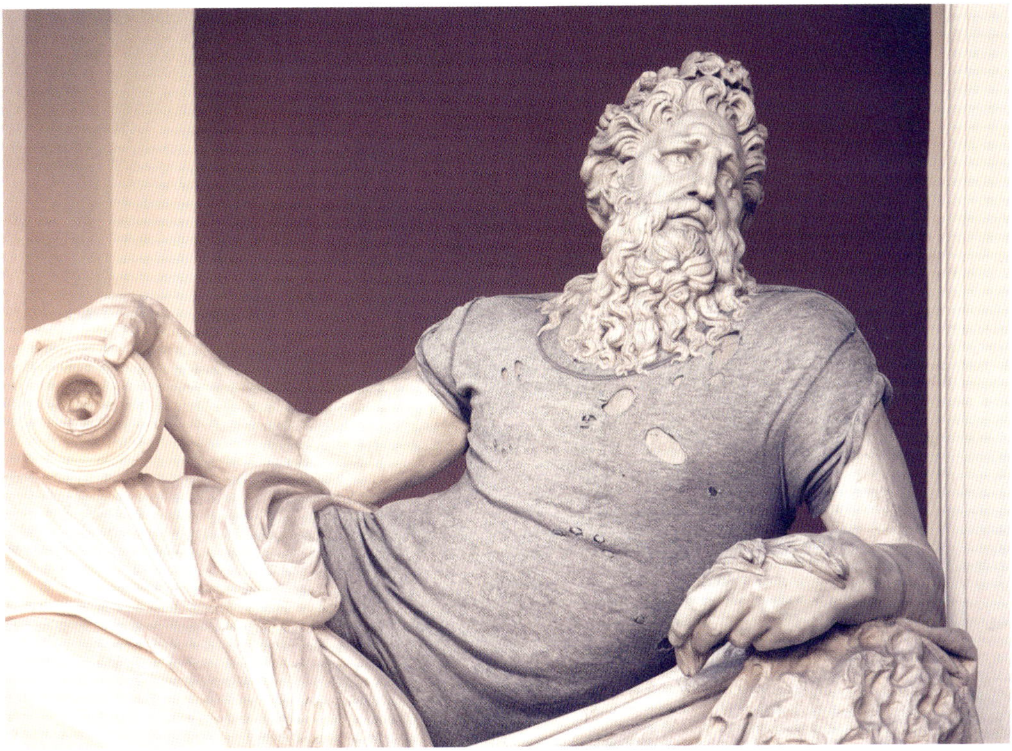

© LÉO CAILLARD, HIPSTER IN STONE 19, 2012-2016

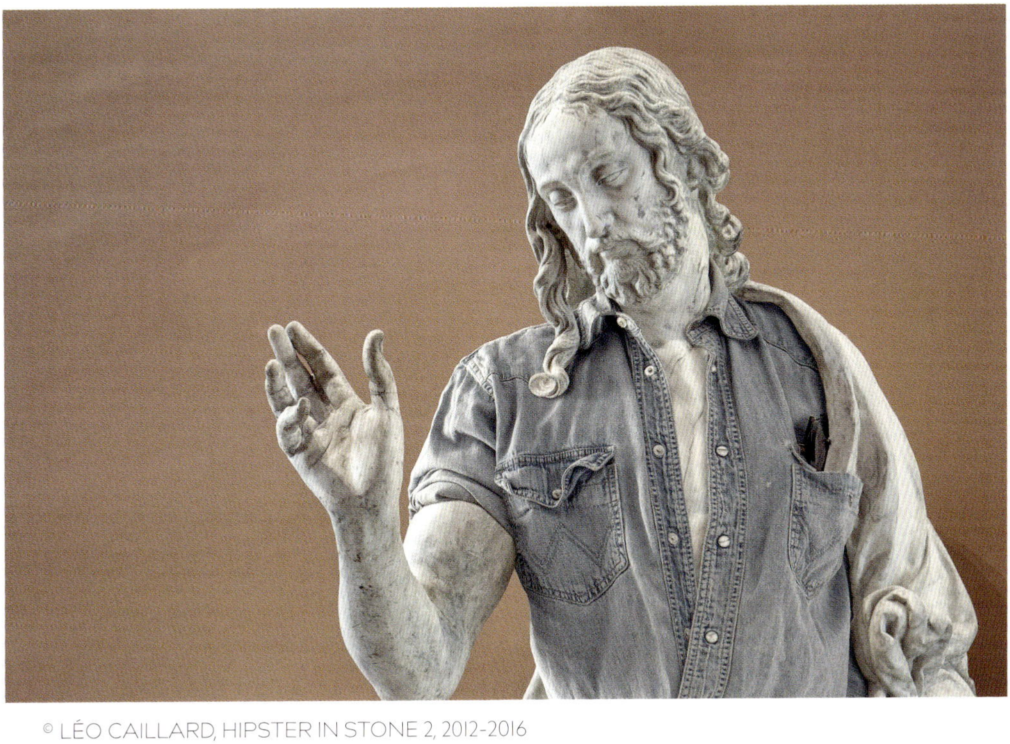

© LÉO CAILLARD, HIPSTER IN STONE 2, 2012-2016

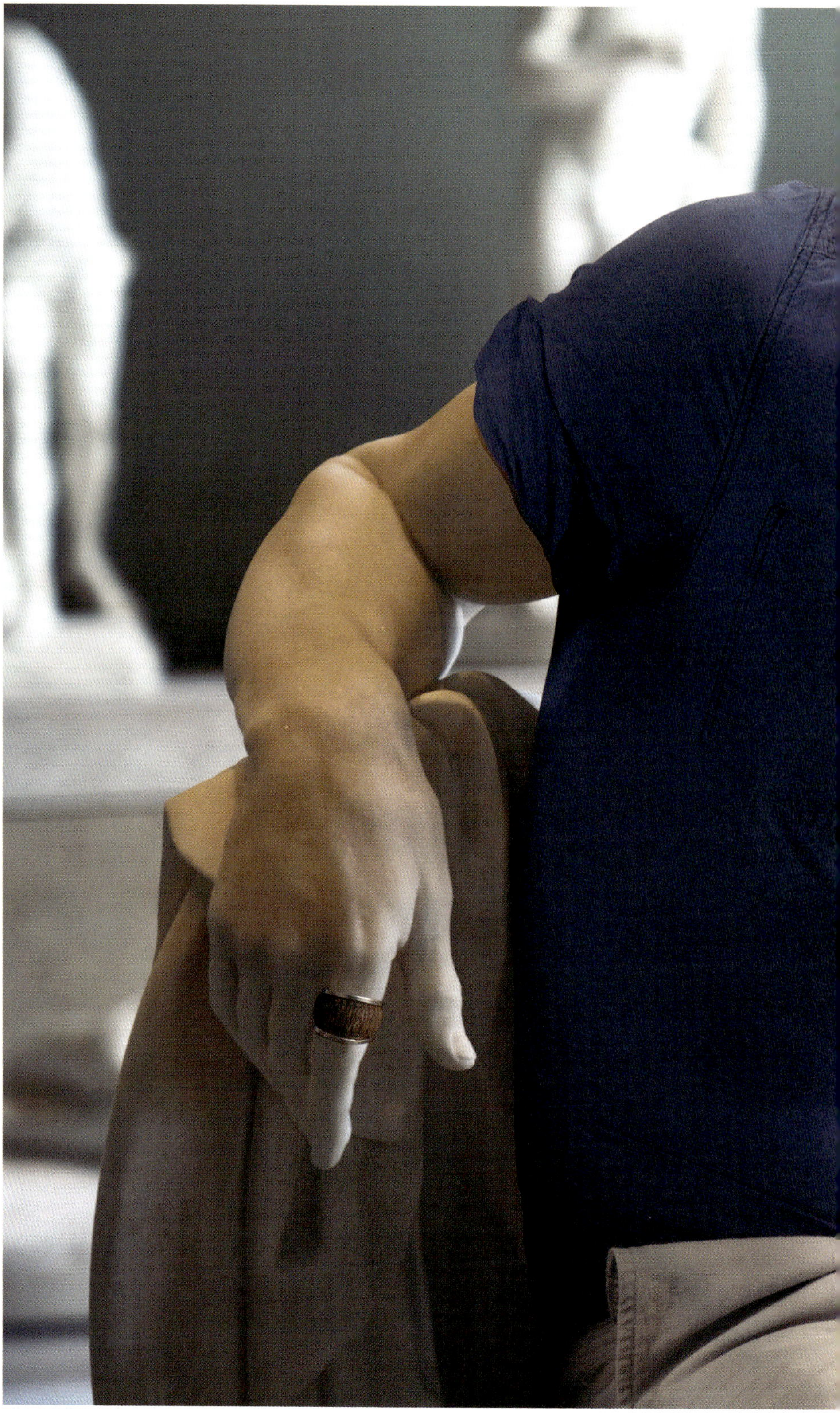

© LÉO CAILLARD, HIPSTER IN STONE 4, 2016

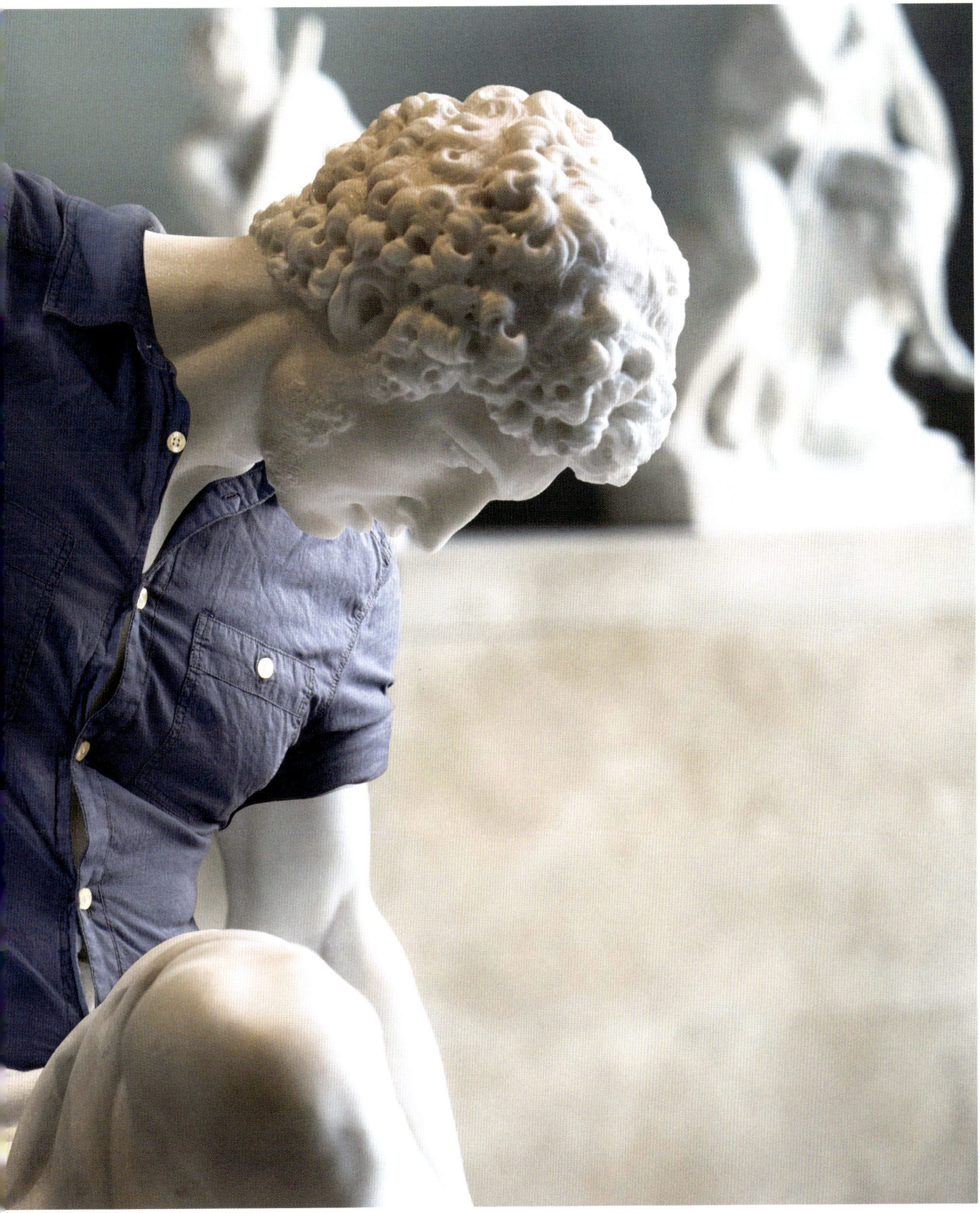

LÉO CAILLARD

FRAN CARNEROS

#BODY

A gigantic walnut as a human brain? A telephone that has an actual mouth instead of a mouth-piece? Málaga-based photographer Fran Carneros expresses absurd ideas not only to cause a visual shock, but also to make the viewer think. His striking and bizzarre images are in large part inspired by surreal art (in childhood the artist was struck by publicity photographs that used surrealism as a form of communication) as well as the aesthetic of Wes Anderson's movies. 'But', as Fran stresses, 'one of the things that motivated me the most were the images of Maurizio Cattelan and Pierpaolo Ferrari from Toilet Paper Magazine.'

The artist's truly crazy visions come to life through the use of collage and digital media in the process of photo manipulation. The atmosphere of weirdness is offset by the pleasing colour palette. Strange and haunting visions that can be read as existential reflections.

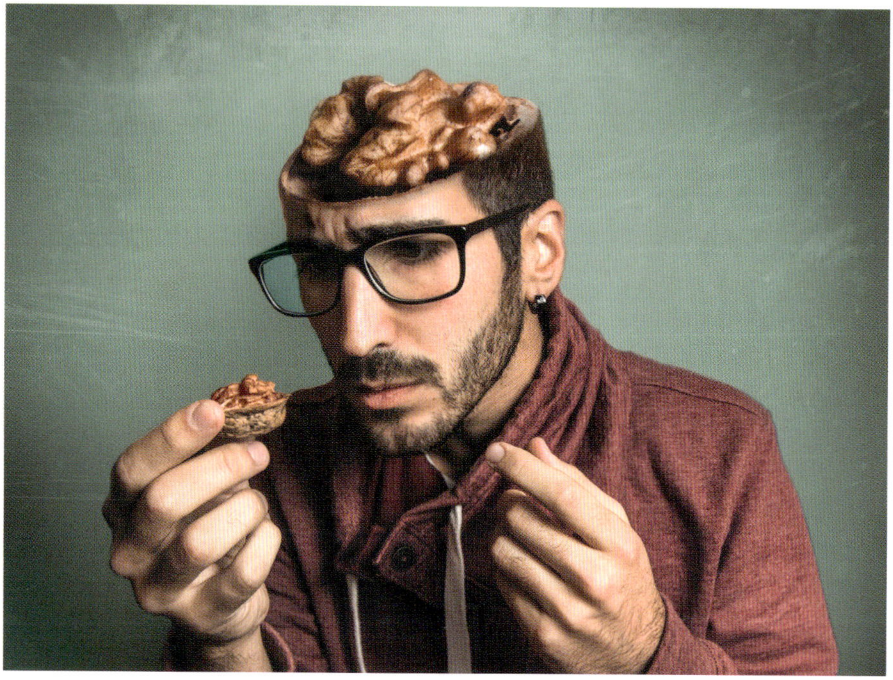

© FRAN CARNEROS, WEIRD

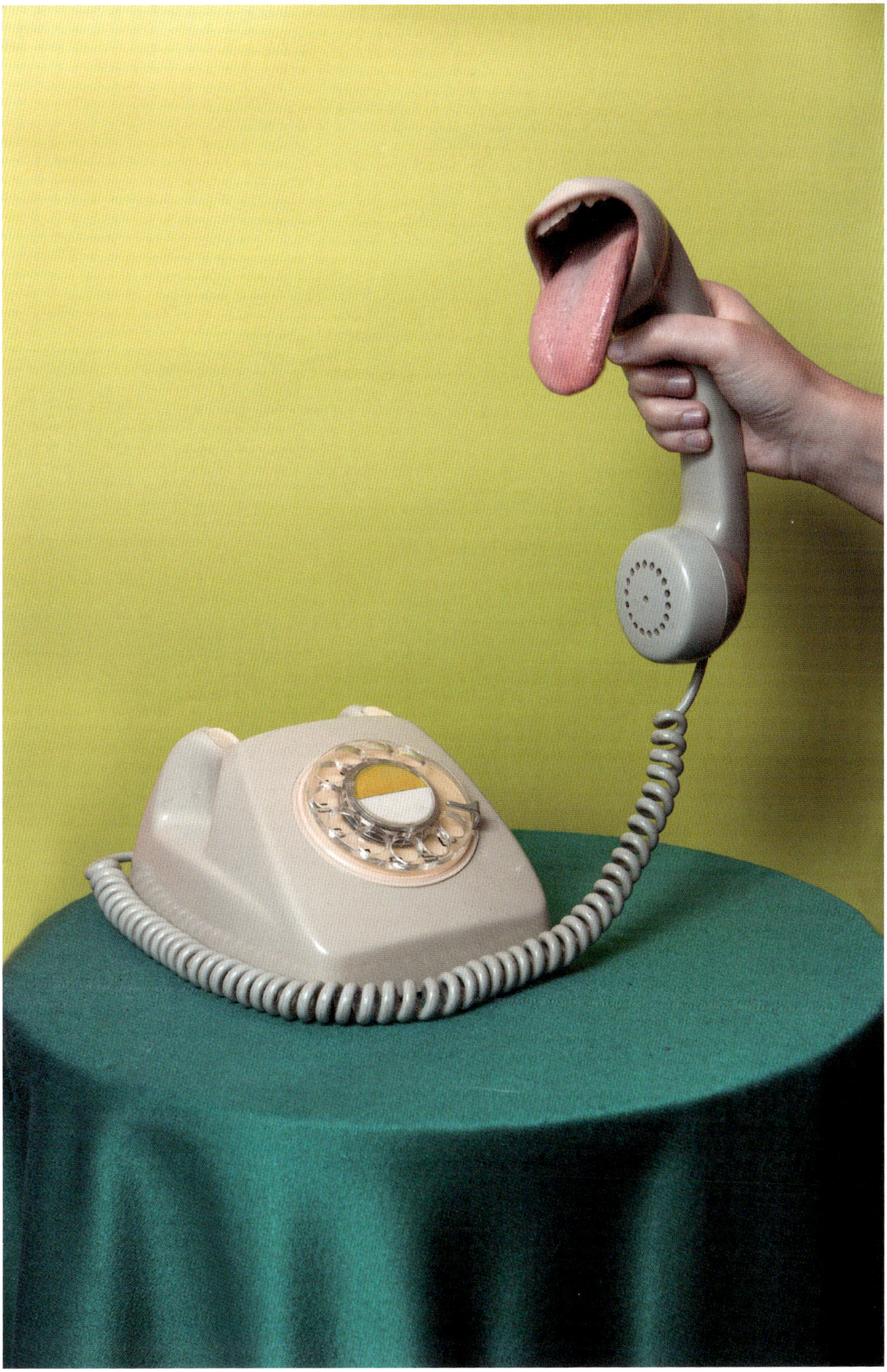

© FRAN CARNEROS, WEIRD

LAURENT CHÉHÈRE

The views of houses floating high in the sky at first glance evoke a fairy-tale atmosphere. Removed from their usual context and featured in pleasant colors, they seem to be part of a fantastic world. In reality, the photomontages are made of images taken in Menilmontant, a poor and multinational district of Paris, where the photographer lives and treats as his playground and source of inspiration.

The photo of each building is created from many details using numerous shots of various locations that are then multilayered. 'The author isolates these buildings from their urban context and releases them from the anonymity of the street to tell the life, the dreams and the hopes of these inhabitants' reads the artist's statement. In the 'Flying Houses' series Laurent Chéhère was also inspired by a poetic vision of old Paris, that of Jules Verne or Jean Cocteau, and these references are visible, too. The effect of these two worlds intertwined produces quite an oneiric vision.

#ARCHI-
TECTURE

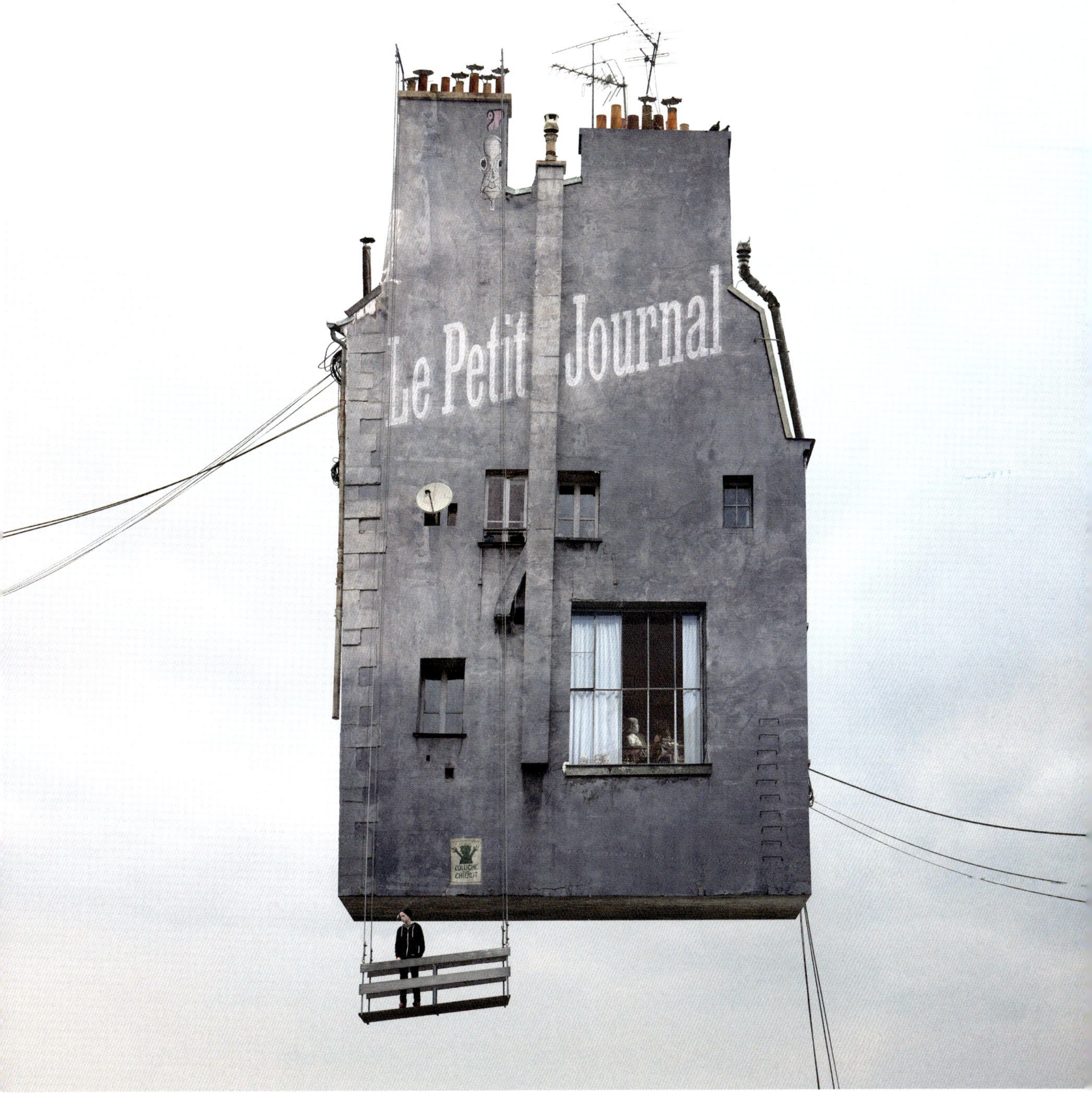

© LAURENT CHÉHÈRE, THE PETIT JOURNAL, 2013

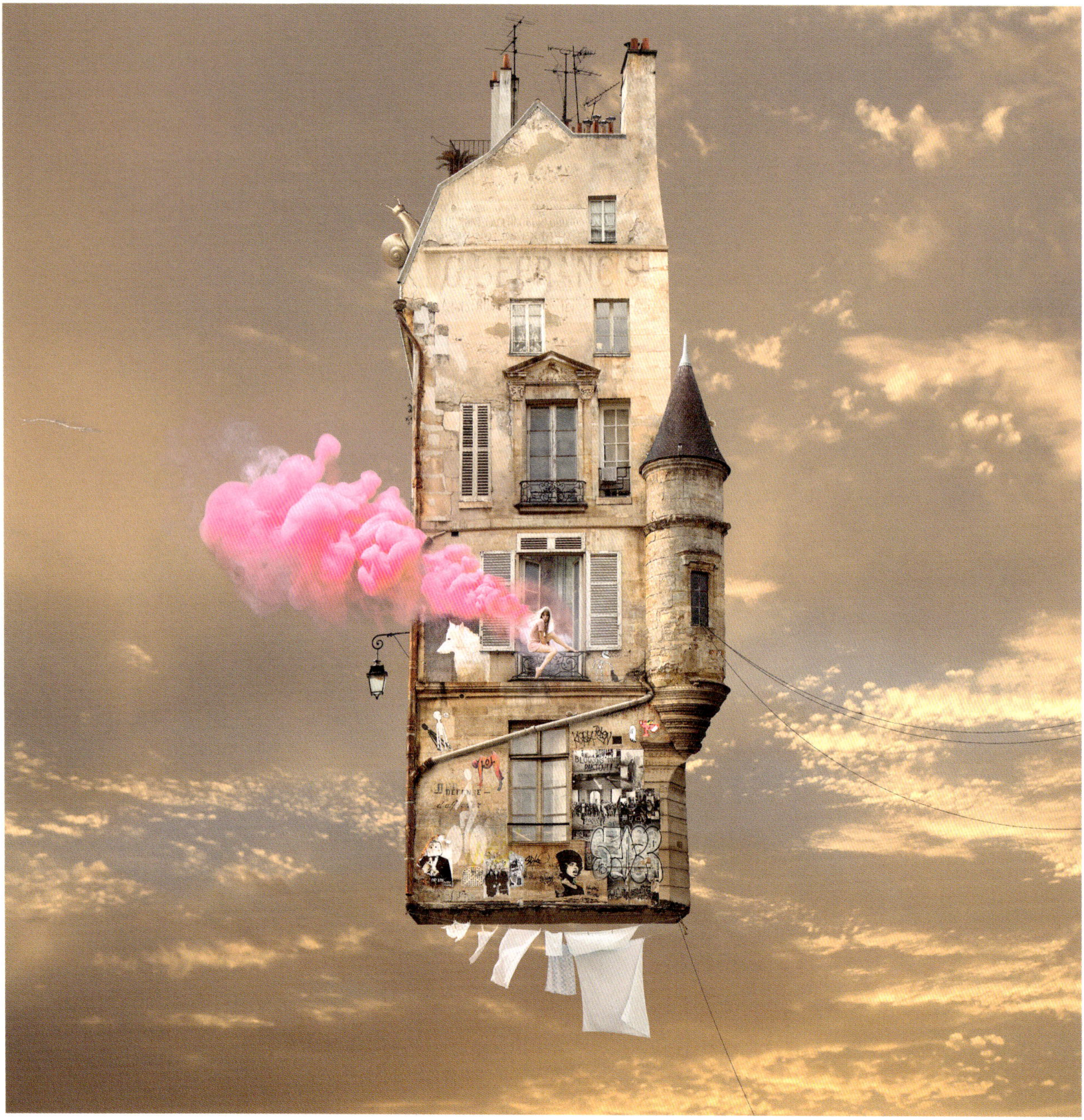

© LAURENT CHÉHÈRE, PINK, 2017

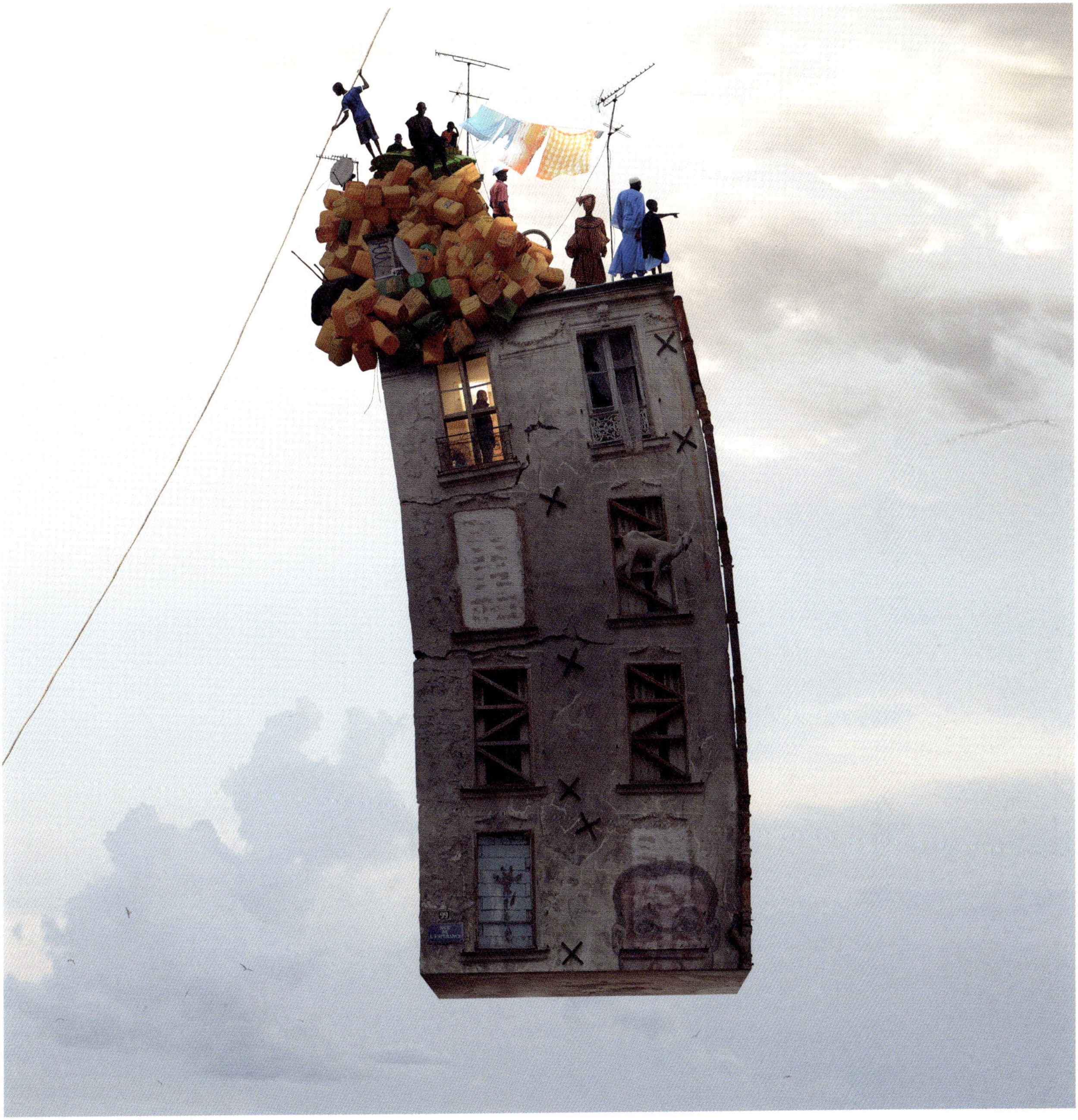

GEORGE CHRISTAKIS

Greek artist George Christakis specializes in landscapes and digital creations. Born in Heraklion on the island of Crete, at the age of 18 he moved to Athens to study public administration. During his second year of studies he became interested in photography and bought his first camera. However, taking photos was not satisfying enough. 'I had pictures in my mind that I couldn't make with just shooting with a camera', George recalls. And so he learned how to manipulate images digitally.

His images have a dreamlike atmosphere achieved either by playing with proportions, surprising the viewer with elements featured out of context or in a very specific palette. Moody, strange environments and unusual colours are main focus for the self-taught photographer. In the future George plans to blend his photographic works with 3D elements to create complex and even more extraordinary compositions.

#LAND-SCAPE

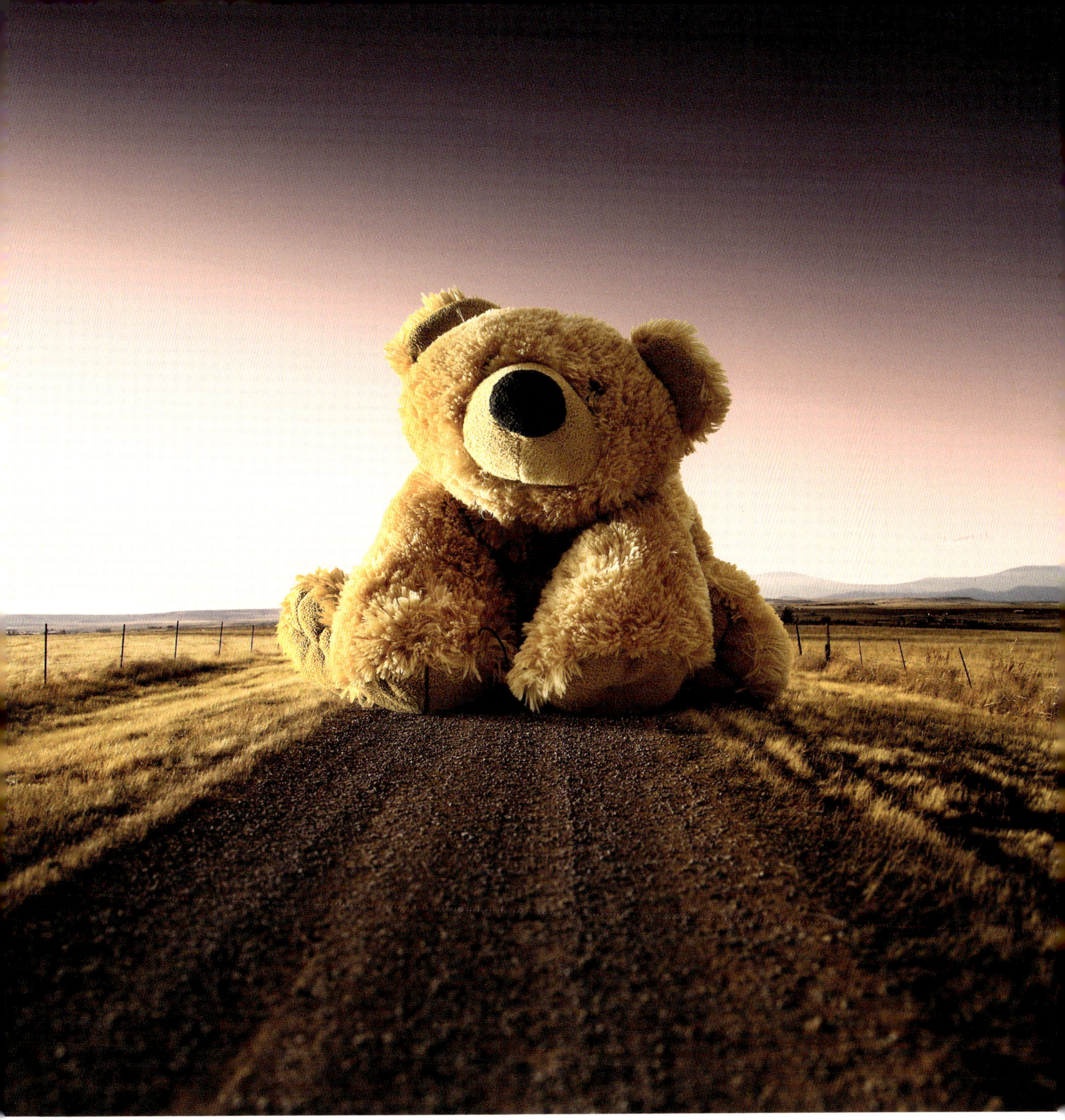

© GEORGE CHRISTAKIS, WHERE THE ROAD ENDS, 2014

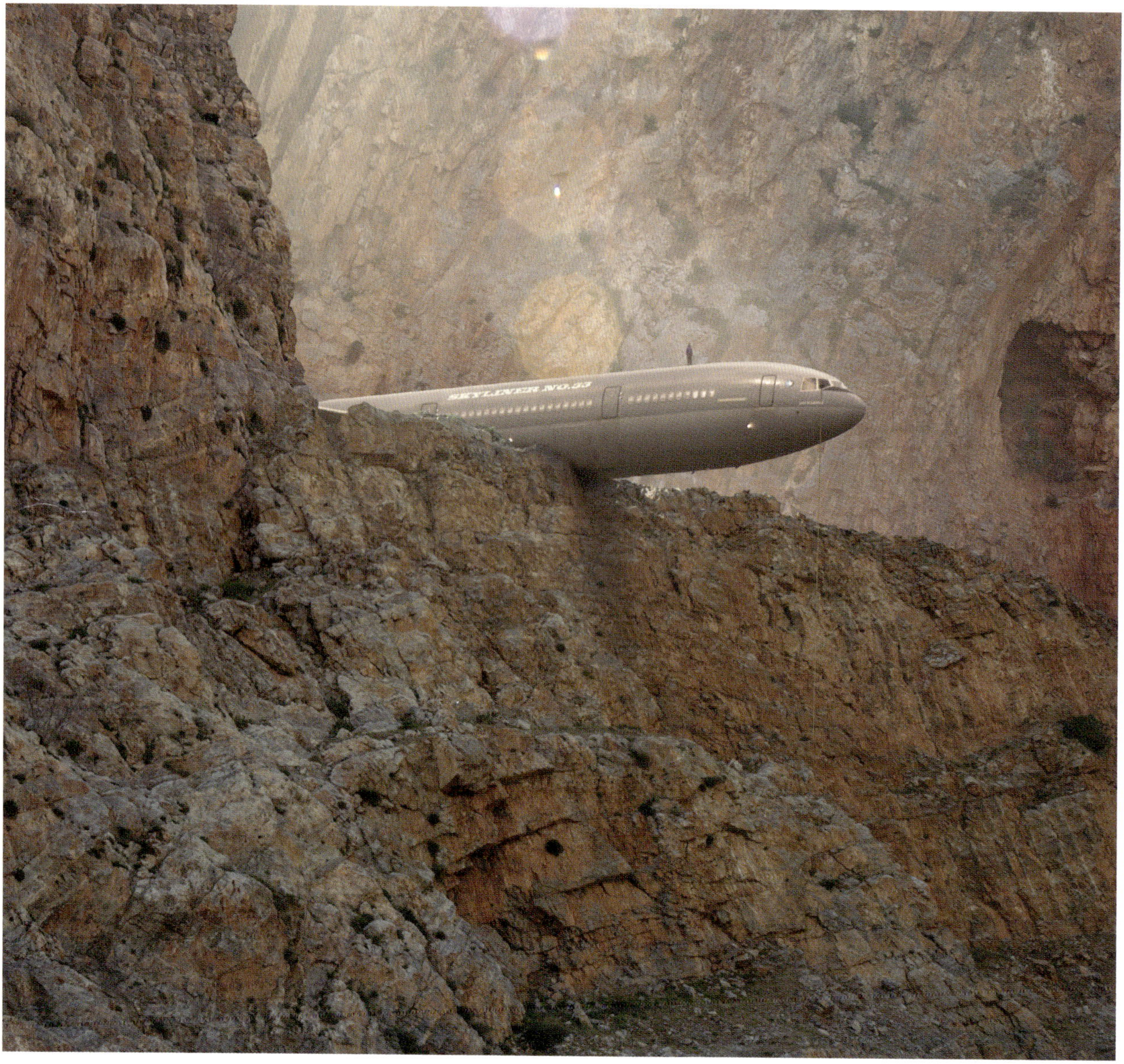

© GEORGE CHRISTAKIS, FIRST DAY OF A MEMORY, 2014

© GEORGE CHRISTAKIS, LANDING, 2012

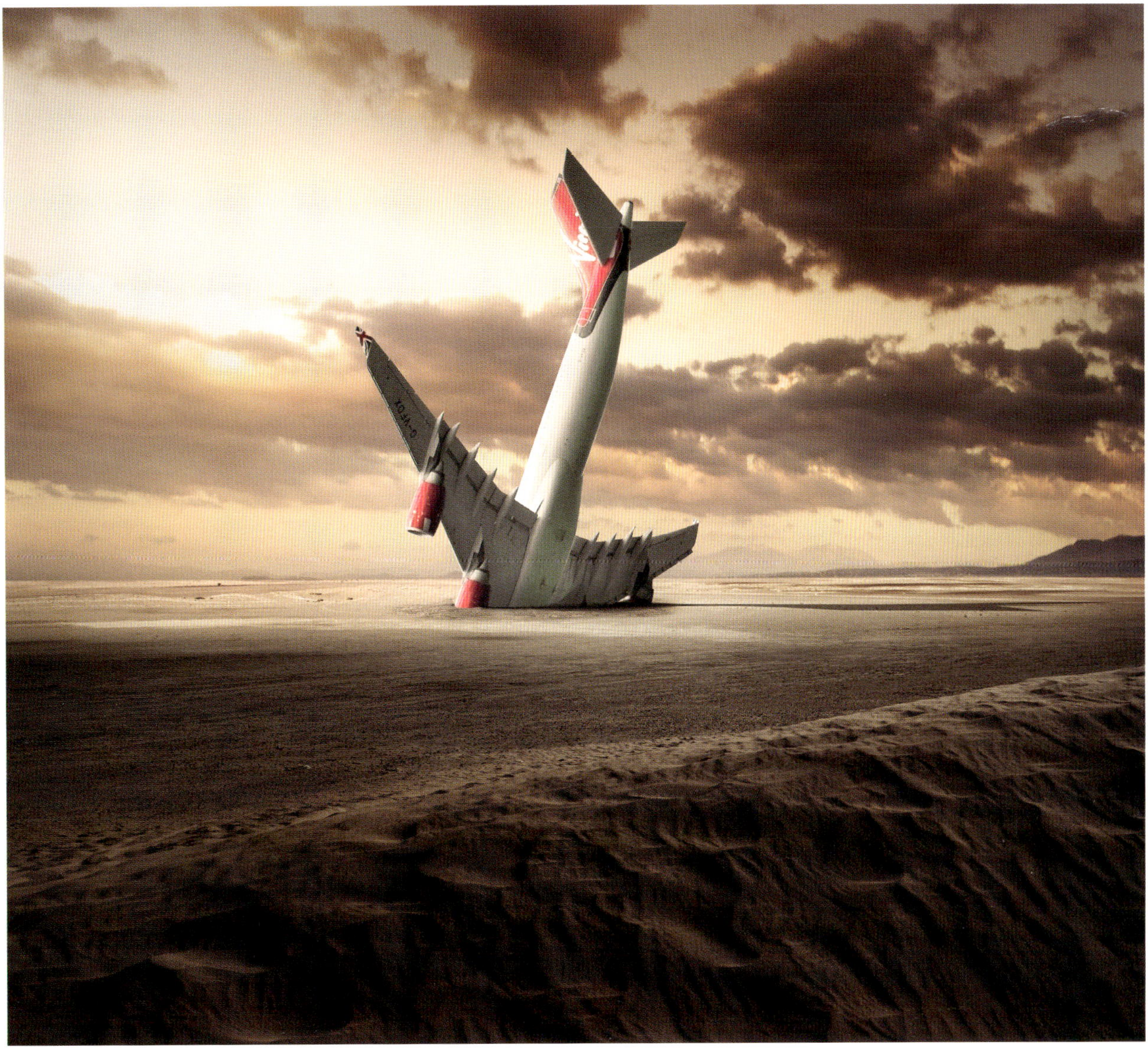

JULIA CHRISTE

When a photographer is also an animal lover, you might expect this result. German artist Julia Christe lives with her family on a farm with donkeys, horses, goats, cats and two dogs. Speaking of the dogs, Julia, inspired by her Frisbee-loving puppy Flinn, decided to put a twist on photographing dogs. The 'Flying Dogs' series celebrates the athleticism and freedom of dogs leaping in mid-air.

As she says, she is interested in canines of all breeds and sizes. In the series, we can admire the tiniest Chihuahuas, Siberian Huskies or German Shepherds. They are portrayed as never before. Captured jumping into the air against monochrome grey backgrounds, the dogs are simply adorable. In this visually sensational collection each dog takes a different pose and has a different, let's call it, facial expression. And just to reassure all readers, no dogs are harmed in the making of Julia's images.

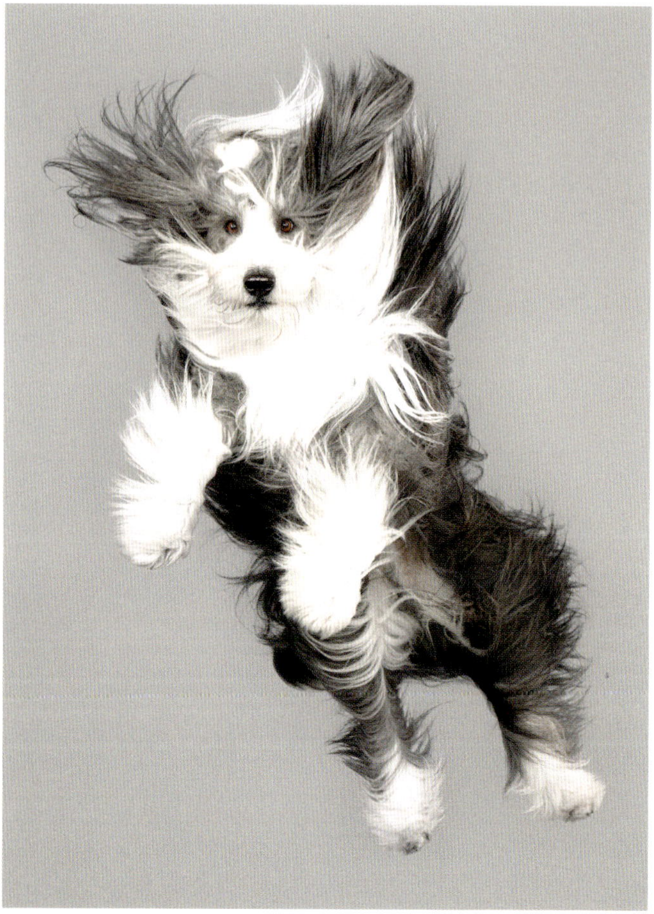

© JULIA CHRISTE, FLYING DOGS I

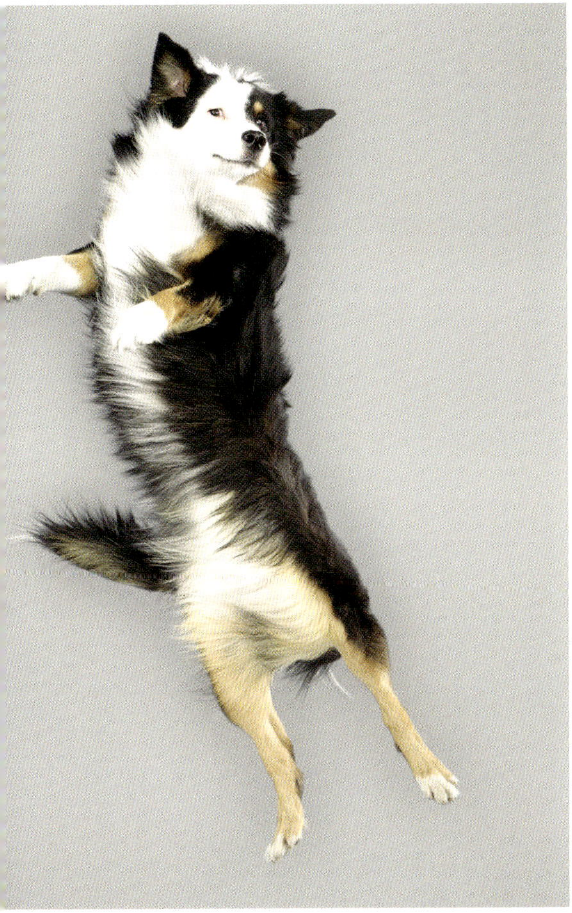

© JULIA CHRISTE, FLYING DOGS 2

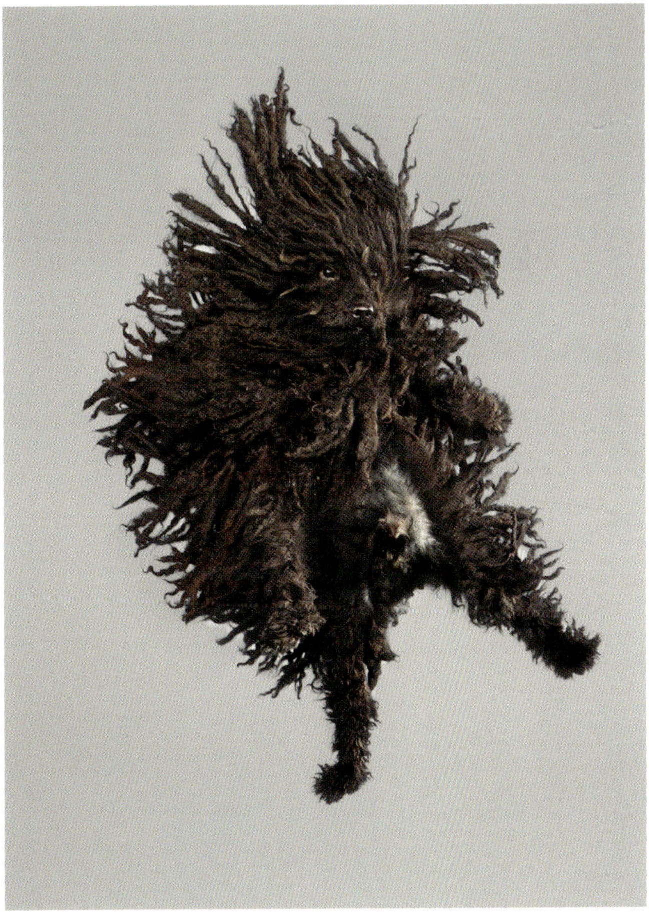

© JULIA CHRISTE, FLYING DOGS 3

DAVID CUBERO

#TOYS

The photos of Barcelona-based David Cubero (nickname Suppa-Duppa) are populated with hilarious and colourful scenes featuring popular toys. 'I have collected all kinds of action figures since I was a kid', says the photographer, 'a few years ago I started shooting pics of my toys in order to get a reference posing guide for drawing my own comic books. Later I realized I had a ton of pics of toys doing funny things and thought I had to do something with that.' David's sense of humour matches his eye for detail to result in stunning snaps of well-known toys in the most original configurations.

Our selection includes works in which the photographer references the history of art. Using Marvel toys, mostly the iron man figures, he playfully recreates some of the most famous artworks. The toy versions of the 'Vitruvian Man' by Leonardo da Vinci, Rodin's 'Thinker' and the 'Creation of Adam' in the Sistine Chapel, among others, are well-executed!

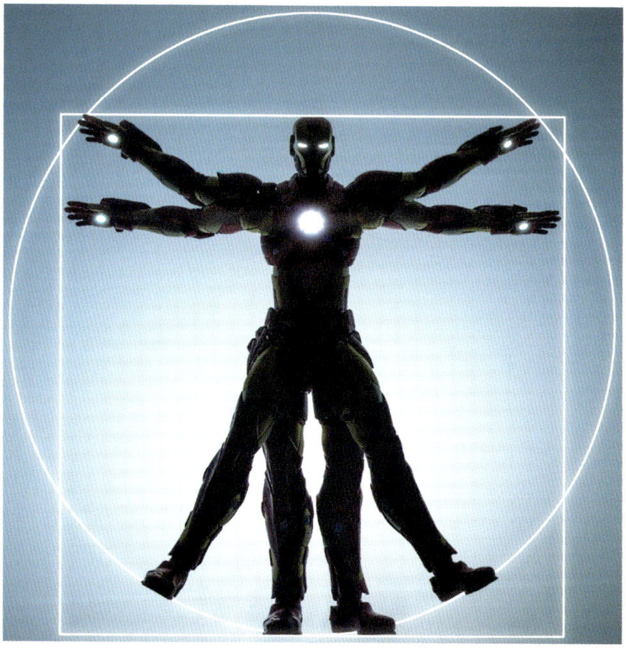

© DAVID CUBERO, VITRUVIAN MAN (LEONARDO DA VINCI, 1490)

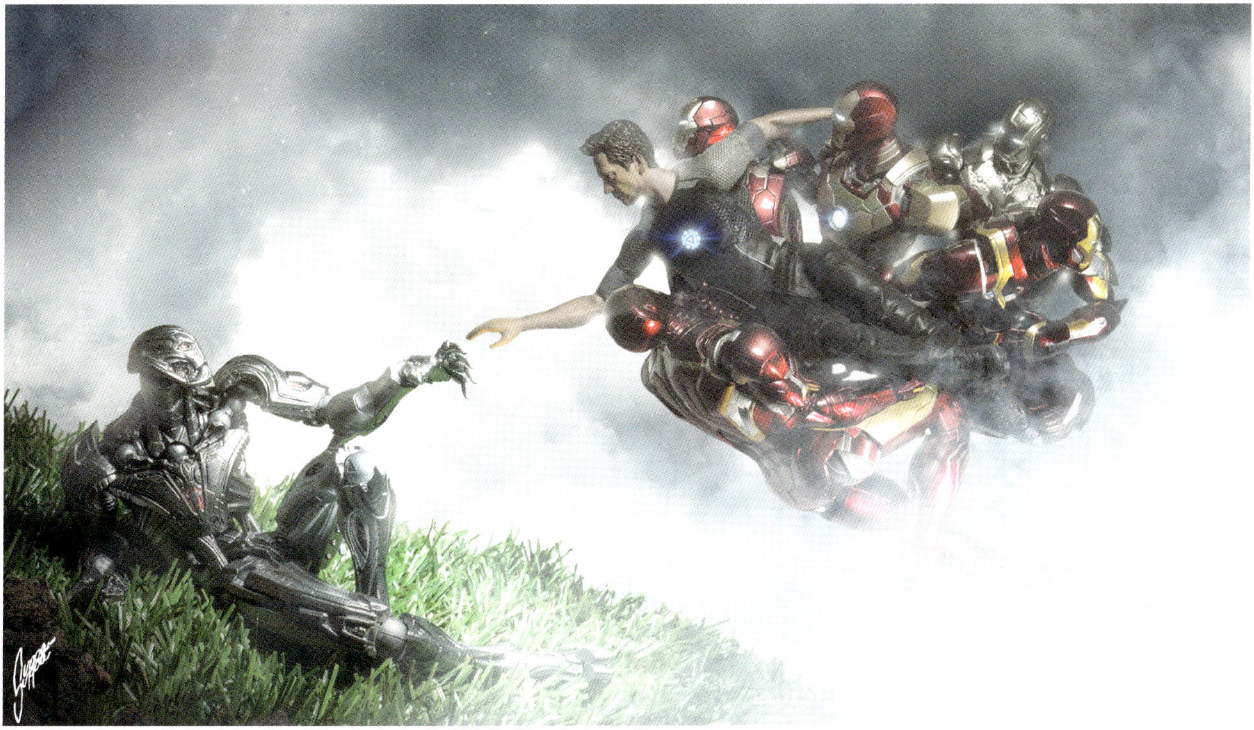

© DAVID CUBERO, THE CREATION OF ADAM, MICHELANGELO (SISTINE CHAPEL, VATI-CAN CITY, 1508–1512)

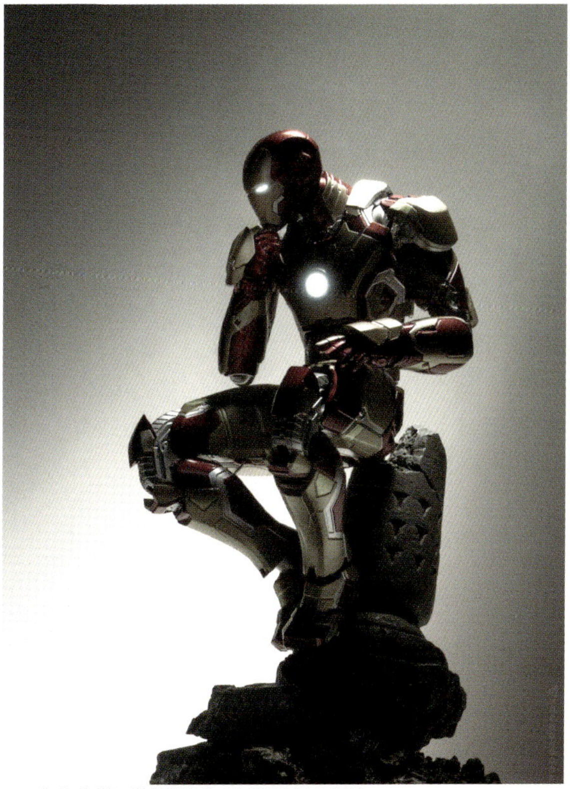

© DAVID CUBERO, THE THINKER (AUGUSTE RODIN, 1880)

BROCK DAVIS

One should not play with food, although in the case of Brock Davis we can make an exception. The Minneapolis-based photographer and graphic designer driven by the less-is-more philosophy, creates comical compositions of what we usually like to eat. In his photos, clever manipulations turn various foods into humorous sculptures. Brock makes new forms by playing ironically with their original shapes or characteristic features.

As often happens with original and good ideas, the series began somehow by accident. The photographer was trying to entertain his two children during breakfast by using a section of the peel as a hat for the banana to wear. Since it worked, he decided to keep transforming food and share it with a wider audience. Brock's style, surely influenced by the advertising industry, is visually effective and full of a sense of fun. 'Any object that begins to appear mundane', he says,' is a good time to start re-imagining it.'

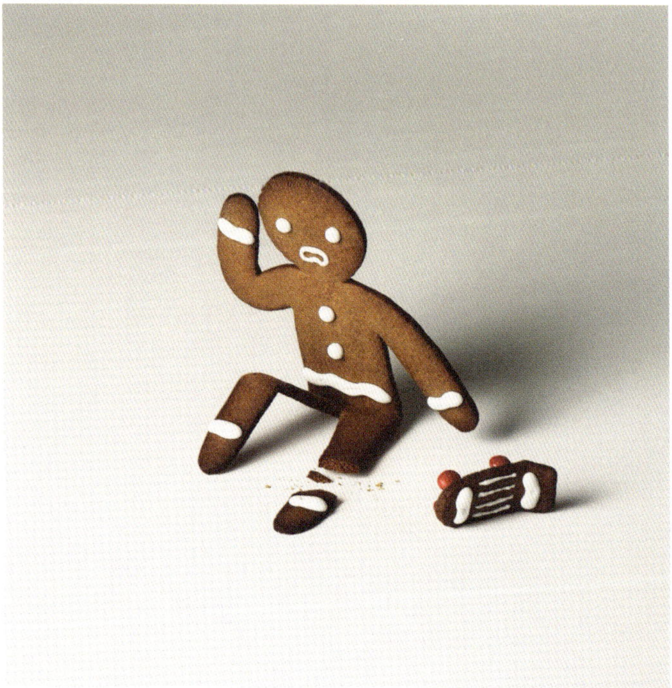

© BROCK DAVIS, THE GINGERSHRED MAN, 2011

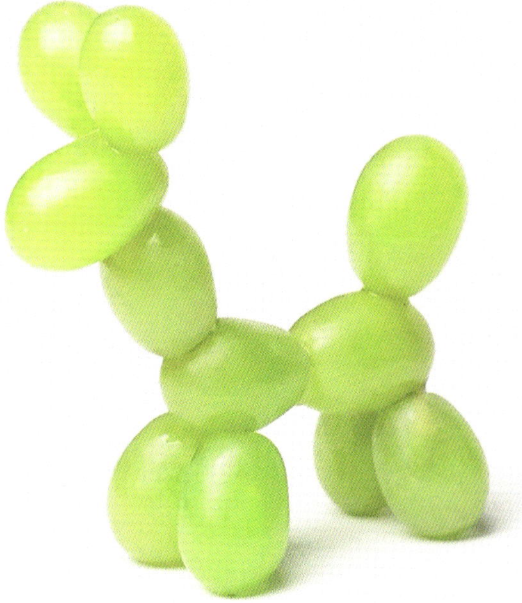

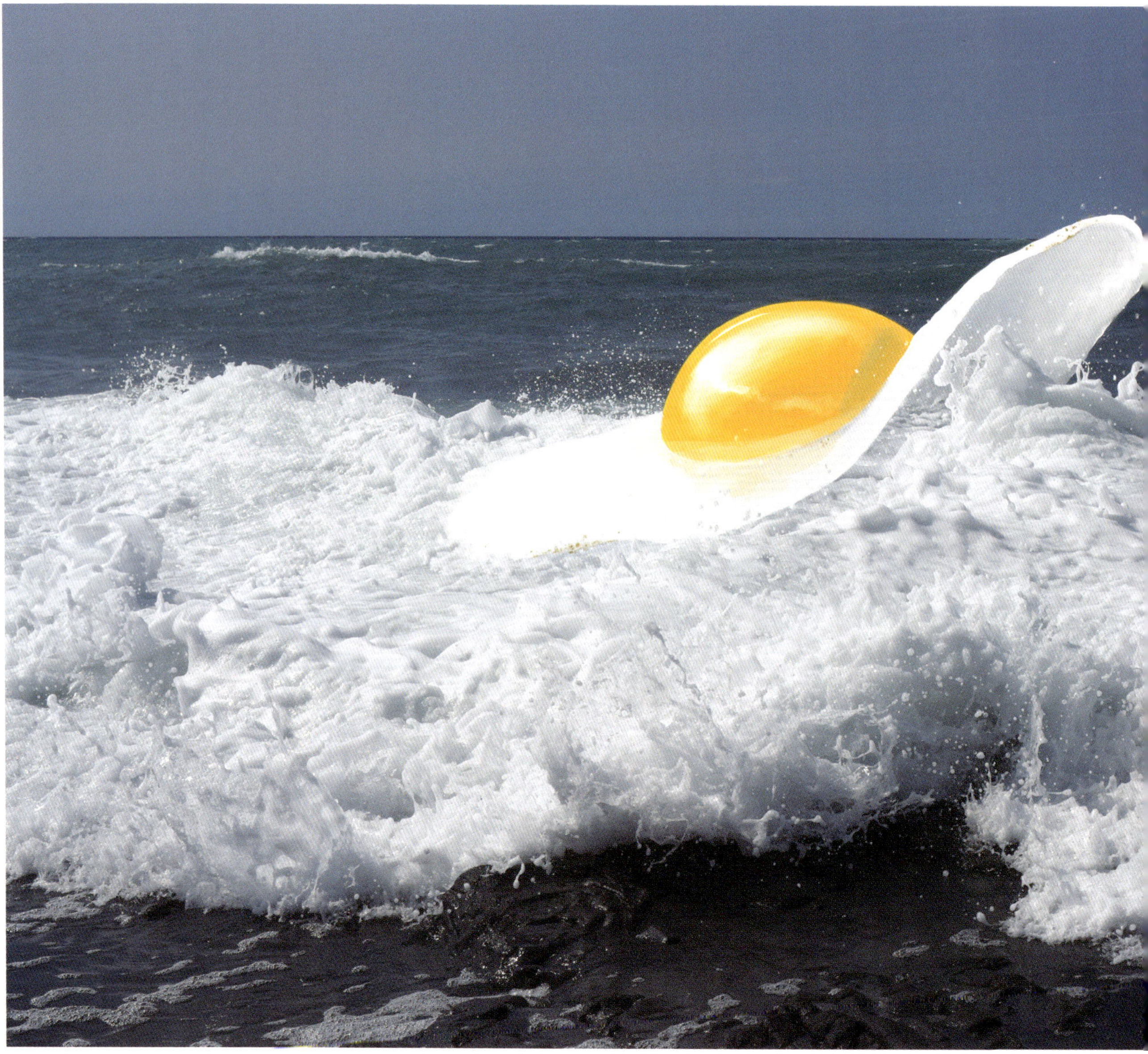

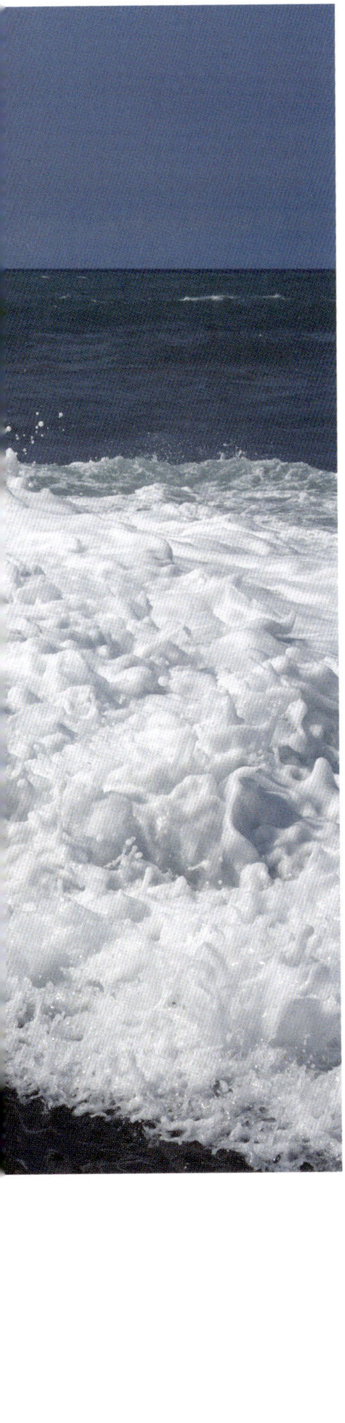

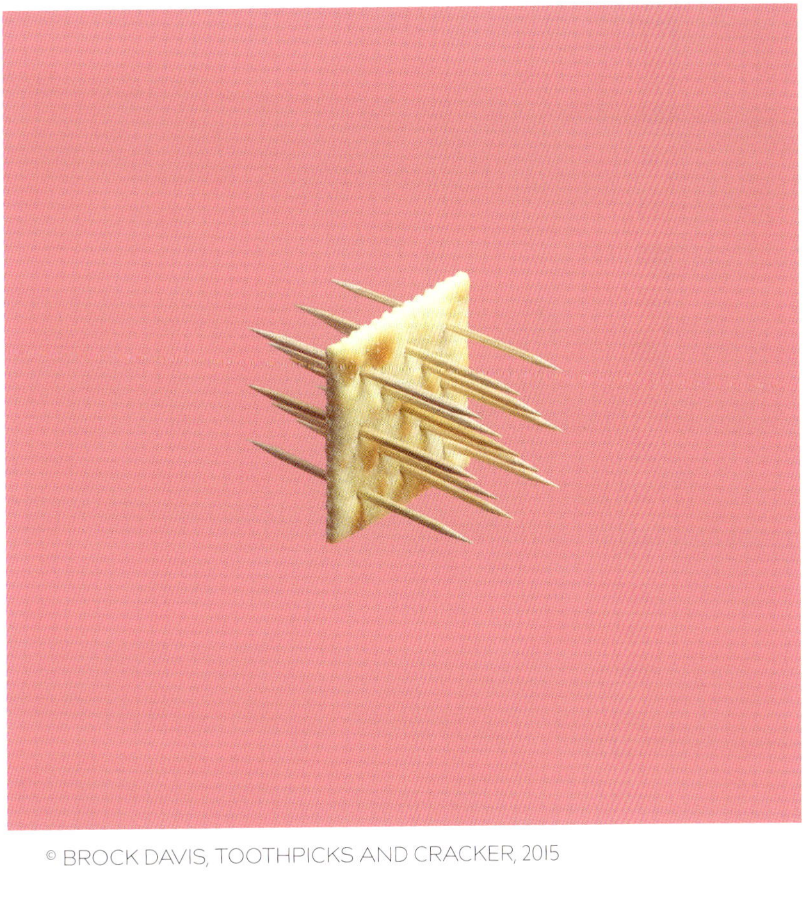

© BROCK DAVIS, TOOTHPICKS AND CRACKER, 2015

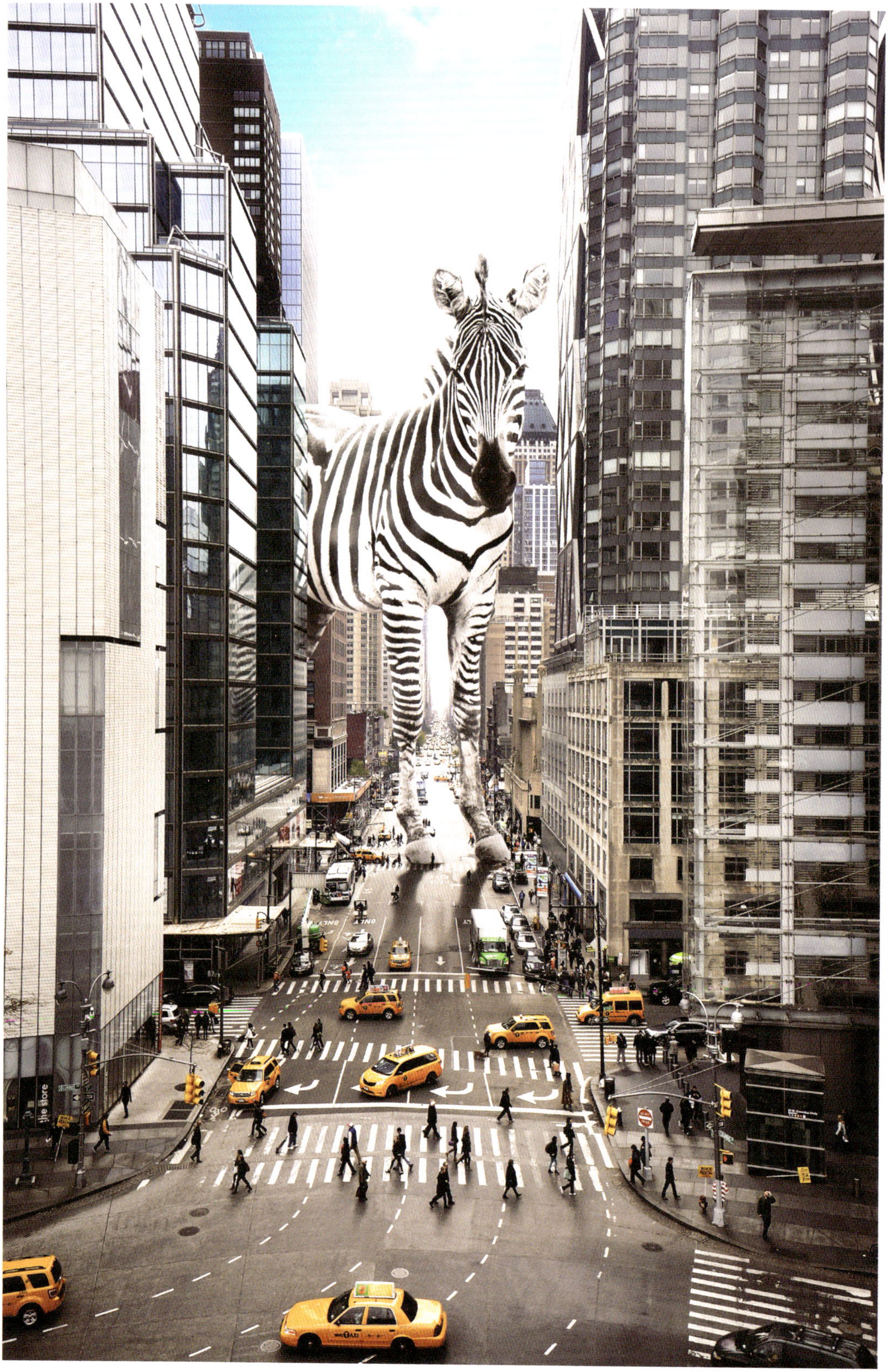

© IGOR DEMCHENKO, ZEBRA

IGOR DEMCHENKO

#ARCHI-TECTURE

#ANIMALS

A deer as tall as Big Ben on the bank of the Thames in London? Pink flamingos walking across the historical center of Paris? Or a zebra trapped in between Manhattan's skyscrapers in NYC? In the vivid world of Igor Demchenko significantly enlarged animals take over the streets of cities around the world. These unusual additions to well-known urban views are each carefully selected – the animals are either characteristic of a particular country or refer to its atmosphere.

The juxtaposition of gigantic creatures with extensive realistic panoramas is striking. Perfectly photographed architecture of megacities is now somehow dominated by animals. 'I'm not a surrealist', says Igor, 'I just share unusual moments from travels. I believe that fantasies are just fantasies. But any fiction is already a reality.' We look forward to Igor's vision of other cities in the world. The digital artist also works internationally as art director and graphic designer on numerous commercial projects..

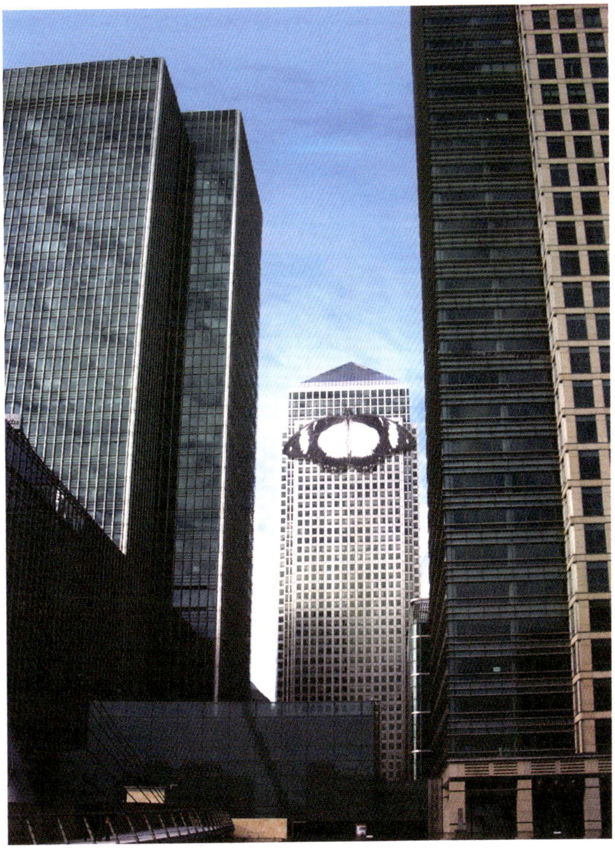

© IGOR DEMCHENKO, BUTTERFLY

next page © IGOR DEMCHENKO , WHALES

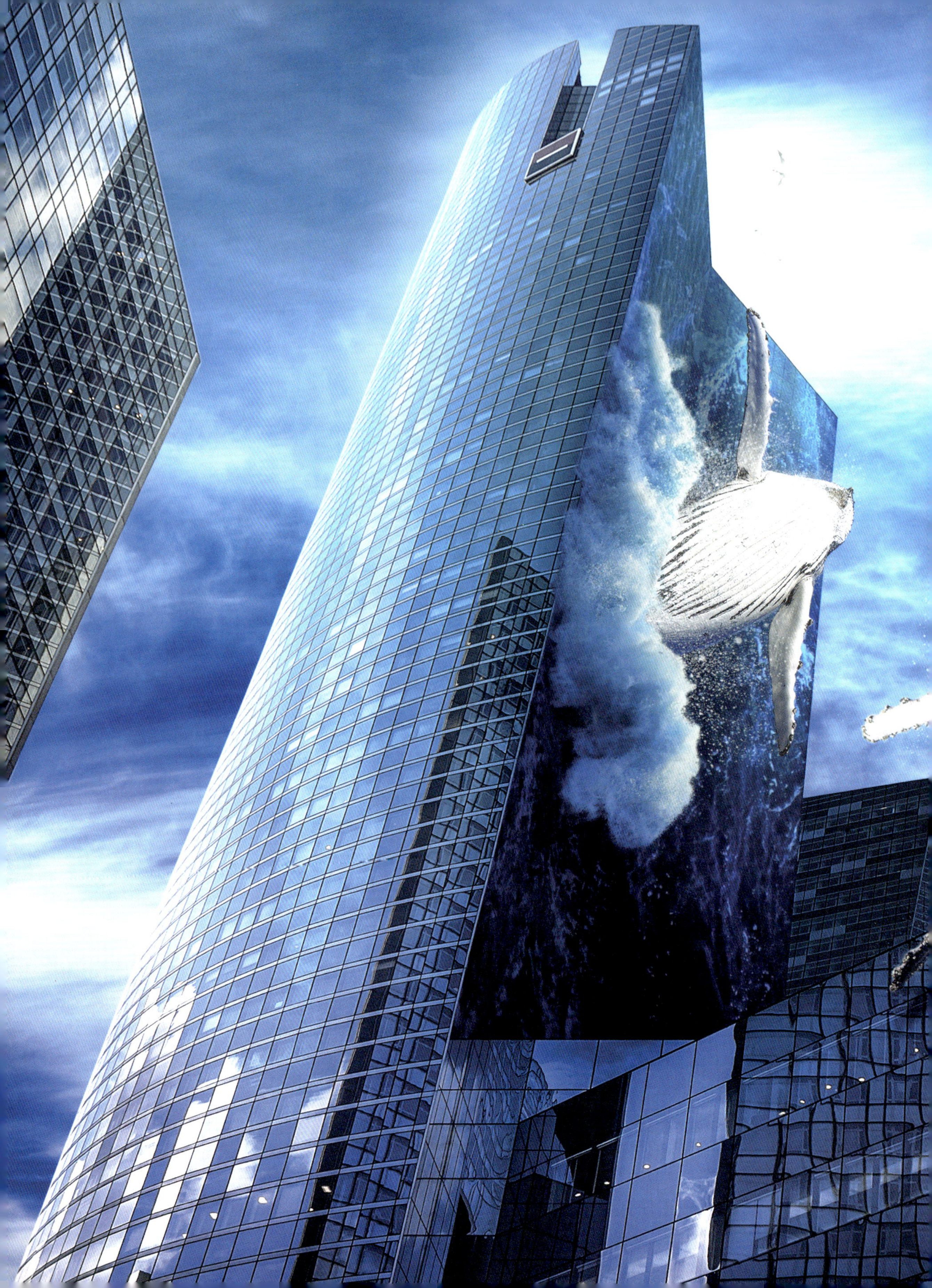

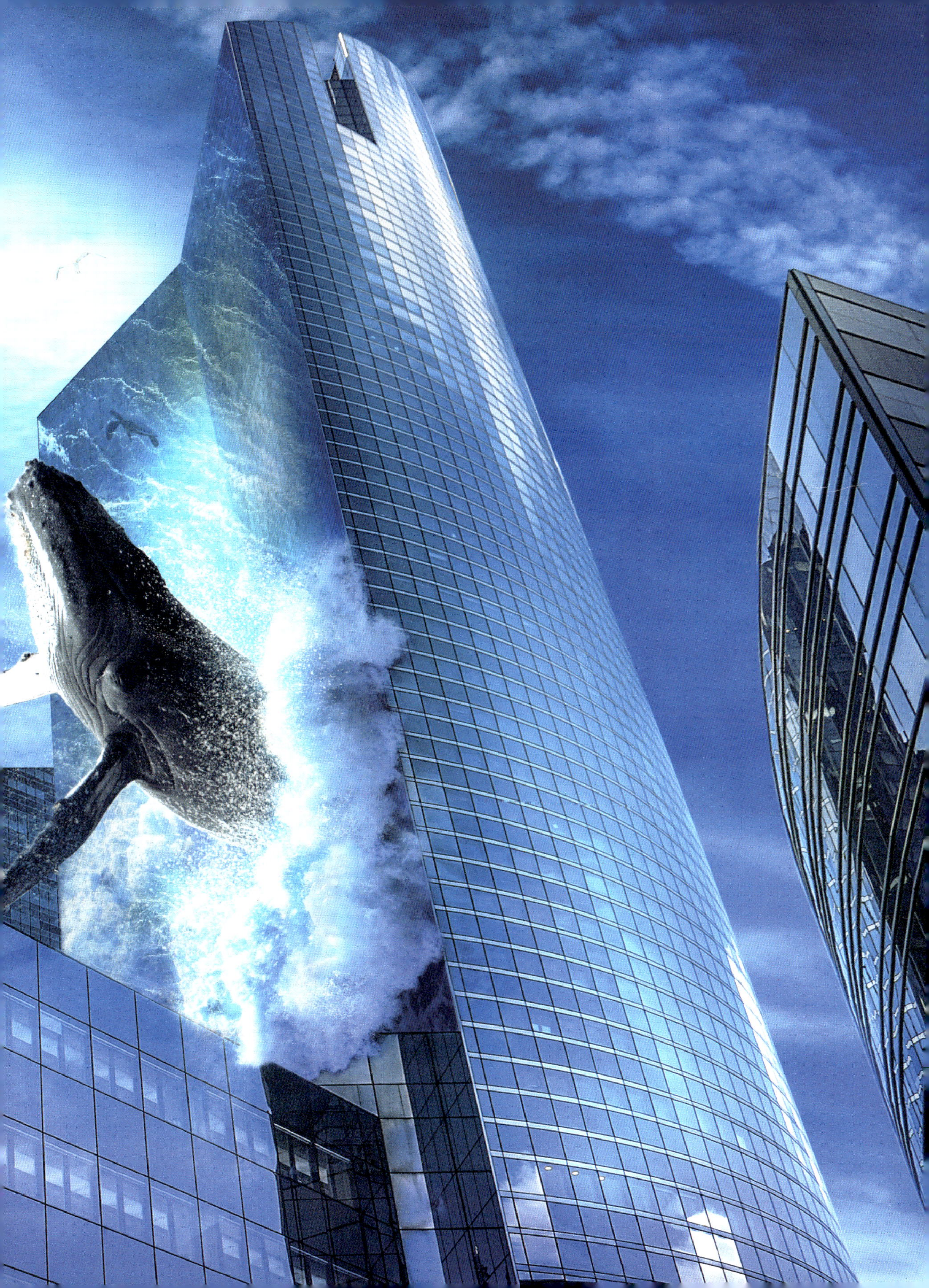

TEZI GABUNIA

#PORTRAIT

Tbilisi-based Tezi Gabunia (b. 1987) graduated in architecture, but he mainly creates series of installations and paints. The artist calls his method 'falsification'. He uses it to reflect upon absolute virtualization, which he claims is the basic feature of the contemporary world. 'An artwork is a result of industrialized production, not creation', states Tezi. 'as the production process is completely industrialized, which makes massive production in a short time possible'.

The concept is explored in the 'Put Your Head into Gallery' series, where the artist creates four models of rooms in famous galleries. In each miniature copy there is a show to see: while in the Saatchi Gallery's room Gabunia installs his own solo exhibition (even if it never happened), the Louvre presents Rubens, Tate Modern Hirst and the Gagosian Gallery Lichtenstein. The mini-versions of the galleries are transportable so they can be brought to the audience who can peep into the spaces, take a photograph and participate as an exhibit.

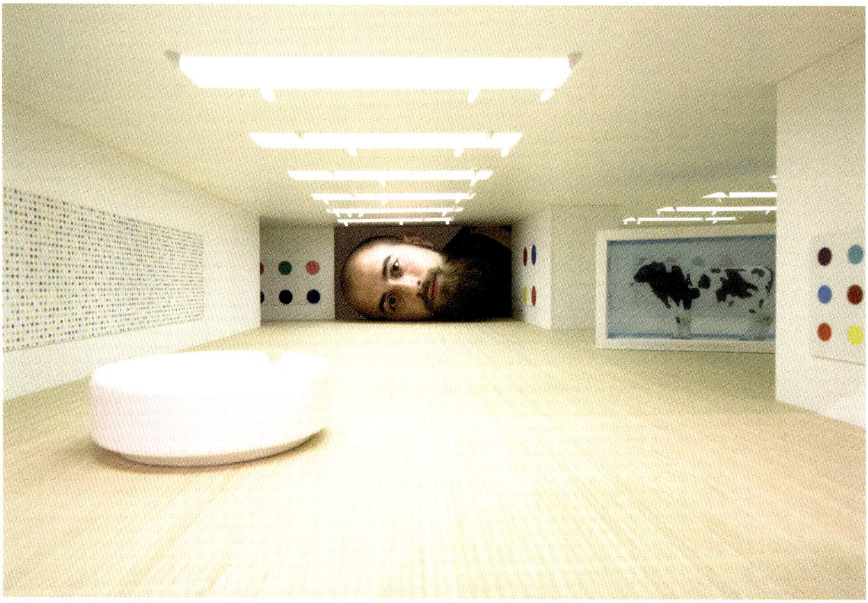

© TEZI GABUNIA, PUT YOUR HEAD INTO GALLERY -TATE MODERN (D. HIRST), 2015-2016
COURTESY OF POPIASHVILI GVABERIDZE WINDOW PROJECT

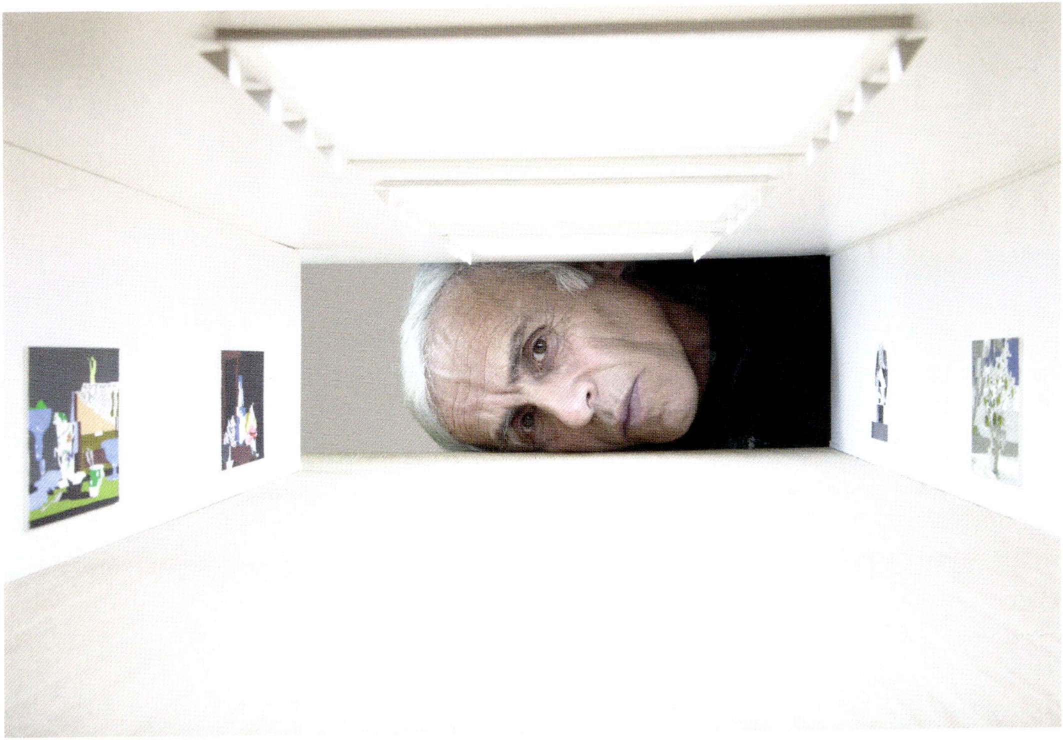

© TEZI GABUNIA, PUT YOUR HEAD INTO GALLERY - SAATCHI GALLERY (T. GABUNIA), 2015-2016
COURTESY OF POPIASHVILI GVABERIDZE WINDOW PROJECT

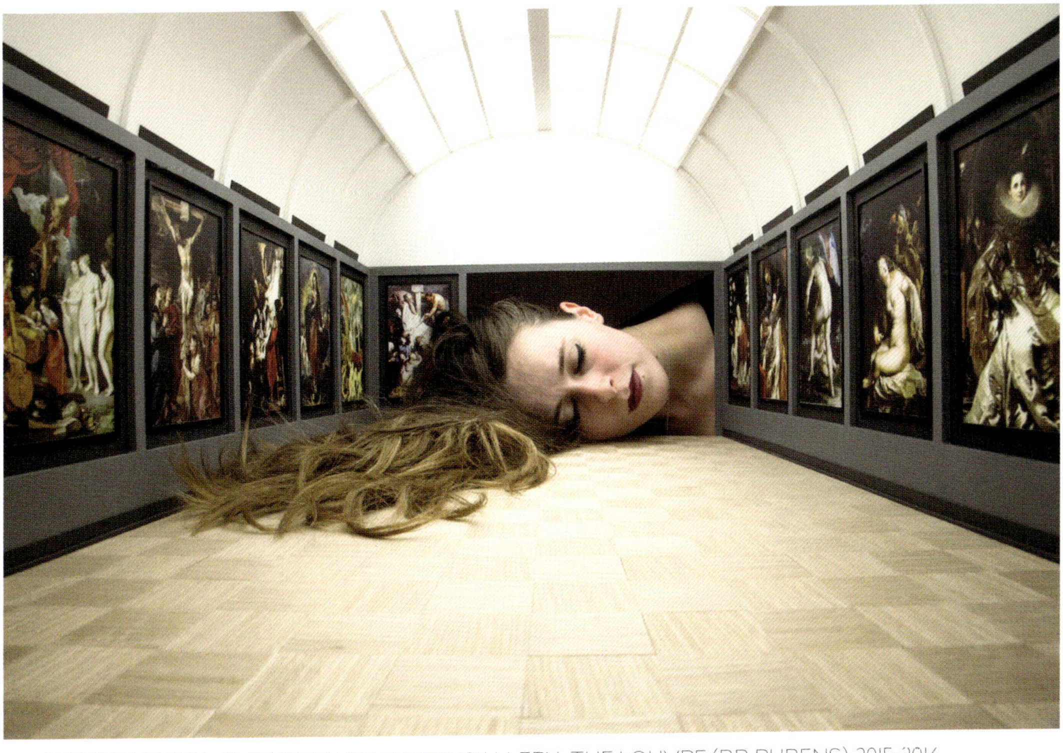

© TEZI GABUNIA, PUT YOUR HEAD INTO GALLERY -THE LOUVRE (P.P. RUBENS), 2015-2016
COURTESY OF POPIASHVILI GVABERIDZE WINDOW PROJECT

CHRISTOPHE GILBERT

#BODY

Brussels-based advertising photographer Christophe Gilbert is a photo-manipulation specialist. As he often stresses, he is a perfectionist as well as a detail-maniac. The way he retouches the pictures and how he plays with forms is impressive. Interestingly Christophe believes that photography is not so much to do with technique, but rather with having a good eye. And 'it isn't about what you see' he says, 'or even how you see things anymore, but about how you want things to be seen. Pictures with a goal.'

According to Christophe a good idea lies at the core of each image and the photographer's role is to capture it satisfactorily. They should have the whole picture in their head before even starting to work. Far from boring, his visual ideas are witty and arresting. Keen on experimenting and re-inventing things, Christophe comes up with some truly exceptional ideas.

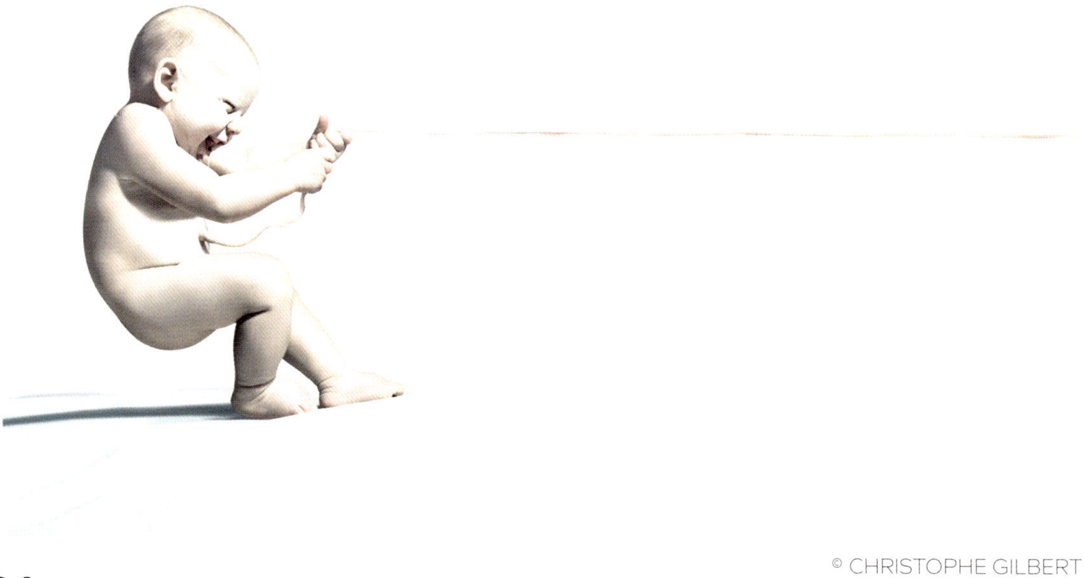

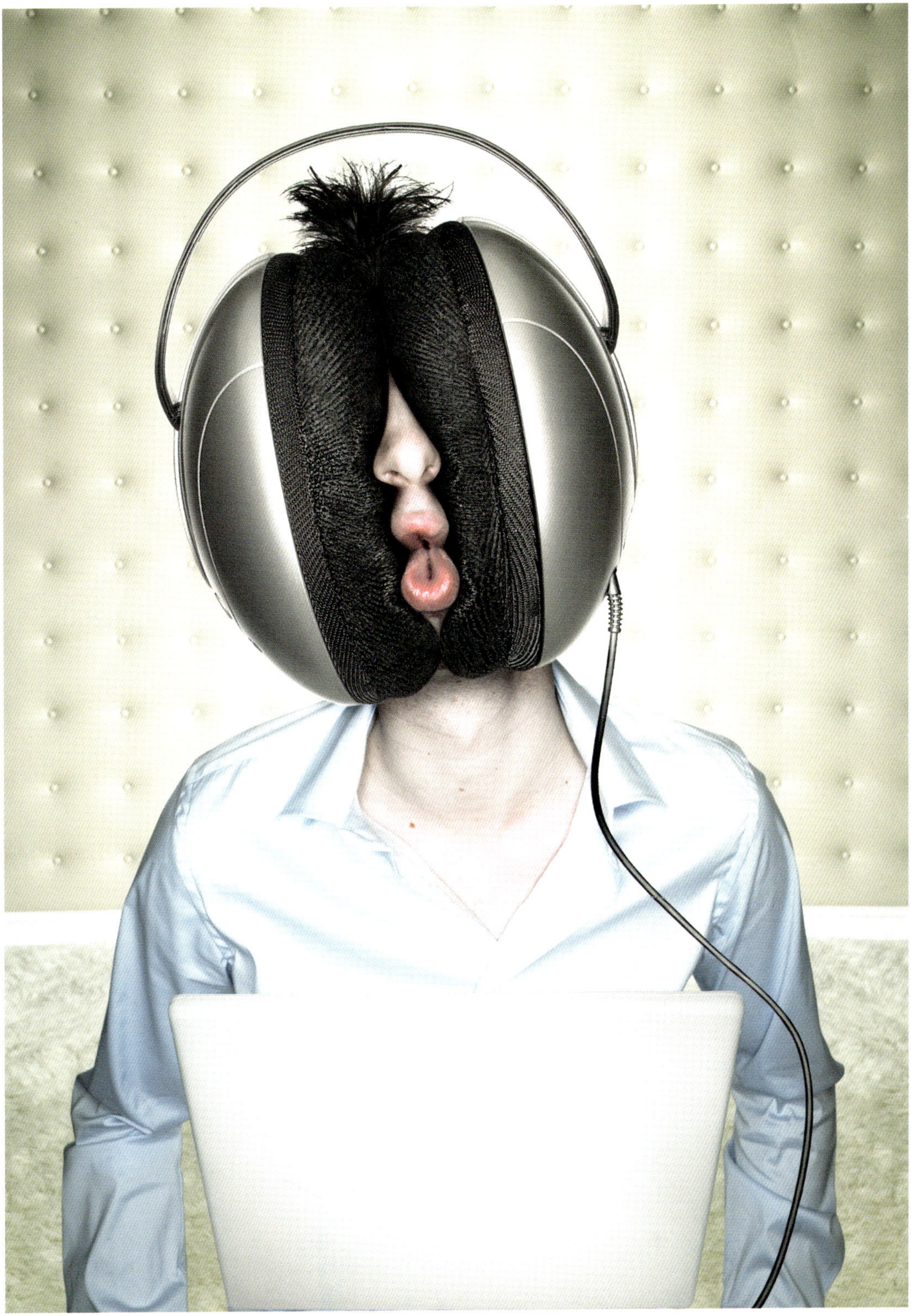

© CHRISTOPHE GILBERT

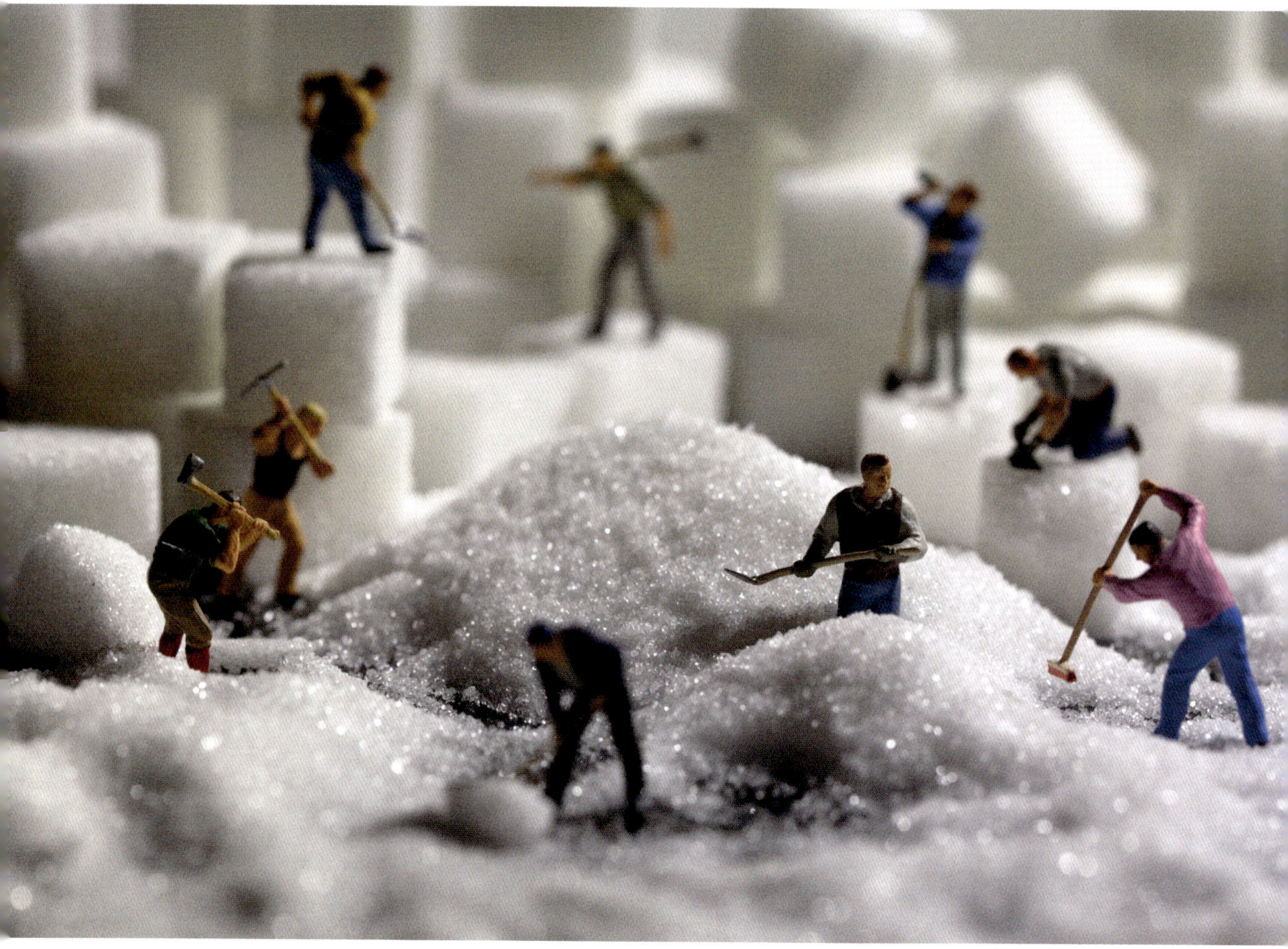
© DAVID GILLIVER, GRANULATING SUGAR

DAVID GILLIVER

#LITTLE PEOPLE

David Gilliver's 'Little People' are only 2 cm (0.8 in) tall, but their tiny world is as complex and colourful as our real one. The Glasgow-based artist has been working on the series since 2001. Playing with proportions and using common objects, the photographer creates miniatures dioramas. 'More often than not', he says, 'I place the figures inside scenarios where they have a gargantuan task to complete which sometimes invokes a sense of sympathy inside me for them'.

In each miniature scene, David comes up with original and humorous ideas. The figurines interact with objects to mimic our everyday life or comment on it in an amusing way. Achieving this effect on such a small scale is impressive. The challenging process starts with finding the characters online, while ideas for compositions are down to David's active imagination. David graduated from the Fine Art Photography course at Glasgow School of Art. Apart from macro photography, he specializes in light painting photography.

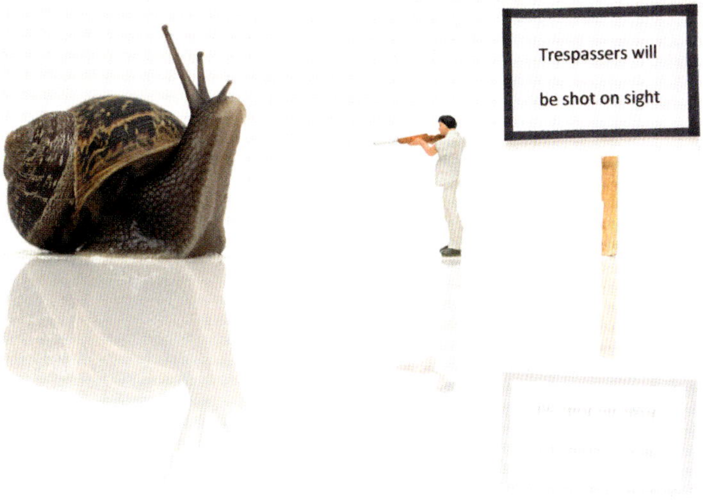

© DAVID GILLIVER, NO TRESPASSING

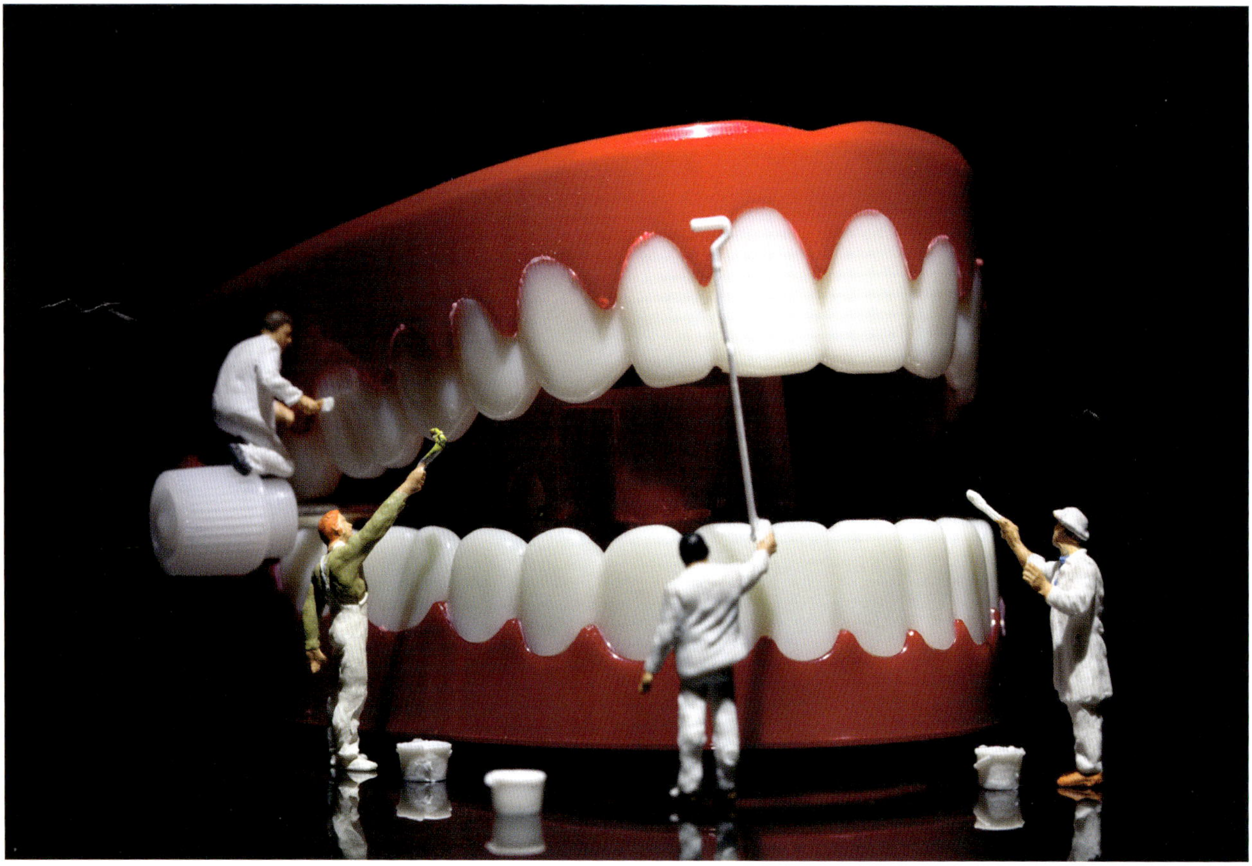

© DAVID GILLIVER, SCALE AND POLISH

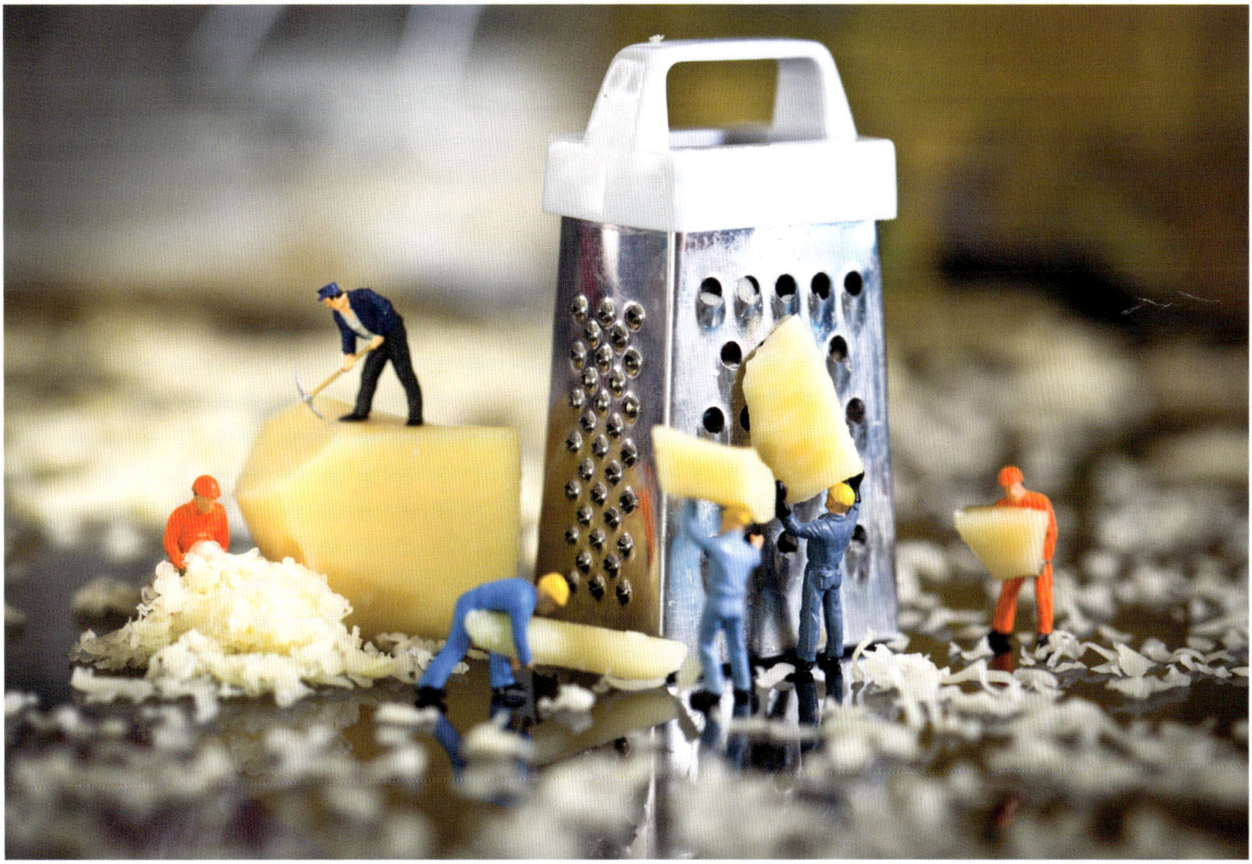

© DAVID GILLIVER, YOU'RE DOING A GRATE JOB LITTLE MEN

FELIX HERNANDEZ

#TOYS

Mexican photographer Felix Hernandez calls his works 'dream-phography' as his works are informed by his dreams and thoughts. To create his imaginative compositions, he uses small toys employing photomontage to show them as if they were part of the real world. Images are taken in the photographer's studio and in various locations, then retouched and combined. A macro lens and a 'focus stacking technique' are used to merge multiple images. The camera shots and digital manipulation are equally important in Felix's practice.

The scenes are very atmospheric, which is often achieved using flour that imitates snow or cigarettes to create fog. Apart from his artistic work, Felix is also a commercial photographer and works as a designer for creative firms and advertising agencies. He also organizes photography workshops and contributes to photography magazines. Felix remarks that his photographs are not 'what exists there, but portray what exists in me'.

HERNANDEZDREAMPHOGRAPHY.COM

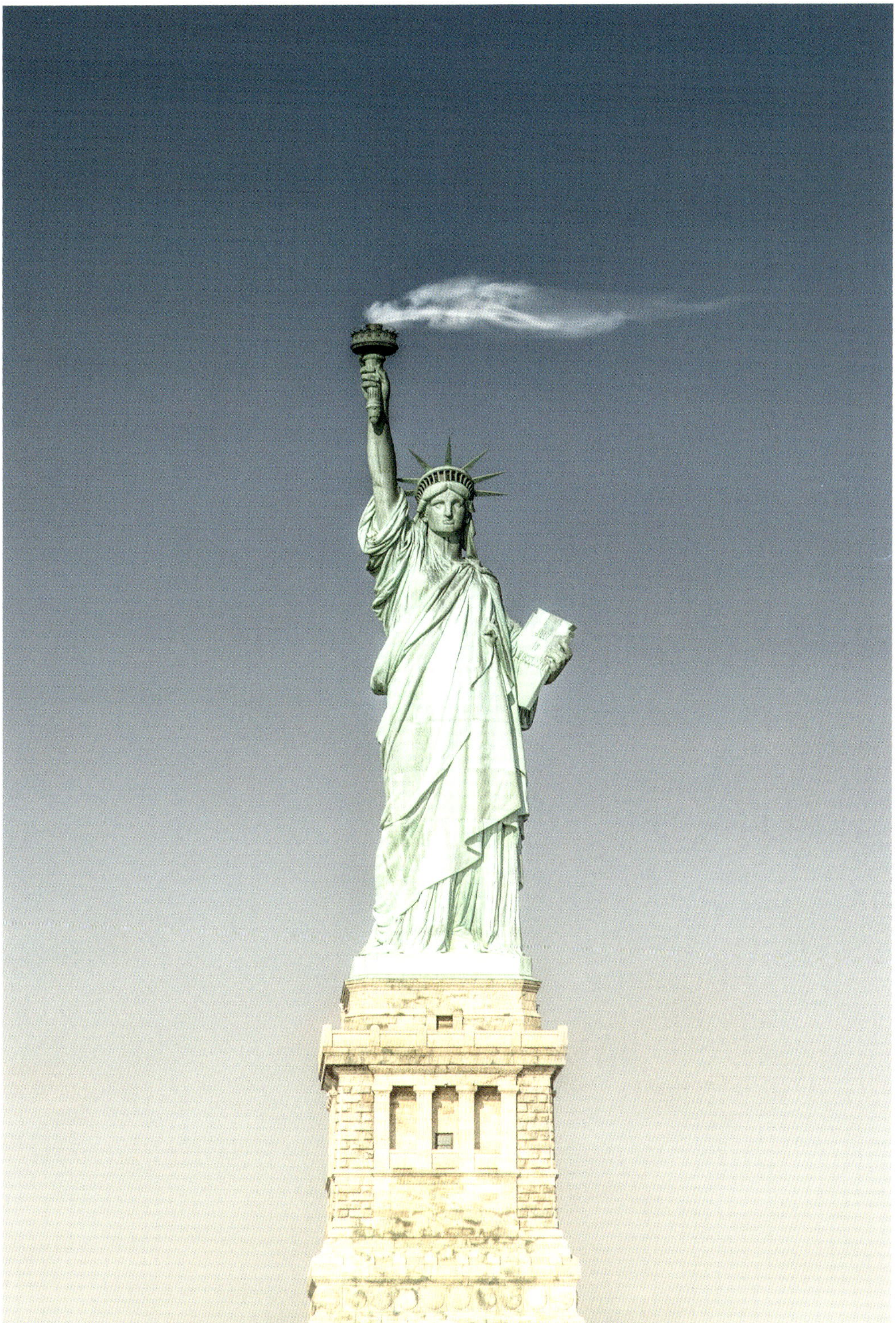

© FELIX HERNANDEZ, LIBERTY EXTINT

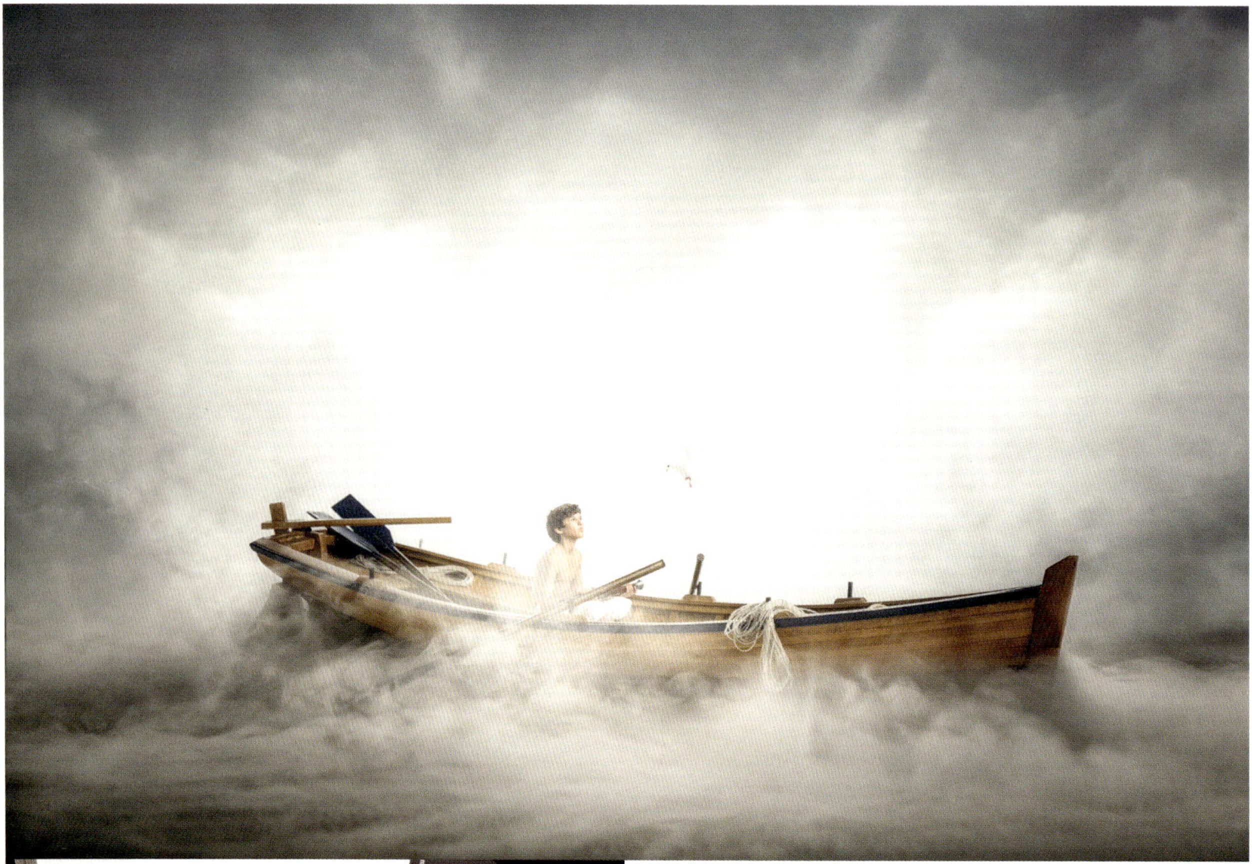

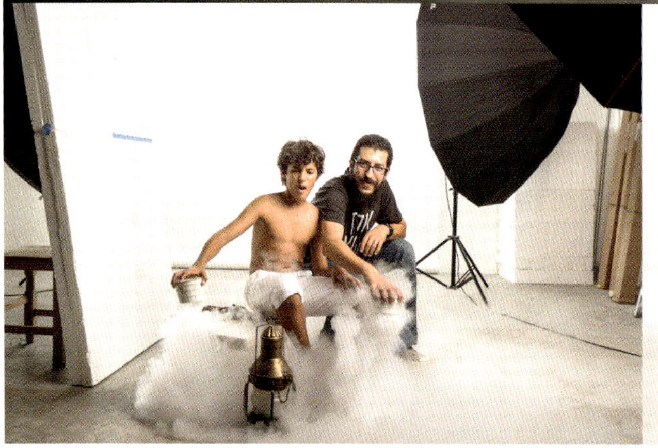

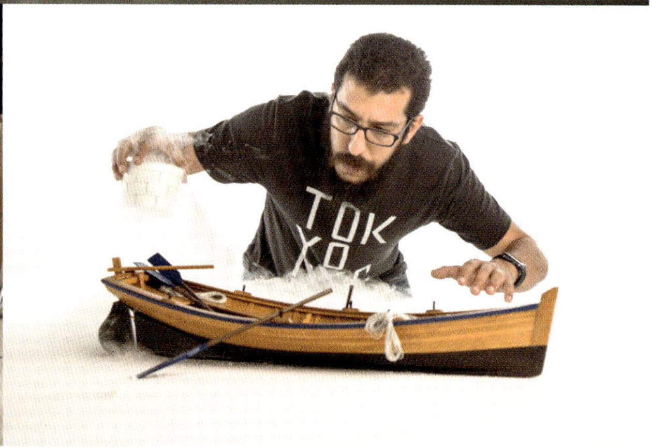

© FELIX HERNANDEZ, THE BOY AND THE DOVE

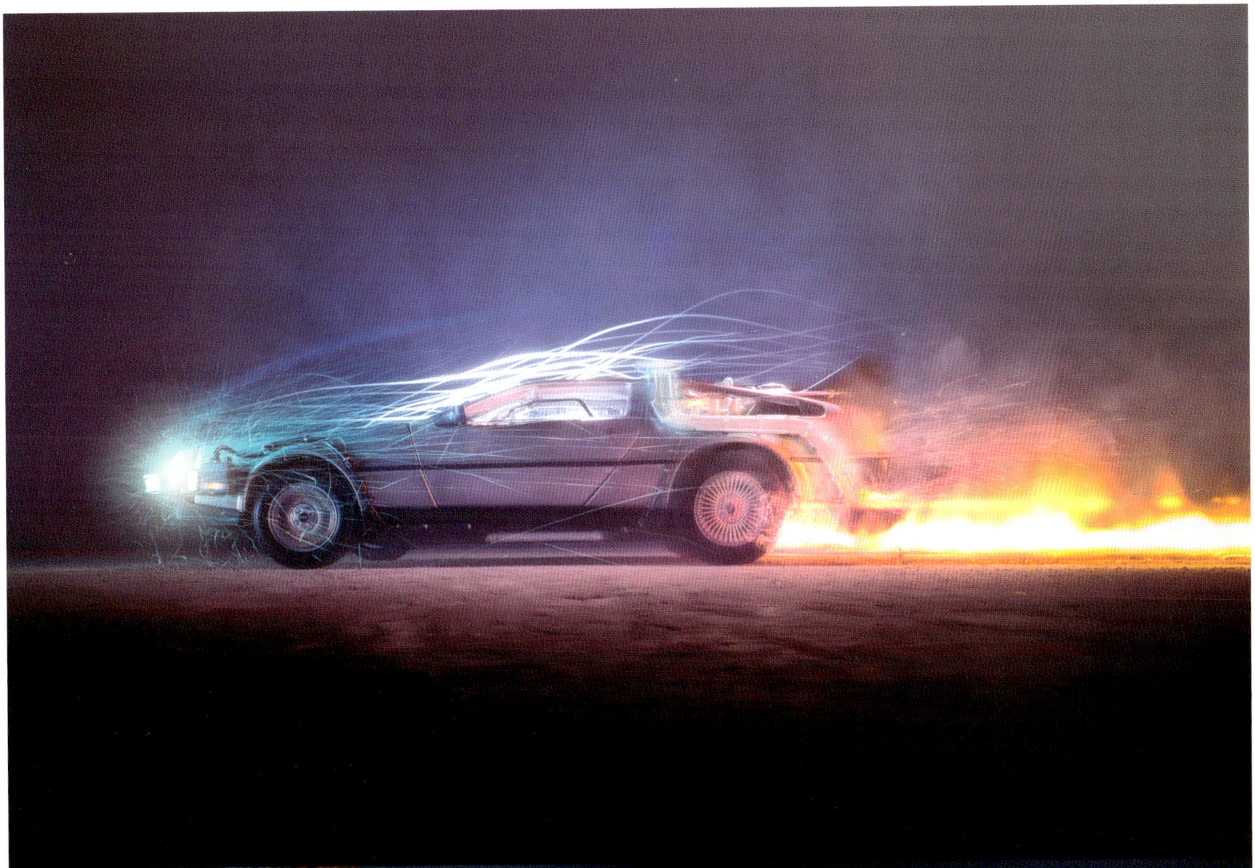

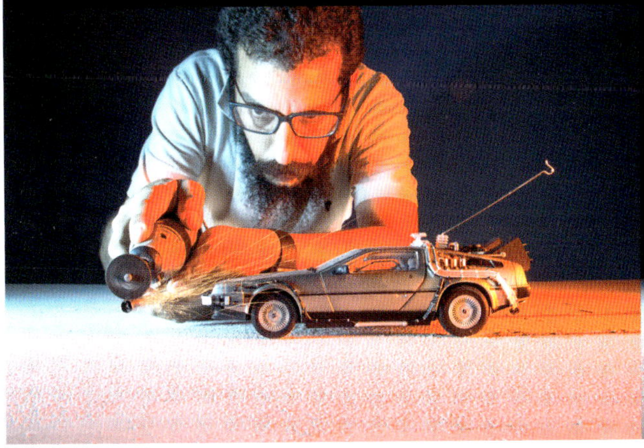

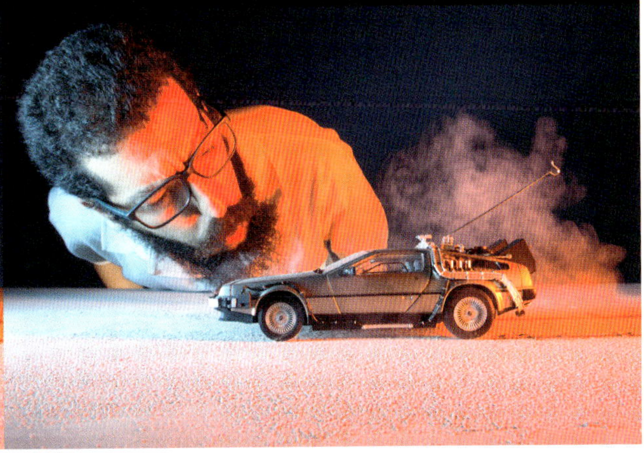

© FELIX HERNANDEZ, BTTF

MICHAEL HUGHES

Michael Hughes (b. 1952) has been photographing since 1973. As he states, he uses photography not only to pose questions about how we live and who we are, but also about the way we look at the world. His 'Souvenirs' series, which started in 1999 on the Loreley and has been developed since in France, Egypt, UK, Greece and Singapore among other destinations, is an example of how he challenges our worldview.

The idea is to capture well-known landmarks around the globe. Small figurines, postcards or tickets that feature images of famous statues or buildings replace the real sites. It's an ironic comment on tourism and modern sightseeing habits. Each composition includes the photographer's hand holding a particular souvenir, stressing his personal involvement so that viewers can imagine their own. Born in London, Michael decided to move to Berlin permanently at the age of thirty.

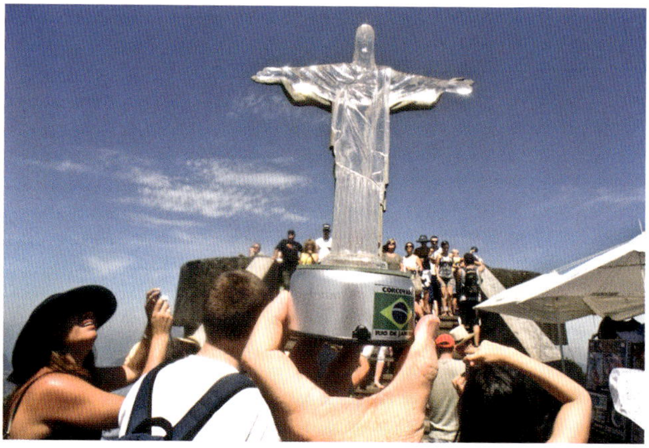

© MICHAEL HUGHES, CHRIST THE REDEEMER LIGHTED ACRYLIC MODEL, RIO DE JANEIRO, BRAZIL

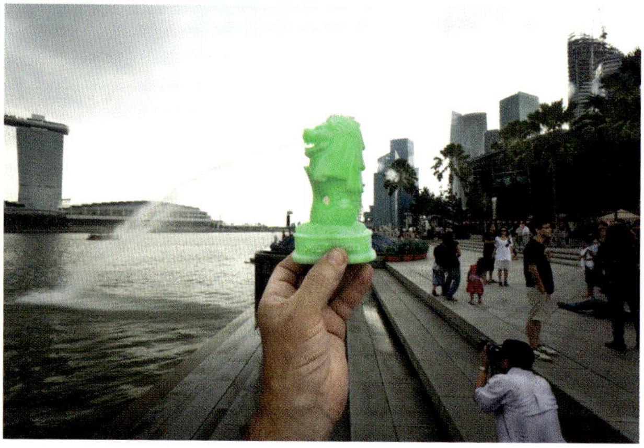

© MICHAEL HUGHES, MERLION STATUETTE, SINGAPORE

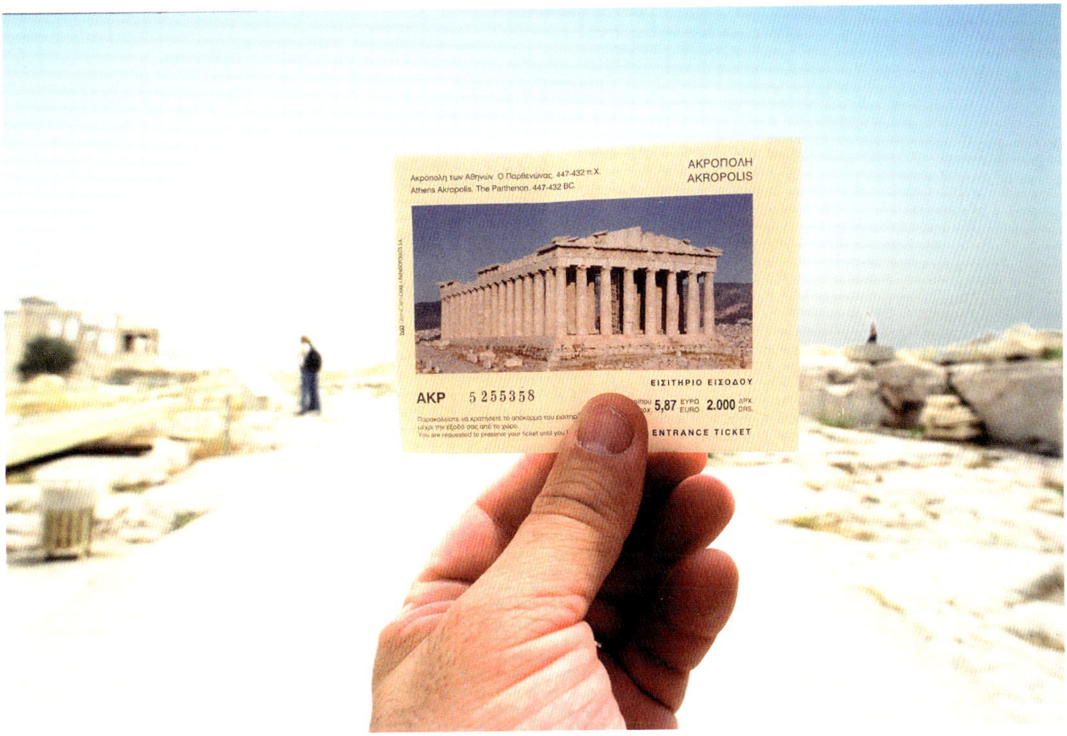

© MICHAEL HUGHES, ACROPOLIS, ATHENS, GREECE

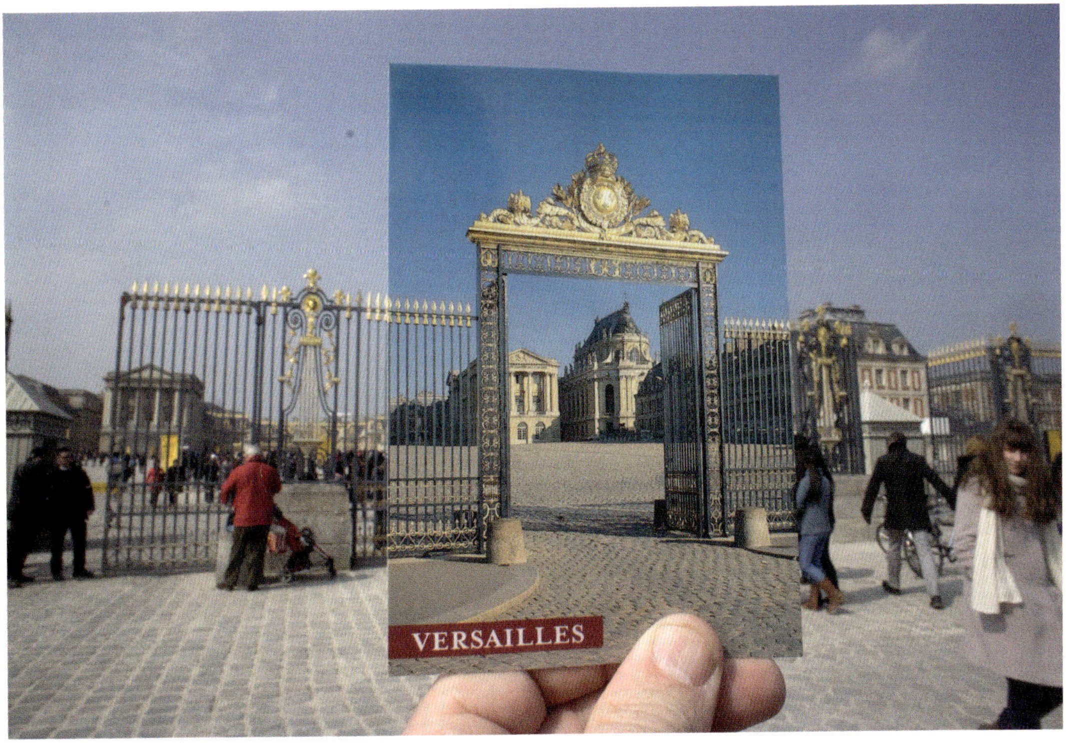

© MICHAEL HUGHES, VERSAILLES, FRANCE

GABRIEL ISAK

Gabriel Isak has an incredible sense of both composition and colour. His images are sharp, both formally and conceptually. The signature feature of his work is that people appearing in the photos are always featured in a peculiar and puzzling way. The images devoid of human presence are rather surreal and seduce the viewers with their atmosphere of mystery. 'Let Go' is a part of 'The Blue Journey' series, which as the photographer states, is an invitation 'to enter a dream world, where solitude is more than just being alone.'

Dream-like atmospheres 'and perplexing scenes mirror psychological states. Similar emotions fuel the image featuring a girl on a staircase, standing as if on the edge of an abyss. Originally from Sweden, the photographer now lives and works in New York. While the medium is a metaphor for experiences of the soul for Gabriel, the photographs are simple in form but rich in ideas and emotions.

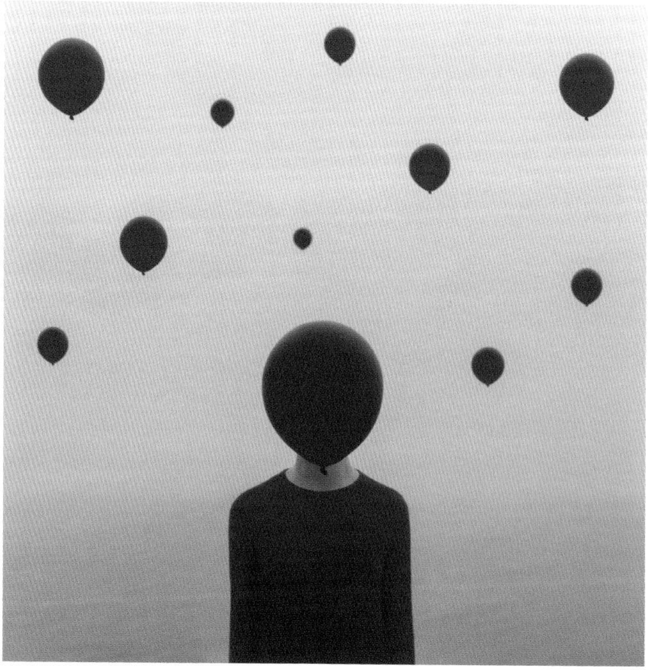

© GABRIEL ISAK, LET GO, 2014

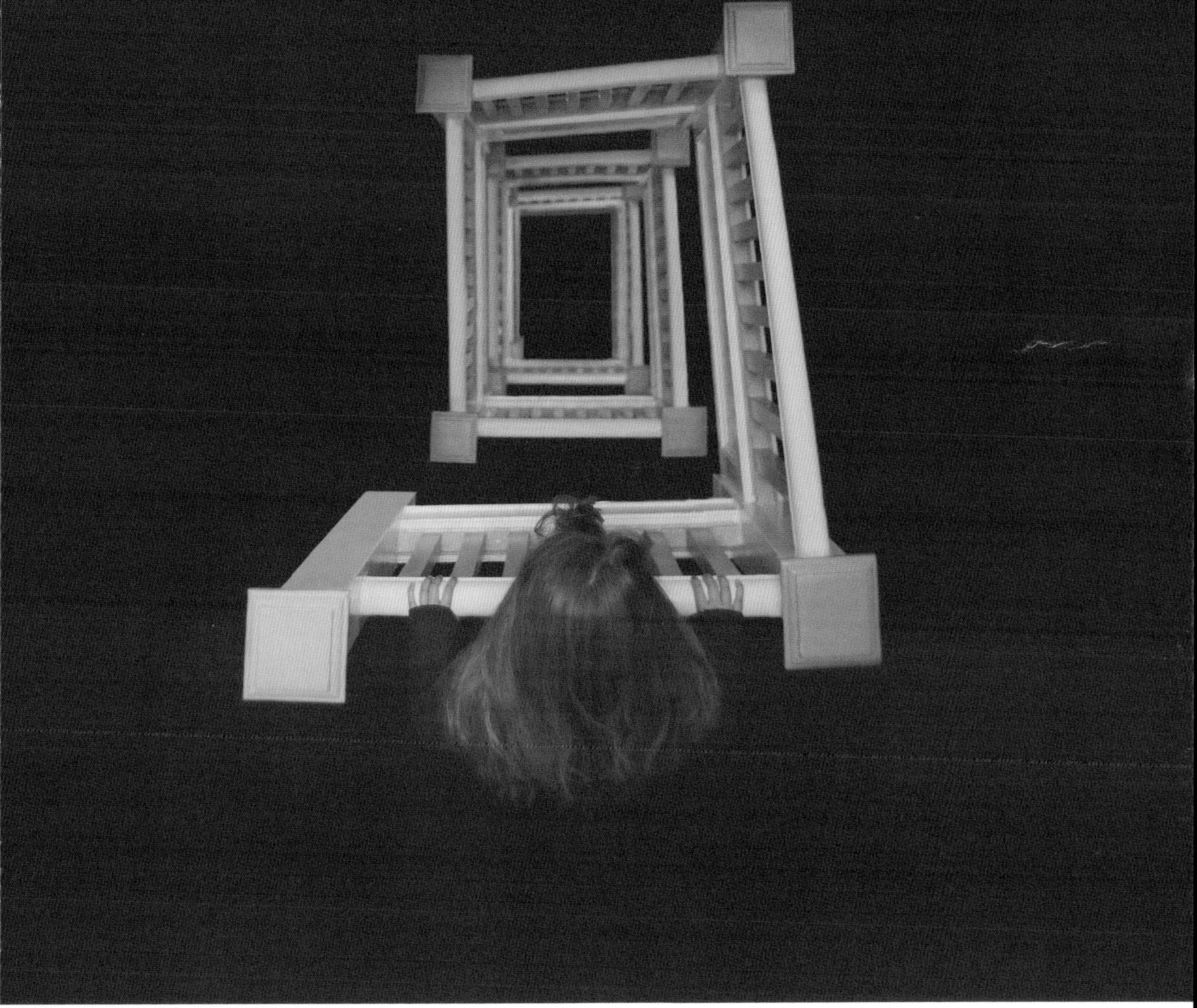

© GABRIEL ISAK, IN A DREAM, 2014

ERIK JOHANSSON

The duet between camera and Photoshop is particularly successful in the works of Erik Johansson (b. 1985). Initially fascinated by drawing, he got his first digital camera when he was fifteen. Pressing the trigger however was not enough, the photographer wanted to do something more with the photos. Computer manipulation seemed the best way to develop his practice. Erik is self-taught both in photography as well as retouching. When mastering illusion, his goal is to make the photos look as realistic as possible. 'For me the realism has always been very important and it's a challenge to make a sketch come to life in a photo', he says and always starts with a sketch of the idea.

Erik was born in Sweden (the Swedish countryside and the northern landscapes are major inspirations), lived in Berlin for a few years and is currently based in Prague. He works on both personal and commissioned projects.

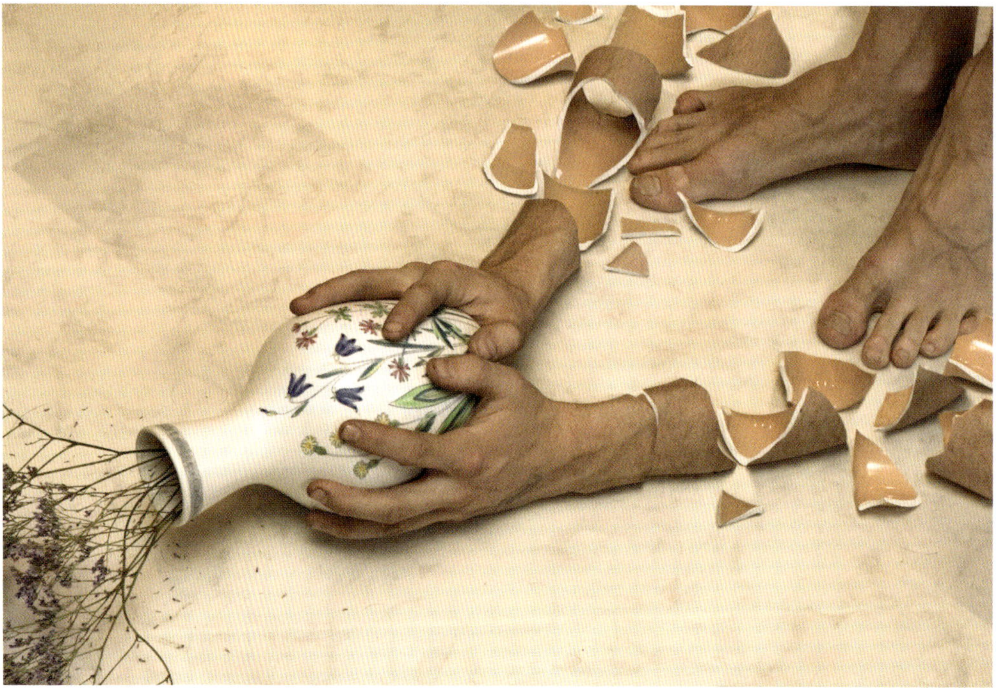

© ERIK JOHANSSON, ARMS BREAK , VASES DON'T, 2008

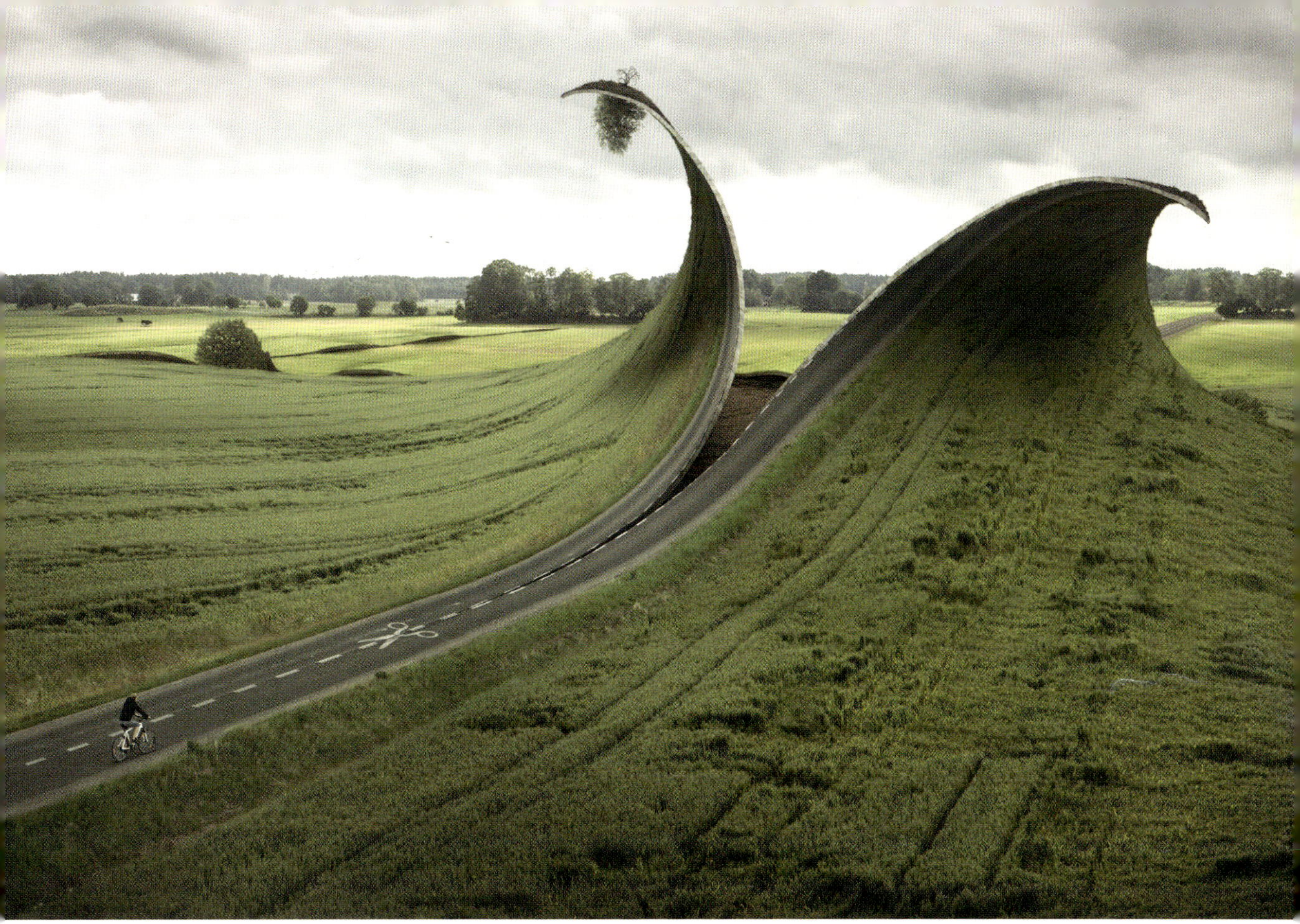

#BODY

#LAND-SCAPE

ERIKJOHANSSONPHOTO.COM

MIKE KELLEY

#LAND-SCAPE

While Mike Kelley is a great architectural photographer specializing in interiors and commercial spaces, his passion is aerial and aviation photography. The inspiration comes from plane-watching at one of the busiest airports in the world in Los Angeles, where the photographer is based. 'My intent was to capture only planes that flew out of LAX', stresses the photographer, 'highlighting and emphasizing what an incredible airport that this city has. It's really fascinating to look at all the planes heading in different directions, ferrying people all over the world, all originating from Los Angeles'.

Mike is particularly interested in photos that are not simply snapshots of a single moment, so his compositions of planes taking off and landing undergo a process of digital manipulation (taking hundreds of single snaps to make the final photo). Surreal as they may look, the images speak volumes about air traffic as well as the scale of air travel today.

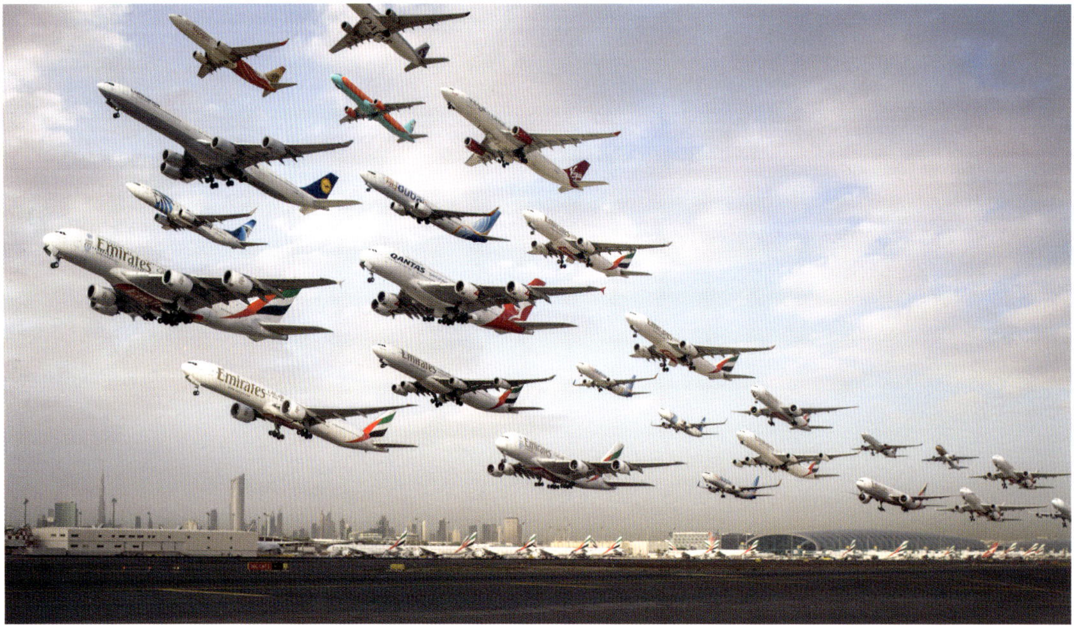

© MIKE KELLEY, DUBAI INTERNATIONAL 12R (MORNING HEAVY DEPARTURES)

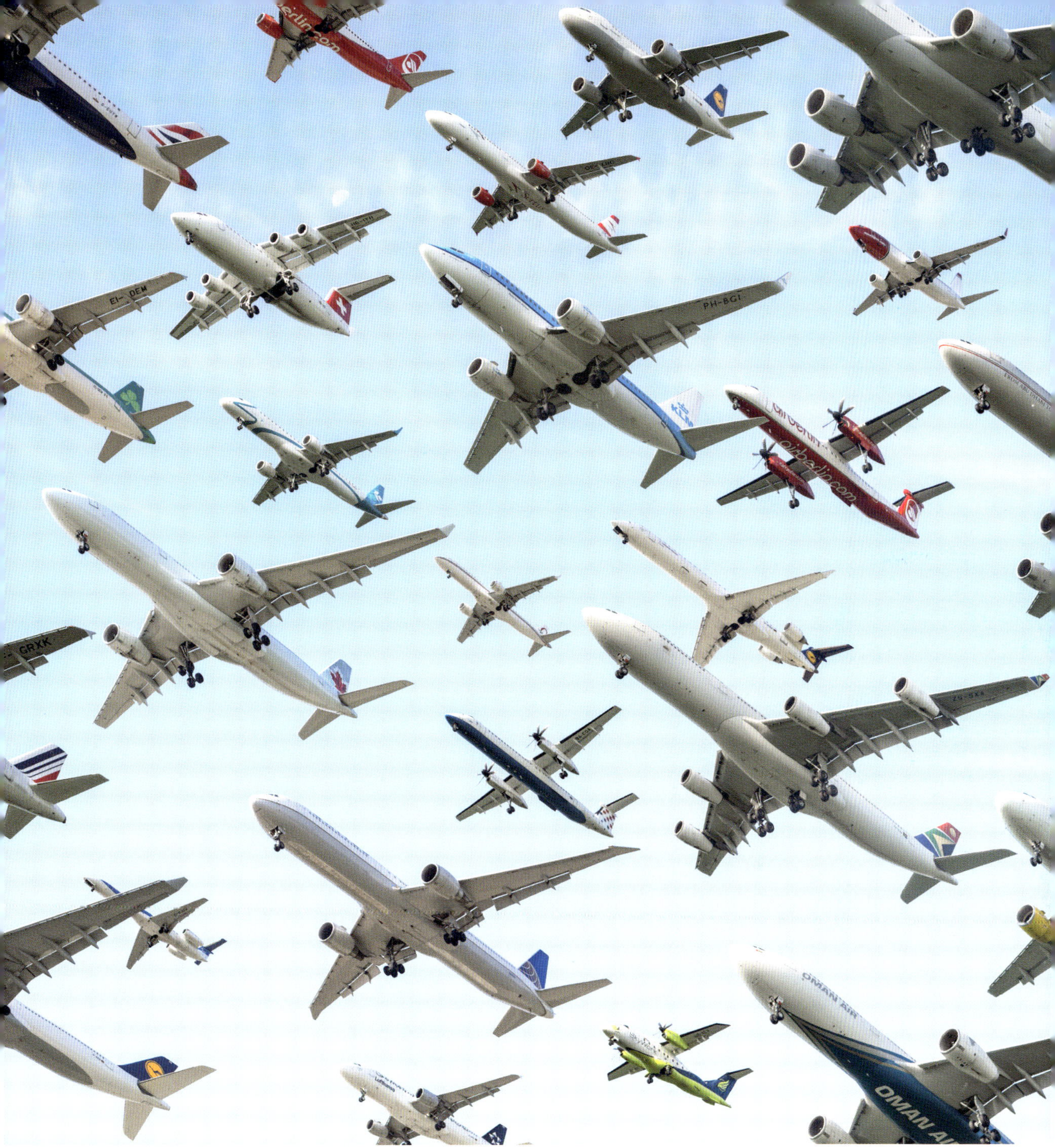

© MIKE KELLEY, FLUGHAFEN MÜNCHEN 08R (DECISION HEIGHT)

JULIEN KNEZ

#NOW &THEN

An art director based in Paris and a graduate of graphic design at Les Gobelins, Julien Knez pays a very sentimental tribute to his city in his photography. It all started when Julien found photos of Paris taken between 1871 and 1968 that inspired him to find the sites and photograph them from the same angle. The historical shot is always a part of the composition bridging the city of today with its fascinating history. 'When historical photographs are inserted into contemporary settings', the photographer comments, 'we open astonishing windows to the past. More than ever, the inquisitive contemporary spectator is plunged into the depths of time, as if given the opportunity to stroll on different stages, at the heart of history in the making'.

Some of Julien's images are atmospheric views of the old Paris, many relate to historical events like the liberation of the city in 1944 (one series celebrated the 70th anniversary of the end of the occupation of the French capital).

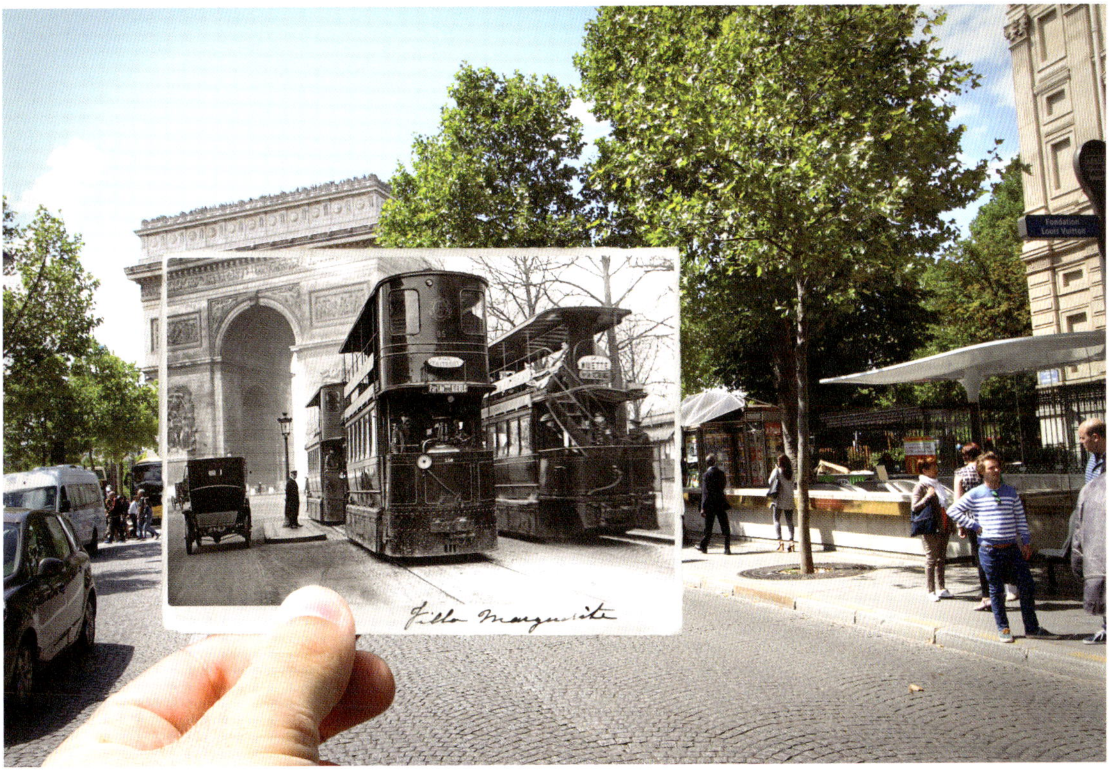

© JULIEN KNEZ, ARC DE TRIOMPHE 1909

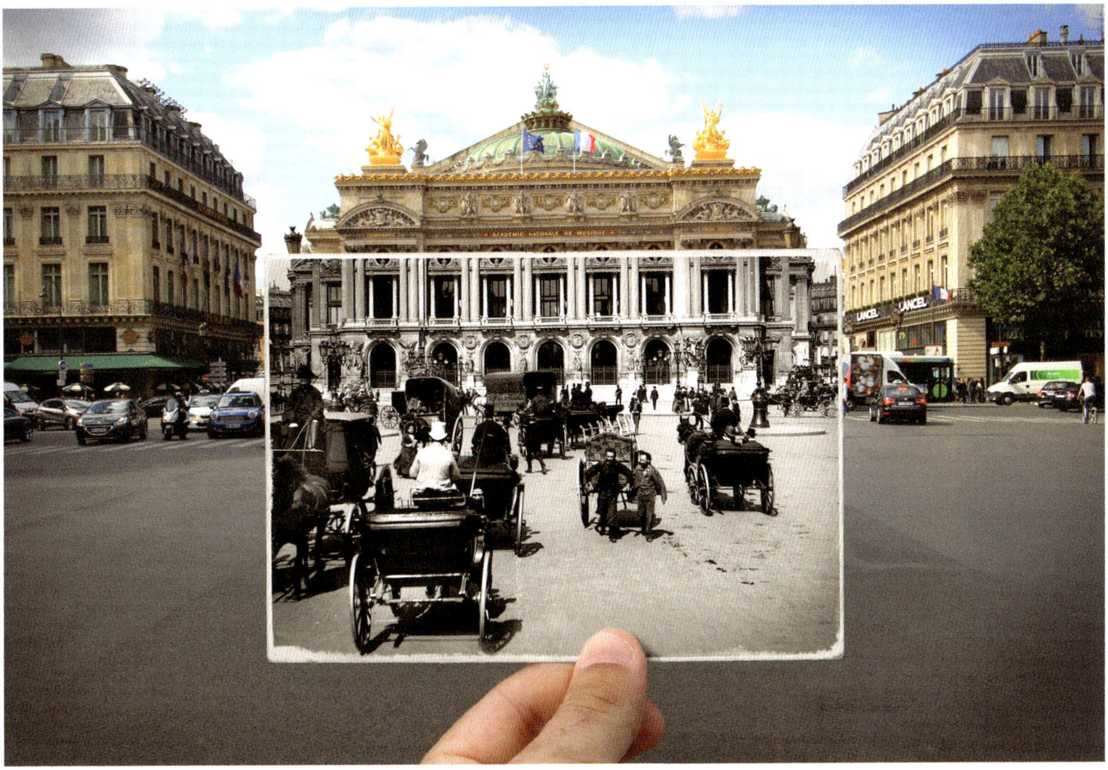

© JULIEN KNEZ, OPÉRA 1900

HUGH KRETSCHMER

Hugh Kretschmer's (b. 1960) photos fuse humour and imagination. As the photographer says, 'they are influenced by my myriad dreams and desires of what life could be, if only...' Hugh discovered photography at the age of thirteen. His father, who was a photo-instrumentation engineer for McDonnell Douglas during the Mercury through Apollo missions, was his tutor in the field.

Inspired by contemporary sculpture and painting, Hugh manipulates the images to trick the viewer's eye with quirky effects. Colour also plays a special role. Brilliantly executed shots, sometimes using irony, reflect on the human condition and issues common to us all. Insight into the photographer's fanciful approach is offered on his blog (hughkretschmer.tumblr.com) with stories on various projects and images from behind the scenes. Hugh lives in Los Angeles and splits his time between his artistic practice and work as an editorial and advertising photographer.

#TOYS #BODY

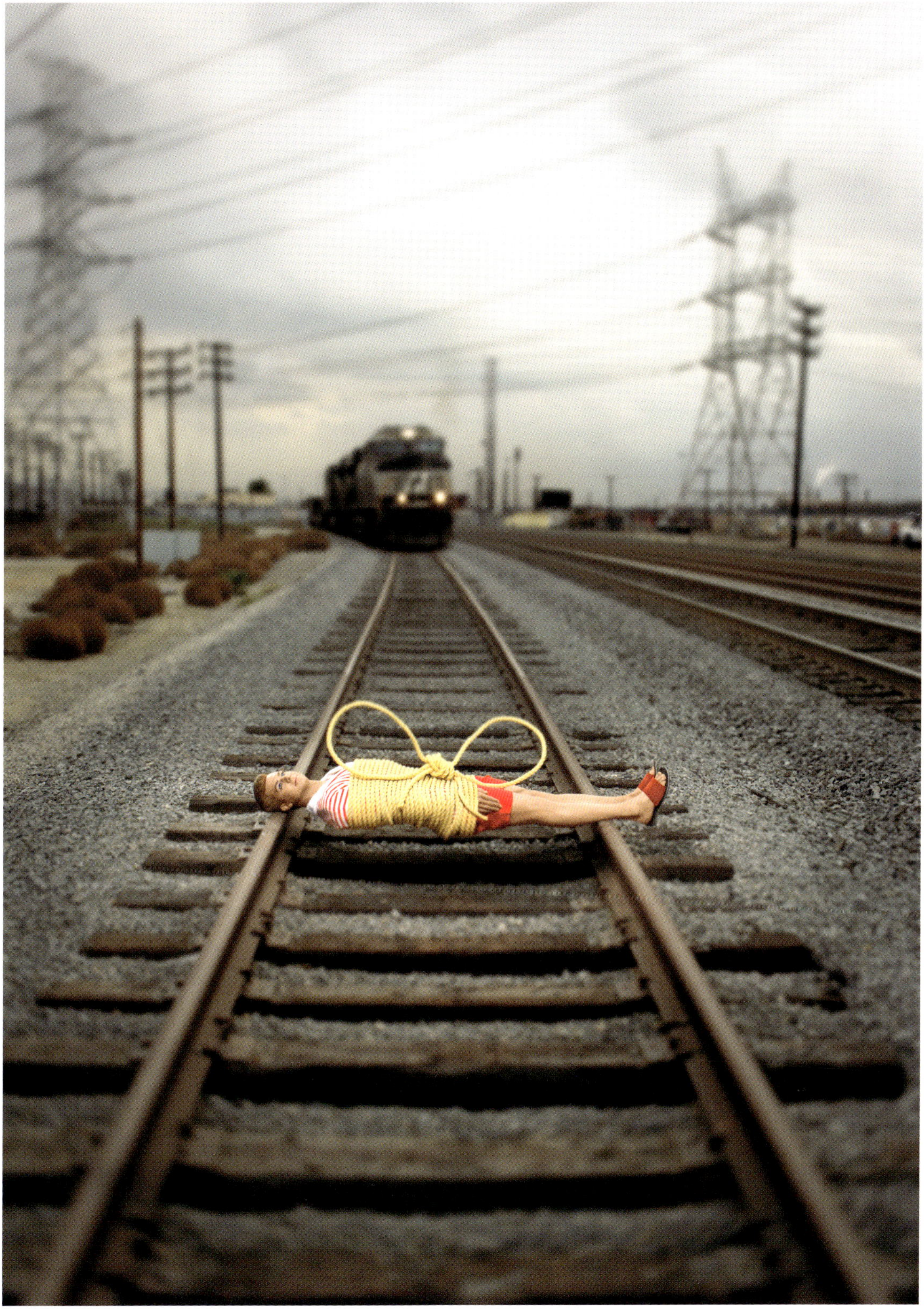

© HUGH KRETSCHMER, MISHAP

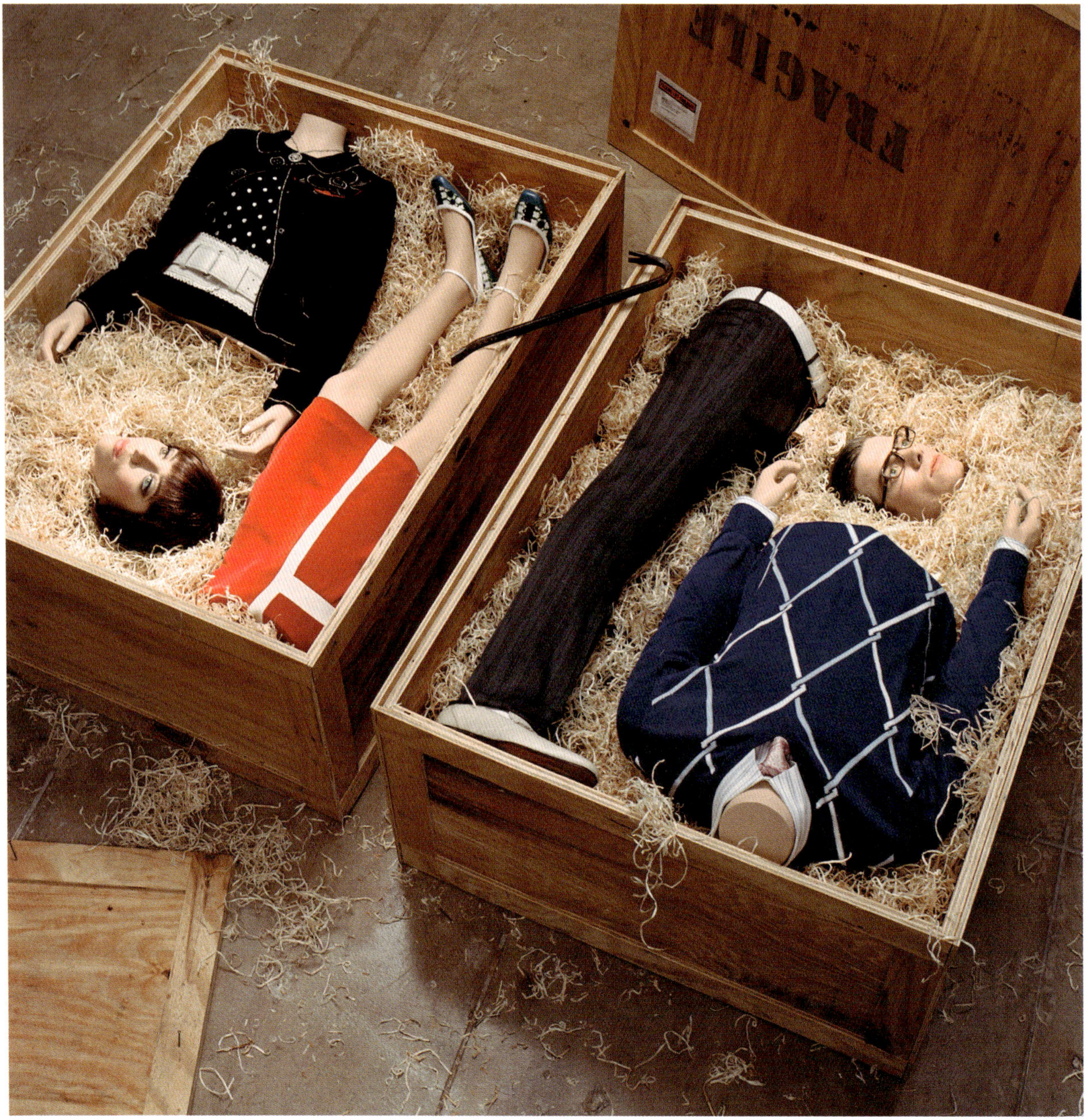

© HUGH KRETSCHMER, SPECIAL DELIVERY

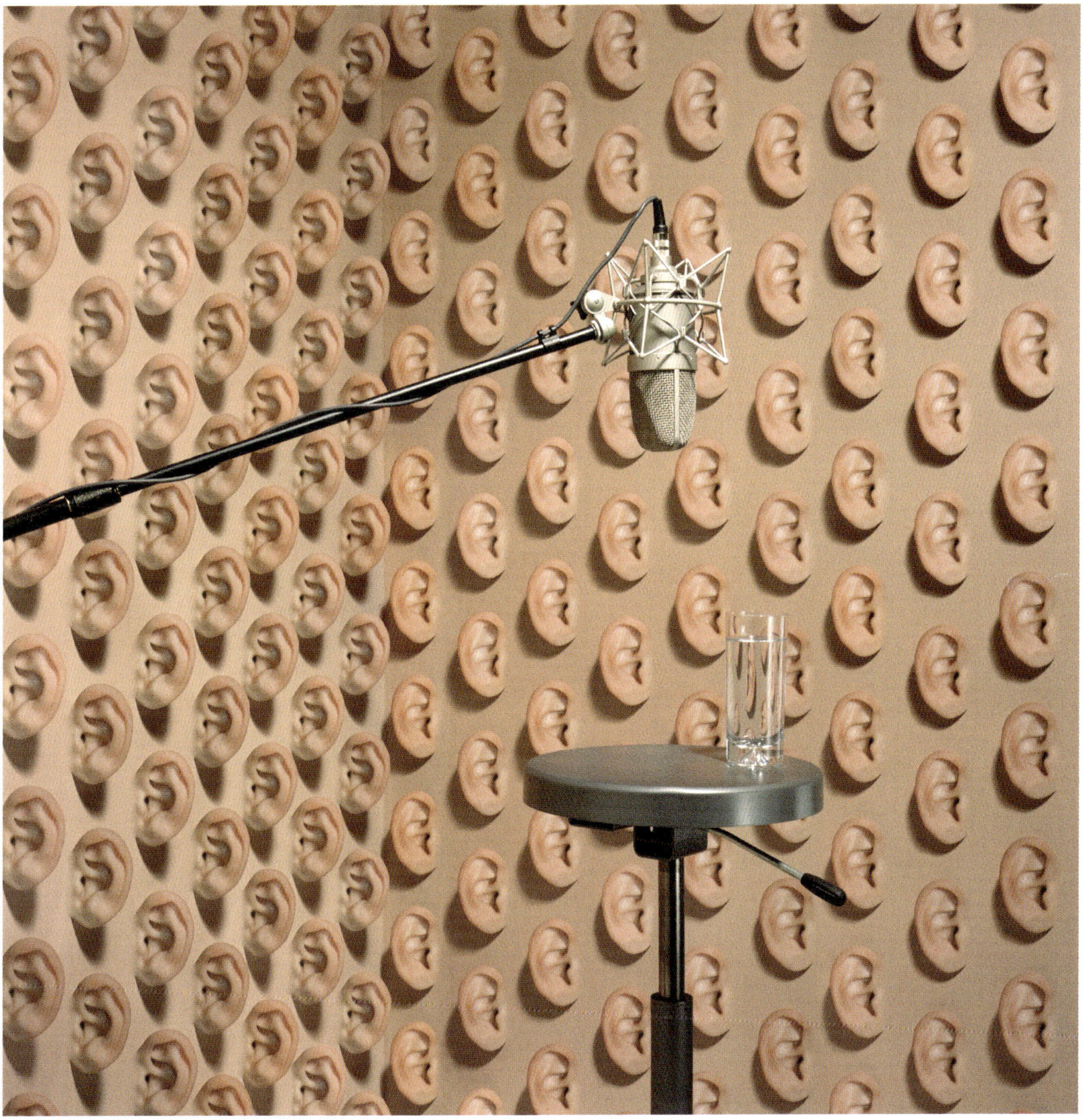

© HUGH KRETSCHMER, ALL EARS

BENOÎT LAPRAY

#TOYS

#ARCHI-TECTURE

Born in 1980, Lapray studied photography in Lyon and since graduation he has worked as an advertising photographer. The year 2010 marked the start of producing his own works. Four years later he decided to move to Paris to pursue his activity as freelance photographer and photo retoucher. He took part in many group shows and states his philosophy as: 'A photograph has to tell us a story'.

His images juxtapose characters from popular culture, which he sets against urban- or landscapes. Significantly enlarged models of super heroes from American comic books, Lego® figurines or dinosaur toys inhabit spaces more natural for human beings. Whether these are Lego® characters invading the Confluence district in Lyon or numerous dinosaurs walking through the La Défense district in Paris before dawn, the effect when two contrasting worlds confront each other is striking.

BENOITLAPRAY.COM

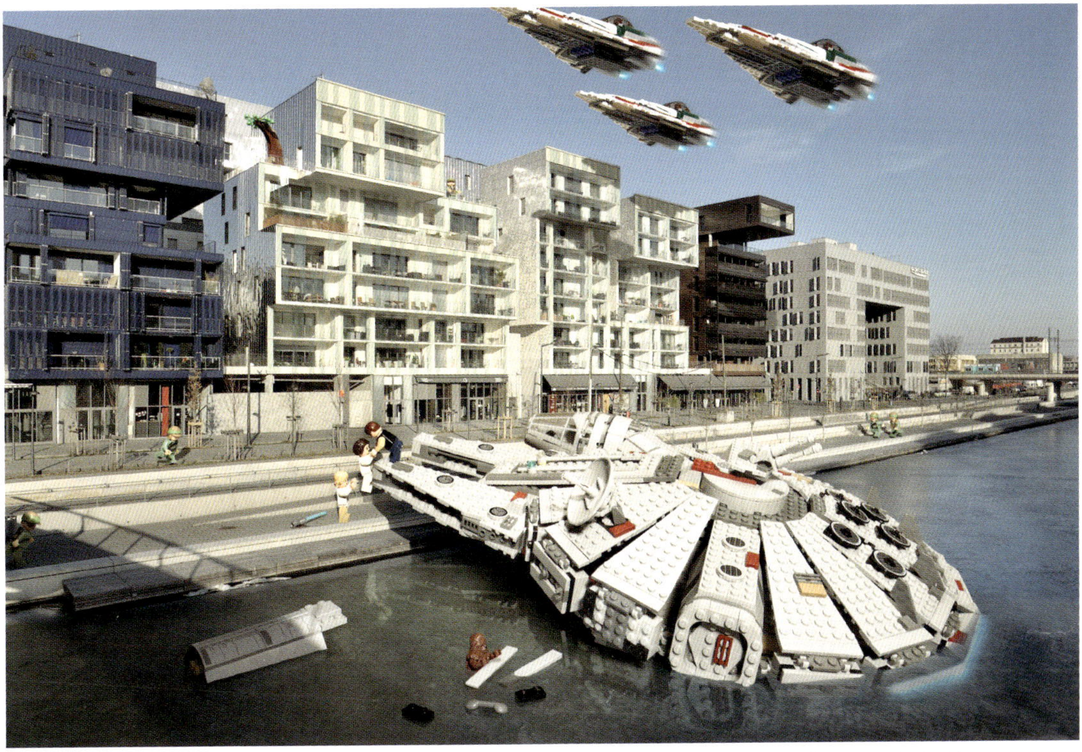

© TOY INVASION #05, BENOÎT LAPRAY (PHOTOGRAPHY), MATHIEU LATRY (RETOUCHING)

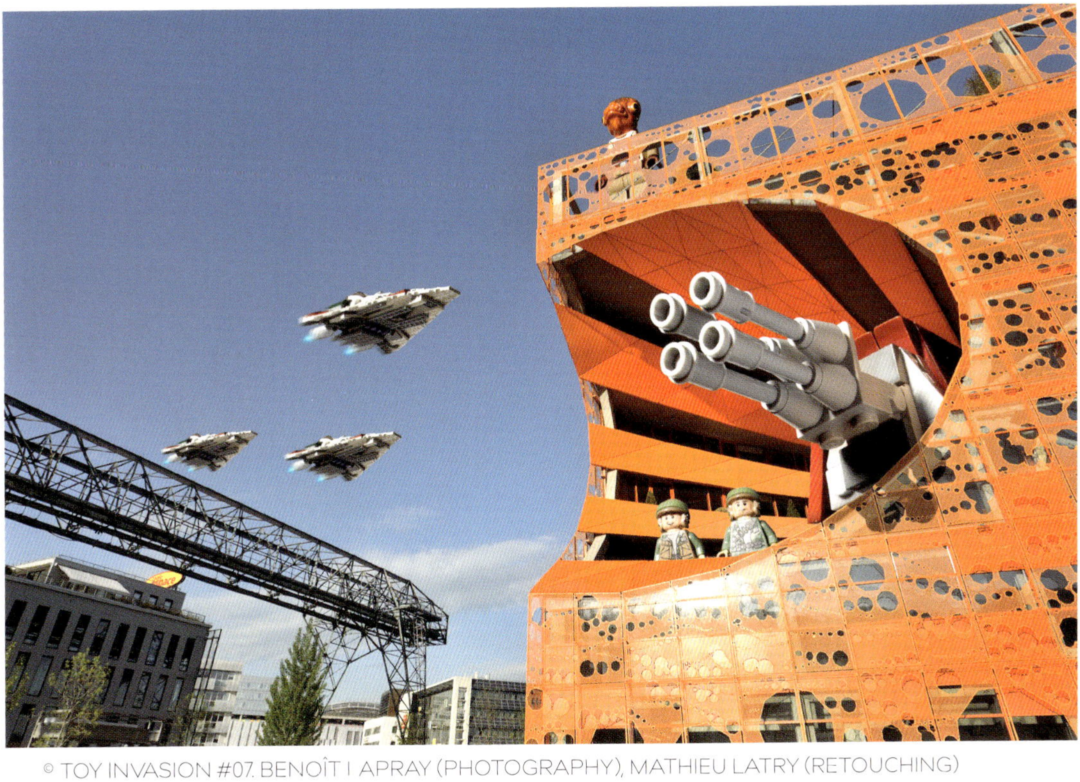

© TOY INVASION #07, BENOÎT LAPRAY (PHOTOGRAPHY), MATHIEU LATRY (RETOUCHING)

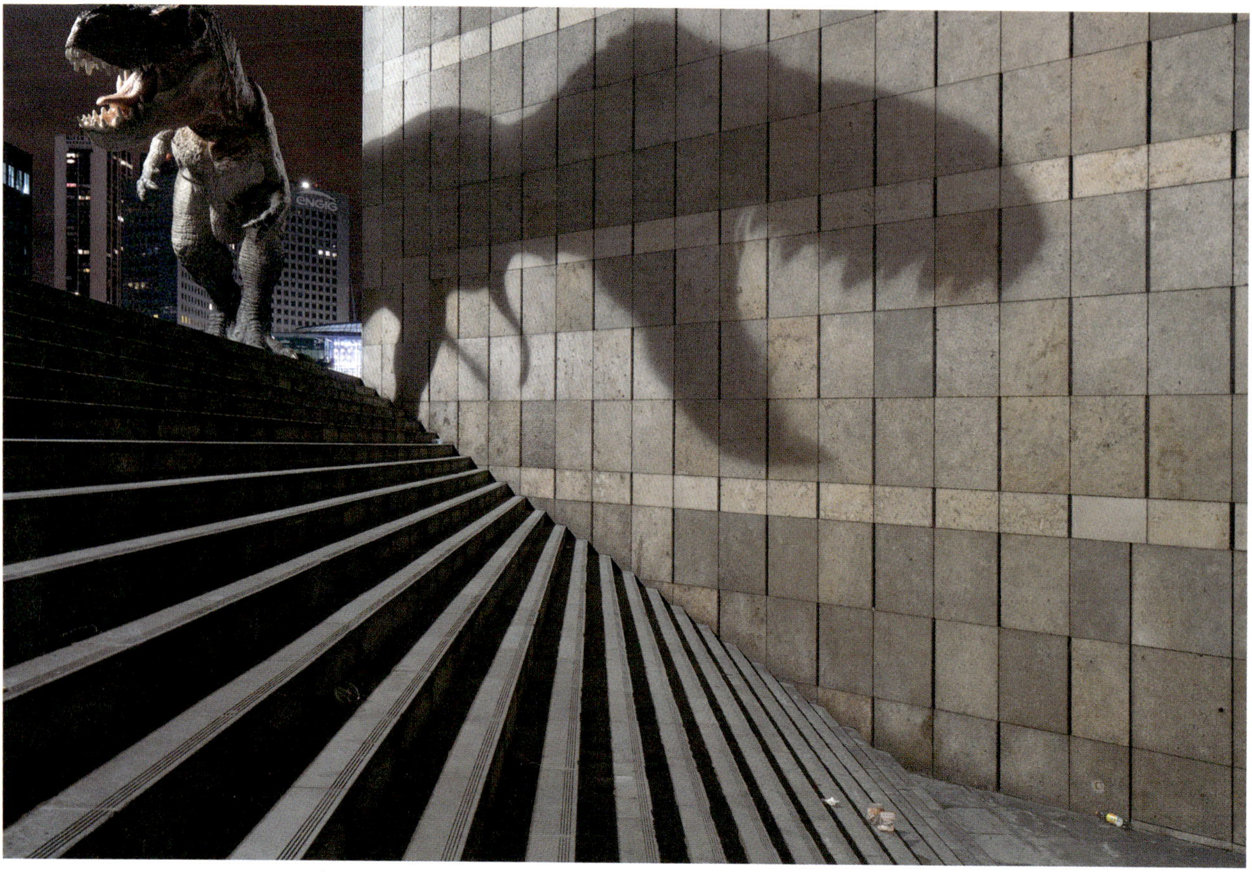

© THE WILDLIFE #25 , BENOÎT LAPRAY (PHOTOGRAPHY AND RETOUCHING)

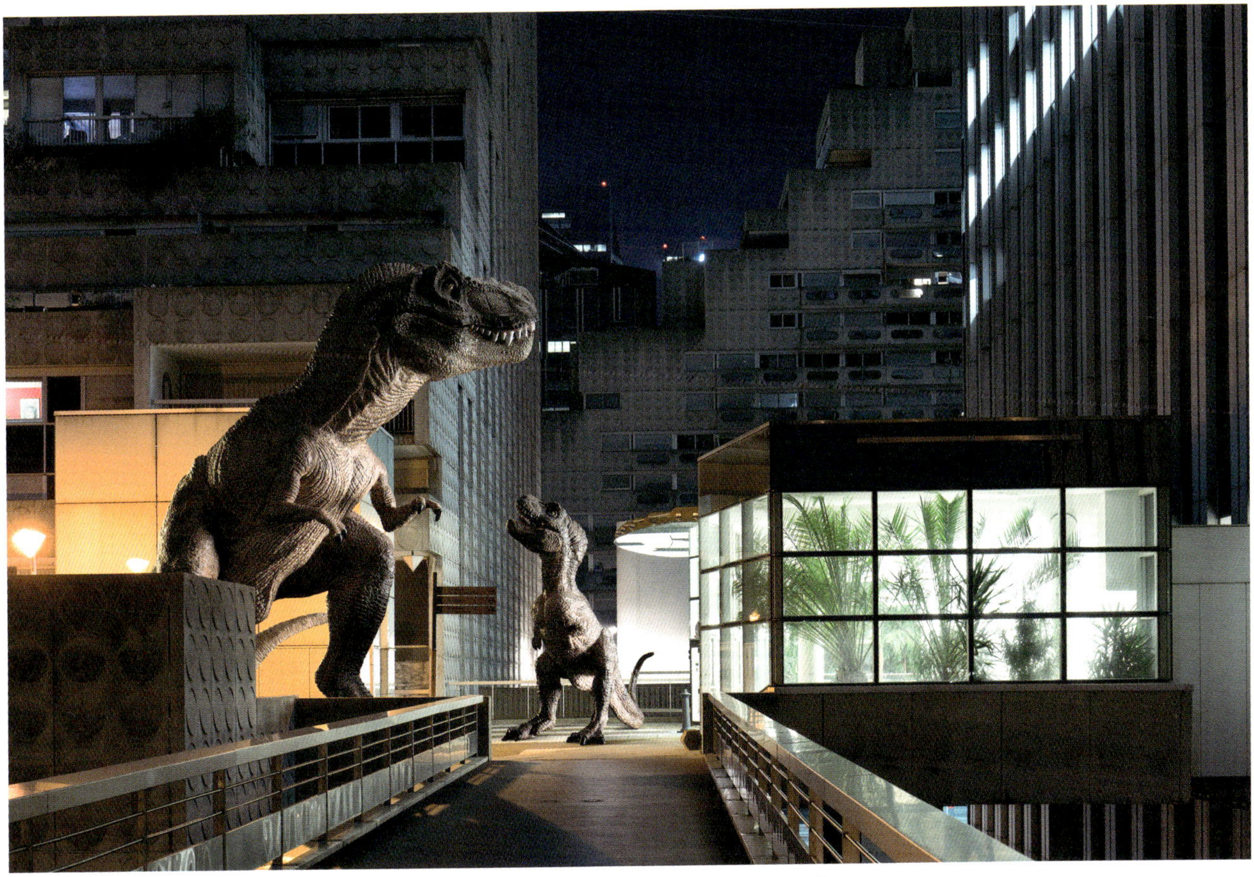

© THE WILDLIFE #01, BENOÎT LAPRAY (PHOTOGRAPHY AND RETOUCHING)

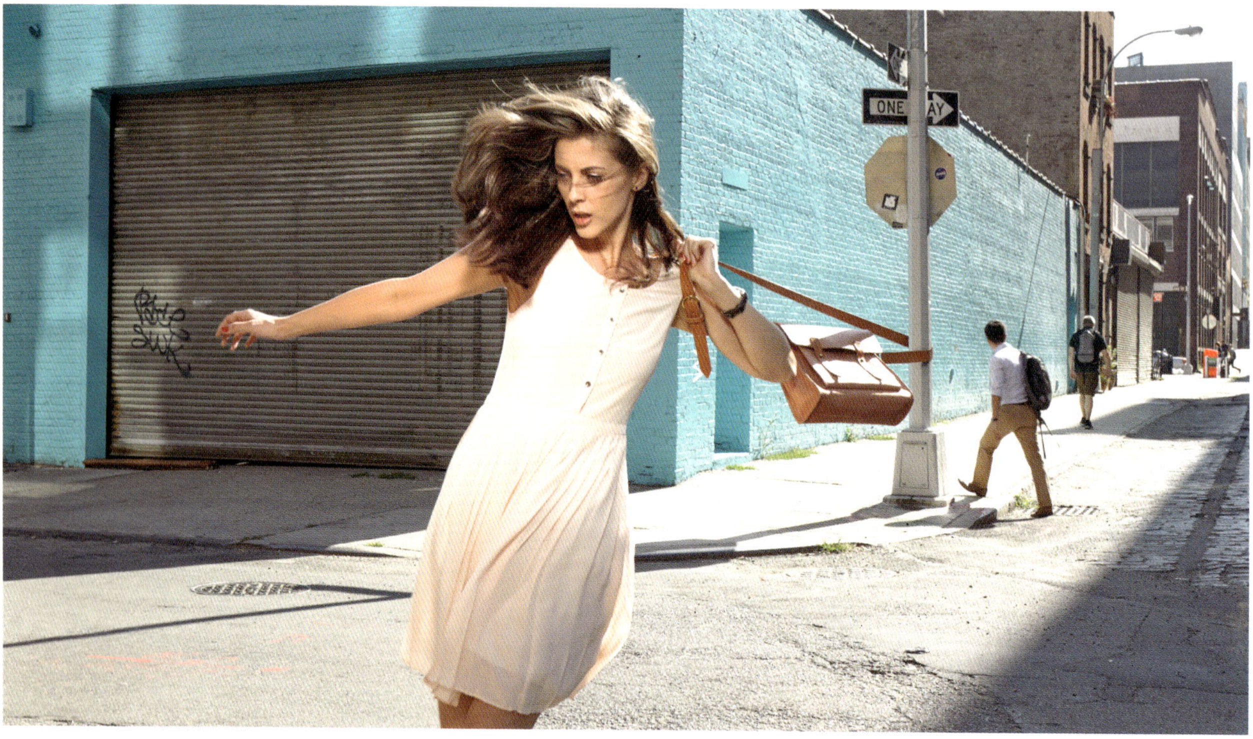

© ROMAIN LAURENT, JENNIFER

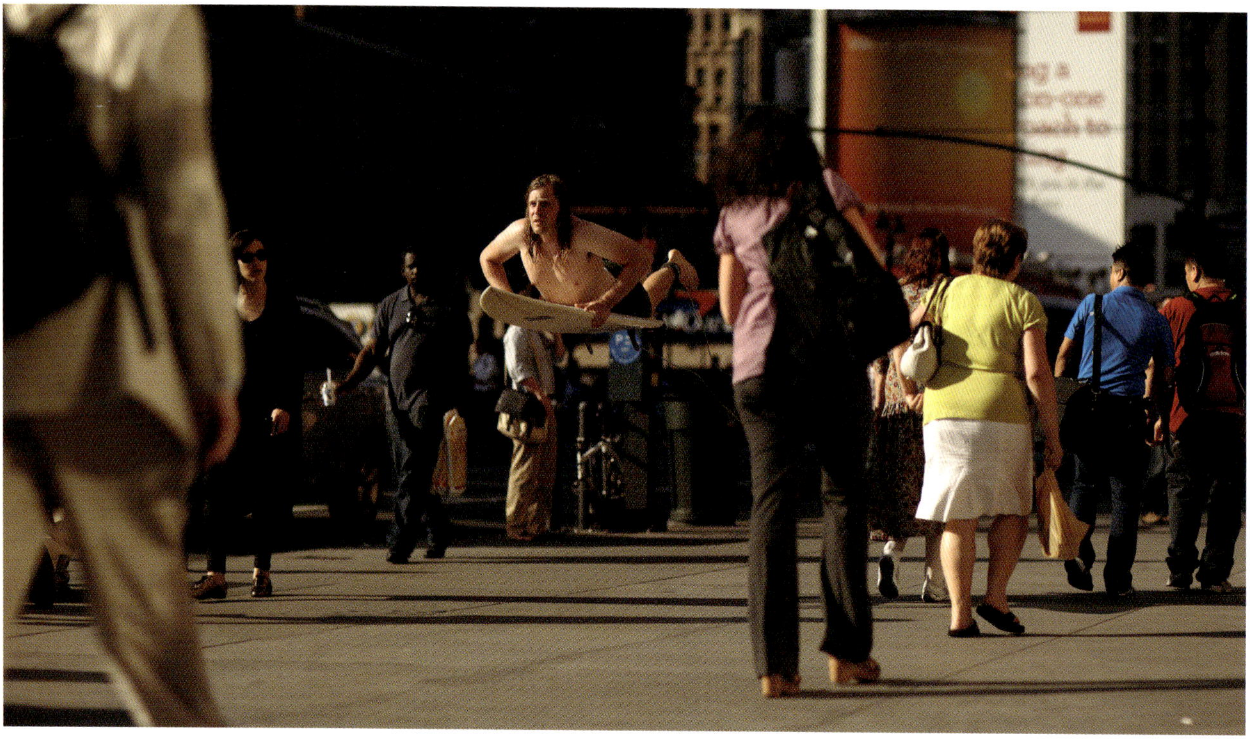

© ROMAIN LAURENT, HORIZON

ROMAIN LAURENT

#BODY

Born in the French Alps, Romain Laurent currently lives in New York City. While working commercially for top brands and magazines, he also dedicates time to his personal ideas. He initially studied product design at the ENSAAMA, National School of Applied Arts in Paris but discovered that conceptual photography would give him many more tools to show people his ideas. So he chose to graduate in photography from Les Gobelins. Romain also specializes in moving image and short movies. Romain's favourite photographers are Sally Mann, Robert Mapplethorpe and Edward Weston. As for inspiration?: 'It's a wide range of interests – from comic books to movies to general art', according to the photographer. Post-production allows him to create the most surprising effects.

Romain calls his aesthetic 'real-world illustration' and his refined works indeed reflect on the human condition in today's reality. The photographer's interventions in these urbanscapes are sophisticated yet take the compositions to a completely different level.

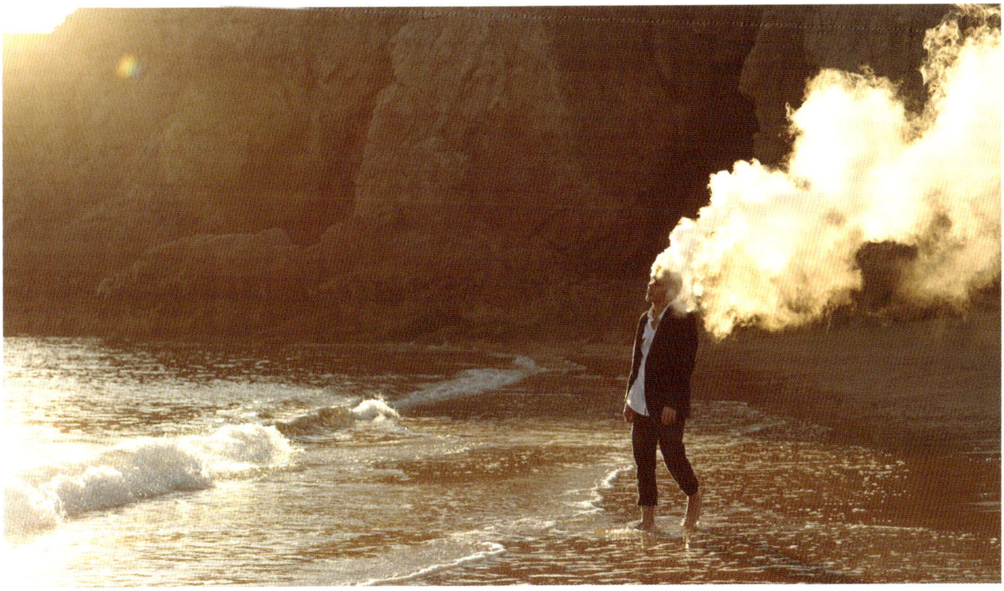

© ROMAIN LAURENT, BURNOUT

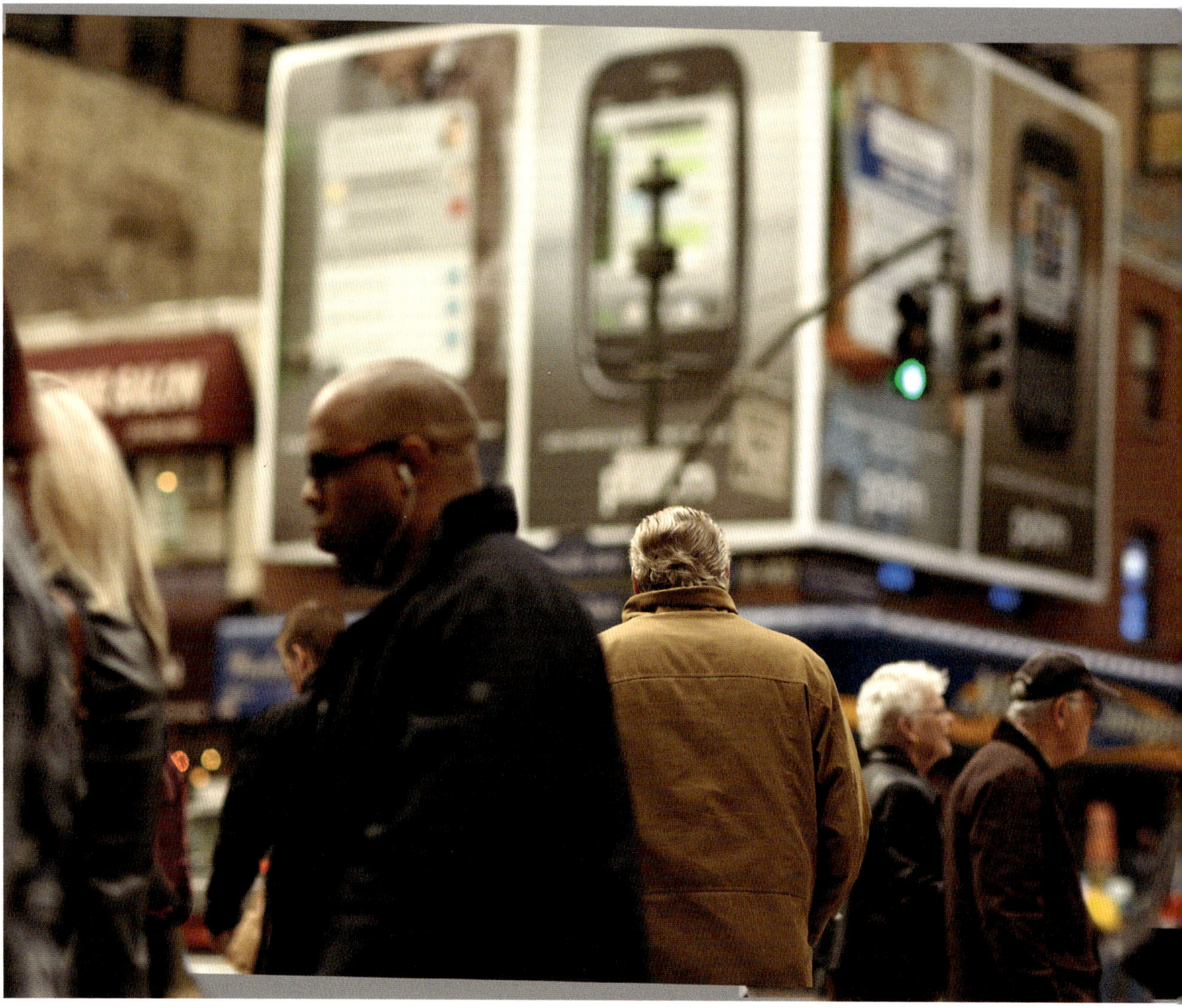

© ROMAIN LAURENT, SOMETHING REAL

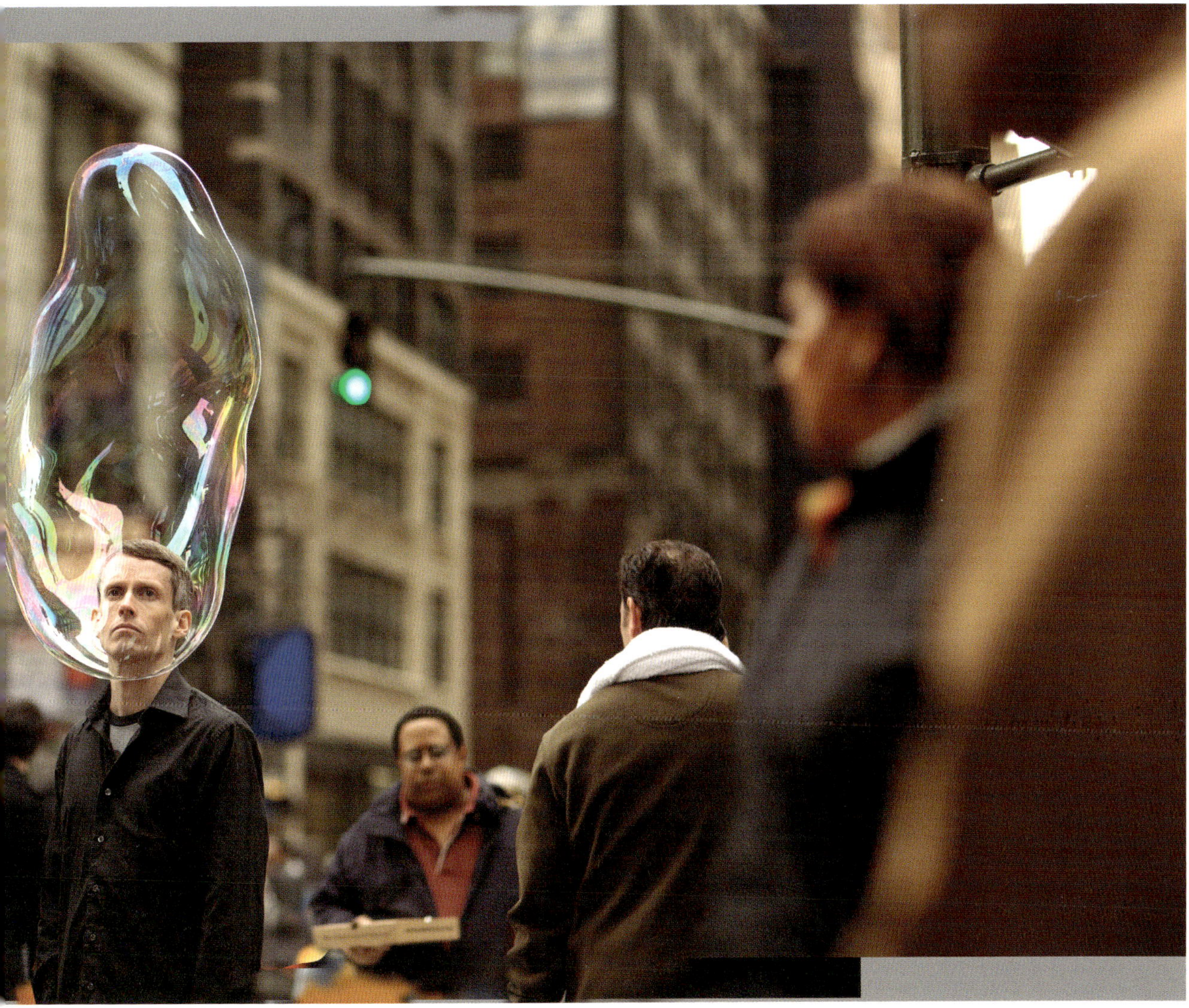

ELIA LOCARDI

#LAND-SCAPE

Elia Locardi is a perpetual traveler always on the move (leading a 100% mobile life) and takes amazing shots of some of the most beautiful locations in the world. In his practice Elia fuses traditional camera techniques with advanced post-processing methods to dramatize his visions. Seeing the world through the artist's eyes is to appreciate its vivid colours, diverse textures and harmonic beauty.

Elia crafts his visions in a very sensual and emotional way. He not only captures the look of the places, but also their atmosphere and energy. The extraordinary Indonesian landscape features Mount Bromo hidden between a dense fog and a starry sky. Cosmic Dance in New Zealand also focuses on the sky. 'I love shooting star trails', admits the photographer, 'because I feel as though it creates a very powerful mood in my imagery'. Elias's photos are visual treasures celebrating the beauty of our planet with a magic twist.

ELIALOCARDI.COM

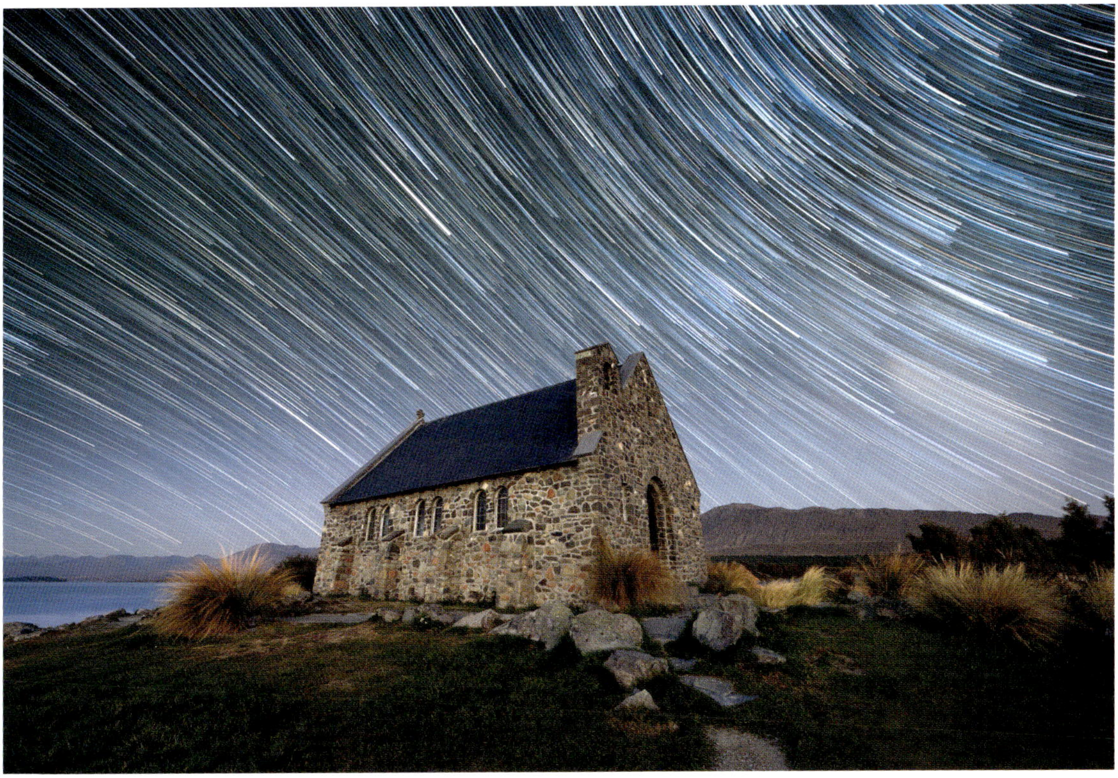

© ELIA LOCARDI, COSMIC DANCE || NEW ZEALAND

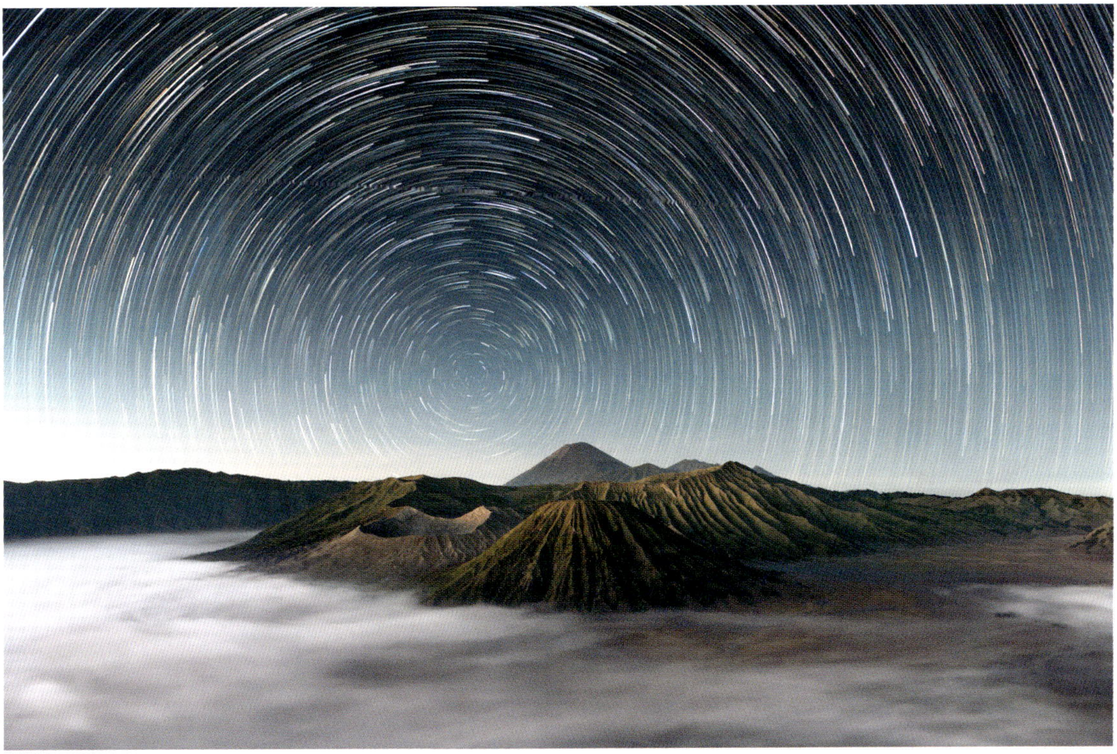

© ELIA LOCARDI, SLEEPING GIANTS || MT BROMO INDONESIA

CHEMA MADOZ

#B/W

Spanish photographer Chema Madoz (b. 1958) provides a view of the impossible. Working exclusively in white and black, he expresses his surreal vision of the world with a great sense of humour. Chema studied art history and specializes in capturing absurd ideas. His signature method is blending two objects that are visually similar in some way (some are freaky, like the eye wrapped as a candy) or showing objects out of their usual context (like putting the plates to dry in a pavement's manhole).

Perplexing compositions surprise the viewer with uncommon ways of thinking about objects we know from our everyday life. We see them anew. Chema likes what is unexpected to try break our habitual view and breathe fresh air into the way we look at things. Sometimes it's just about a witty juxtaposition, such as a half-burnt match that is part of a thermometer indicating the temperature.

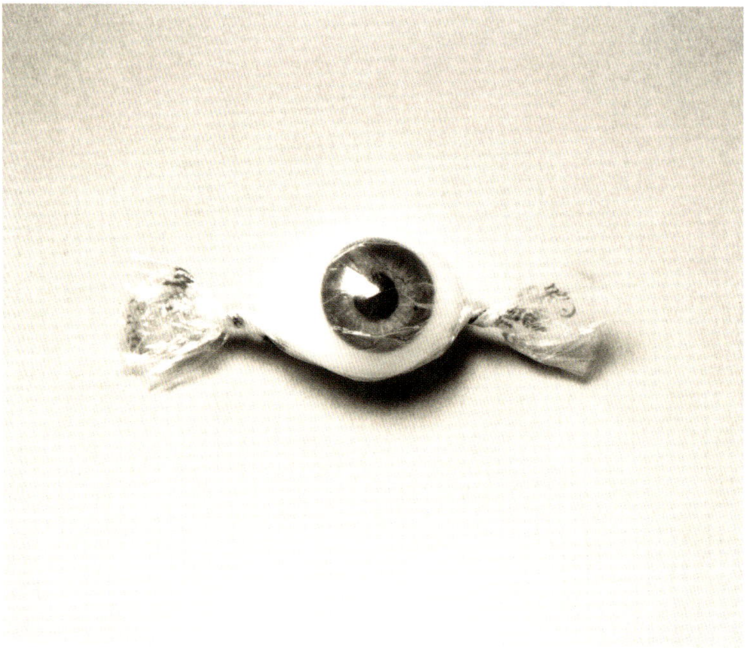

© CHEMA MADOZ

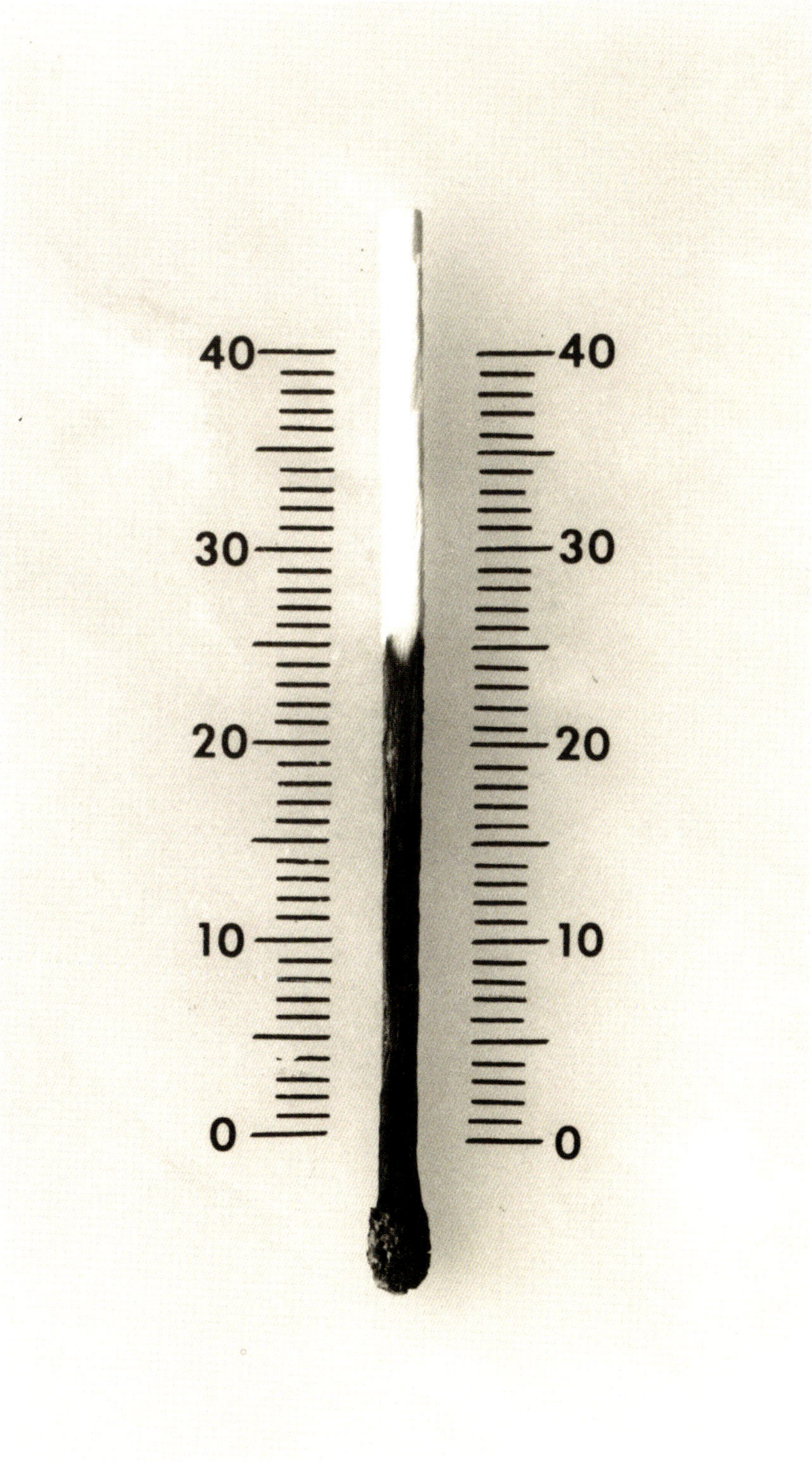
40
30
20
10
0
40
30
20
10
0

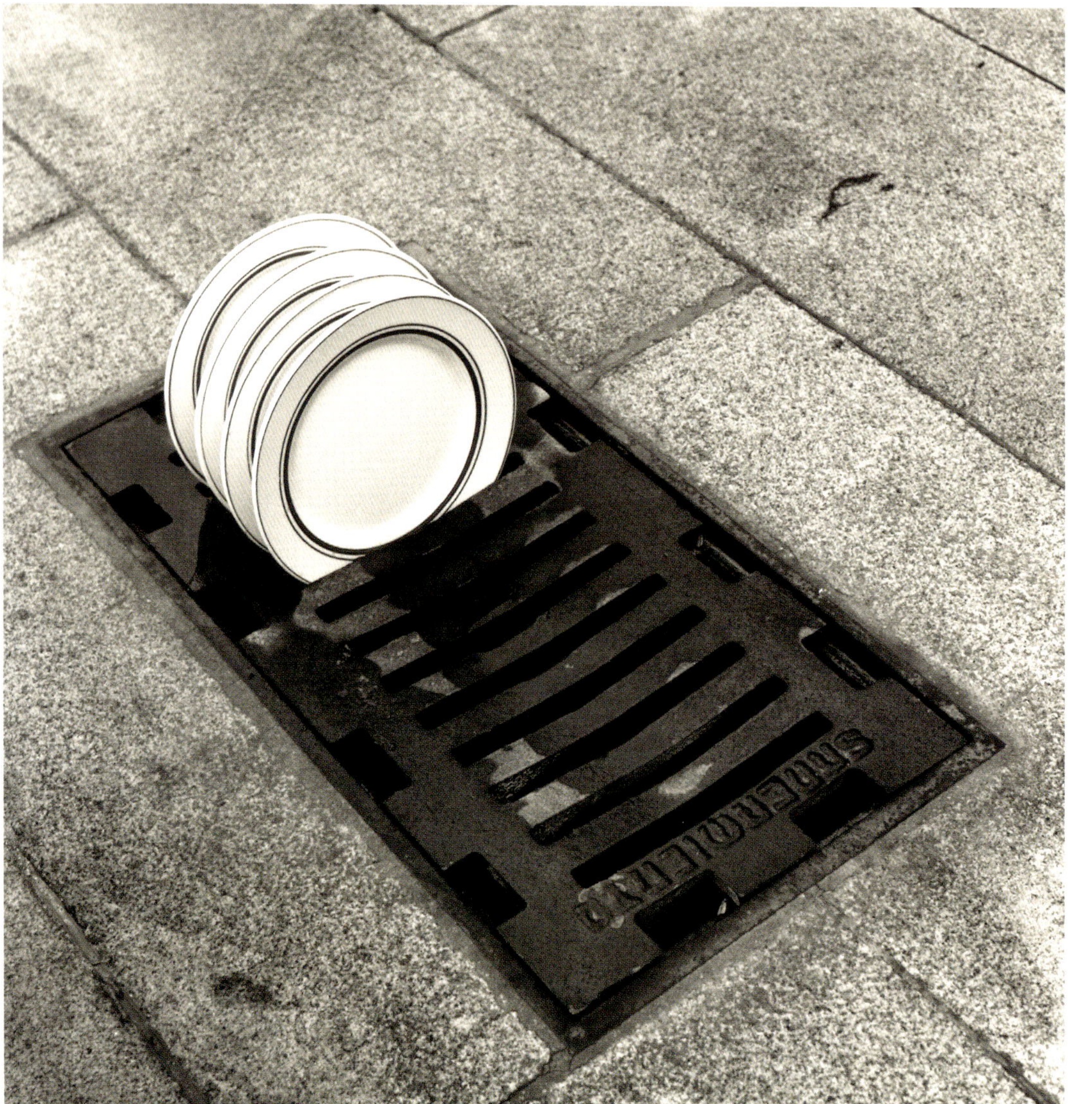

© CHEMA MADOZ

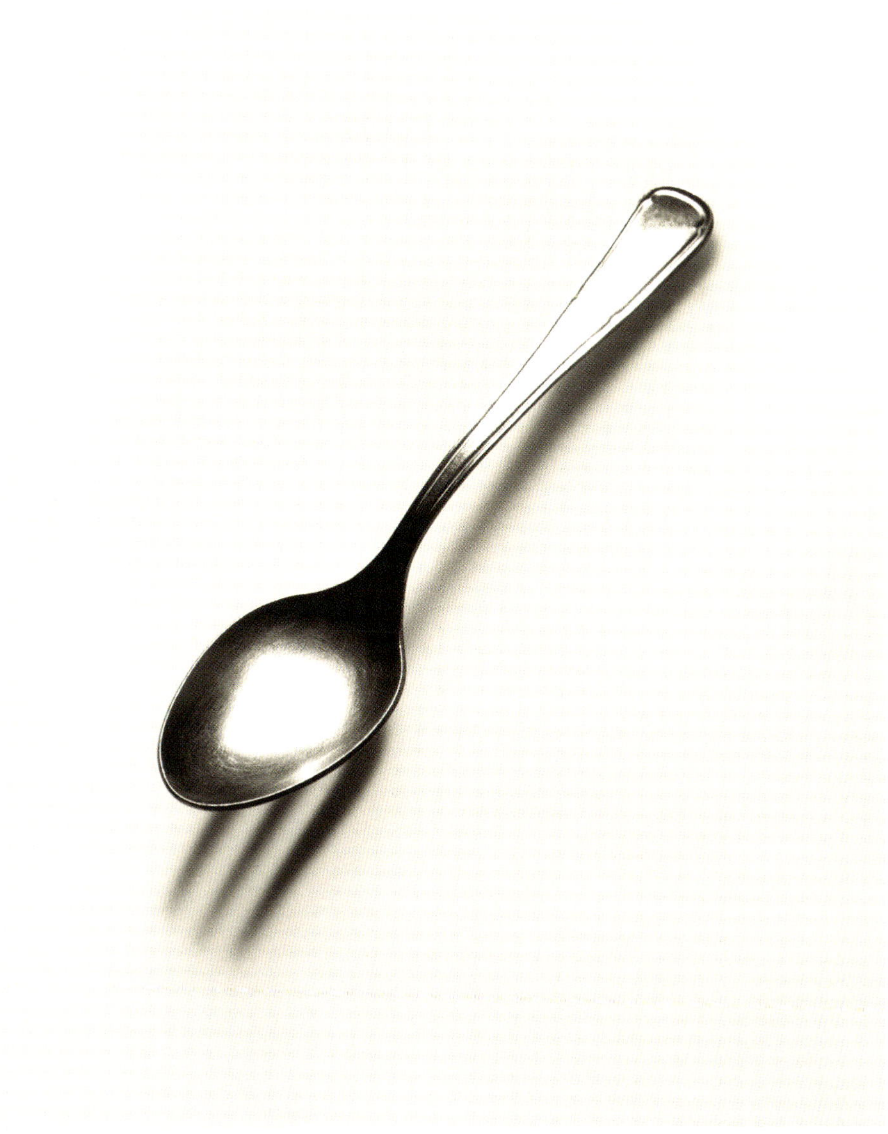

© CHEMA MADOZ

RICH McCOR

#LAND-SCAPE

#ARCHI-TECTURE

British photographer Rich McCor (b. 1987) needs black cardboard, a pair of scissors and a camera to create some of his most original photos. On his Instagram account (paperboyo), followed by the impressive number of nearly 300,000 fans, he says: 'I see things you don't see' and with his black cut-out silhouettes he transforms famous locations, iconic buildings, recognisable landmarks and familiar sculptures.

It all began with a series of photos from London, but then Rich left his job at a creative agency to travel around the world for his art, journeying across Europe to the Far East, to the United States and it continues. The more places he visits, the more ideas come into his mind. Full of humour and surprises, the photographer's imagination is endless. Holding up the cut outs in front of his camera he adjusts the silhouettes to the sight resulting in optically fascinating effects.

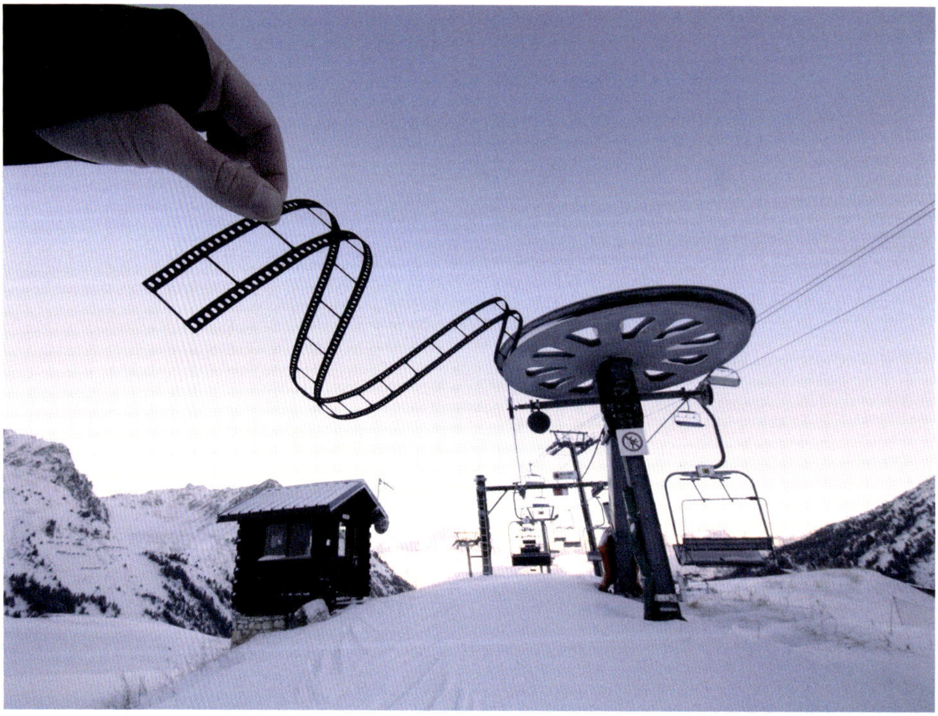

© LES ARCS SKI LIFT FILM REEL, 2017 BY @PAPERBOYO

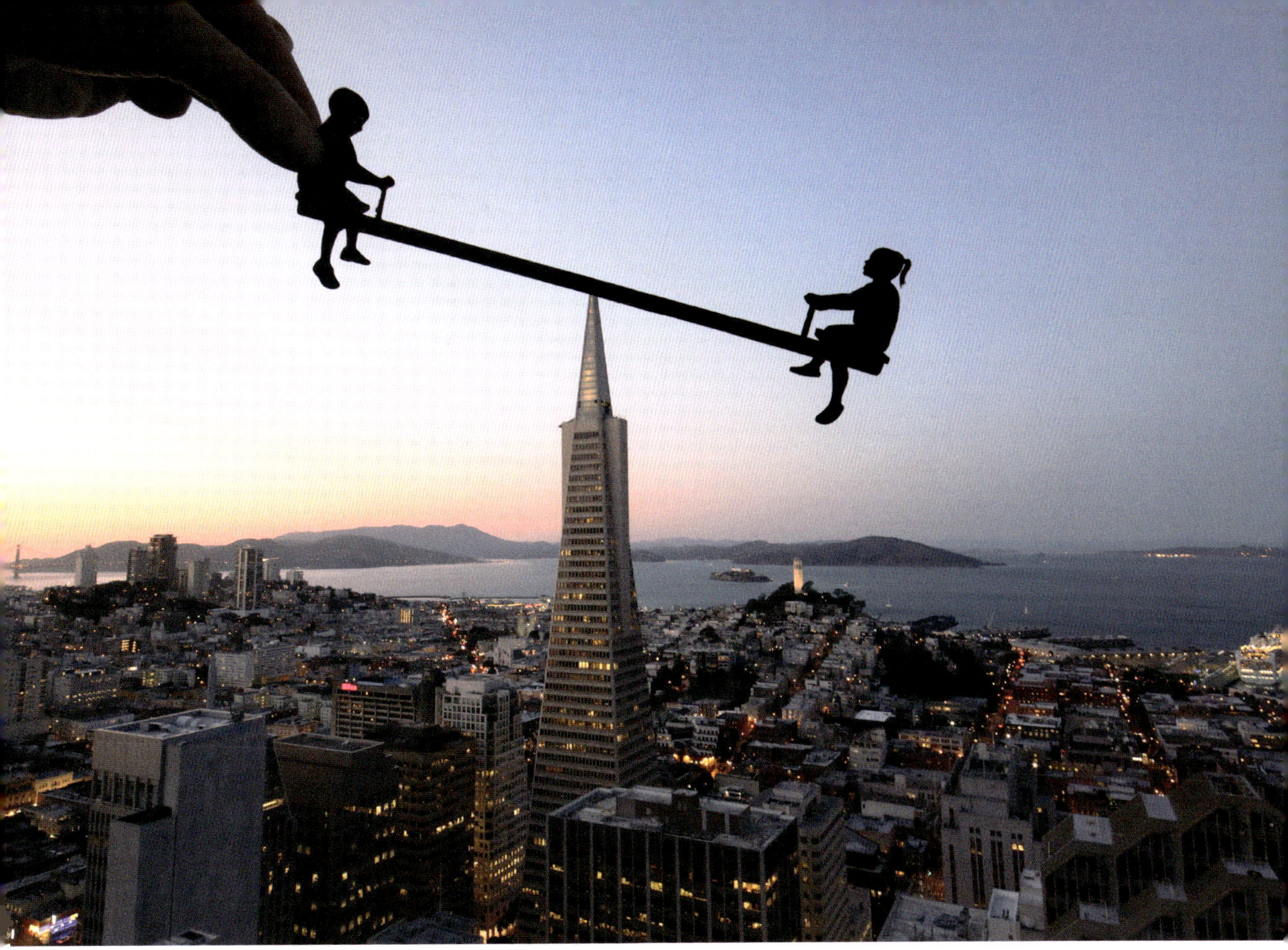

© TRANSAMERICA BUILDING SEE-SAW, 2016 BY @PAPERBOYO

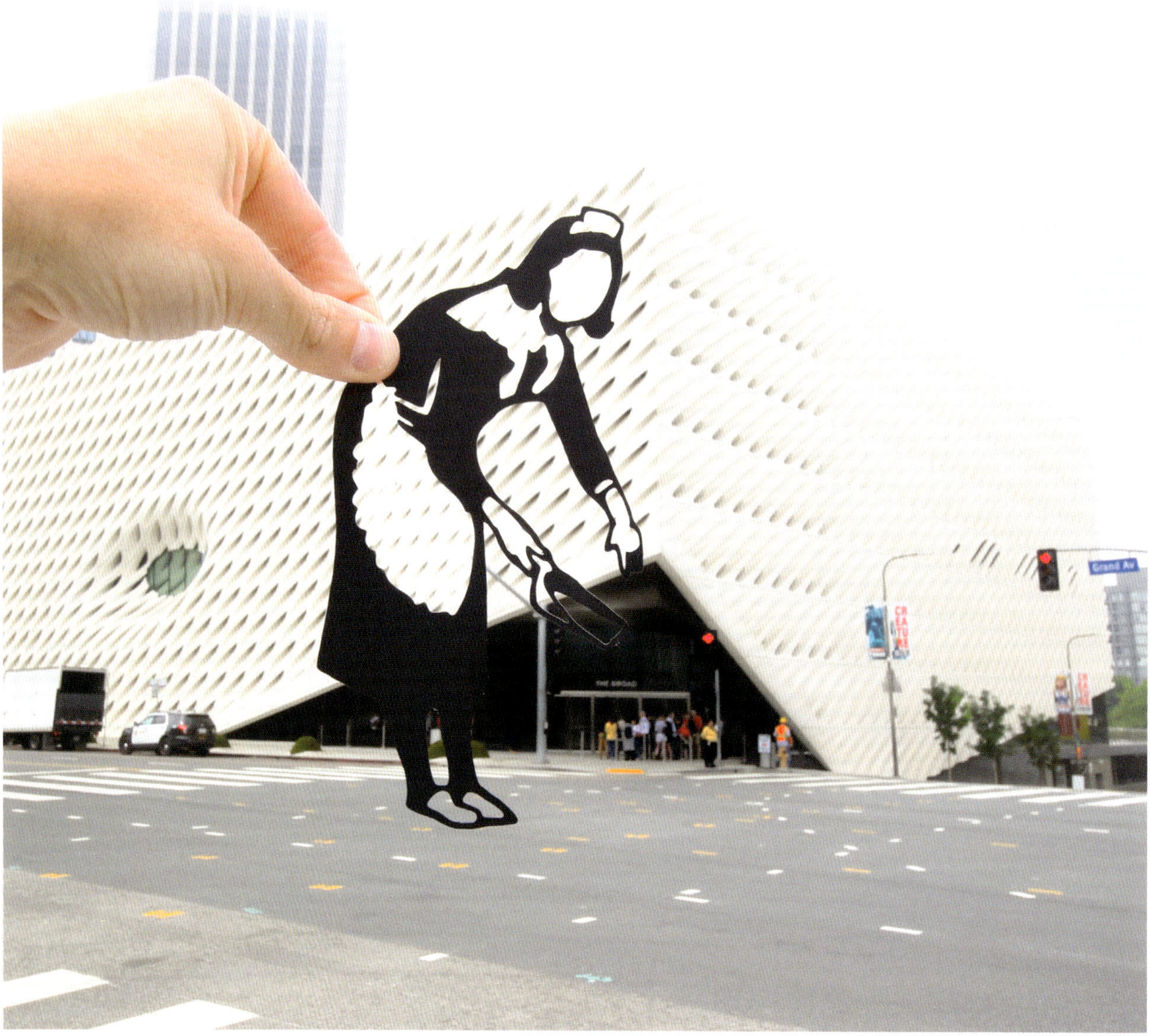

© THE BROAD AND BANKSY MASH-UP, 2016 BY @PAPERBOYO

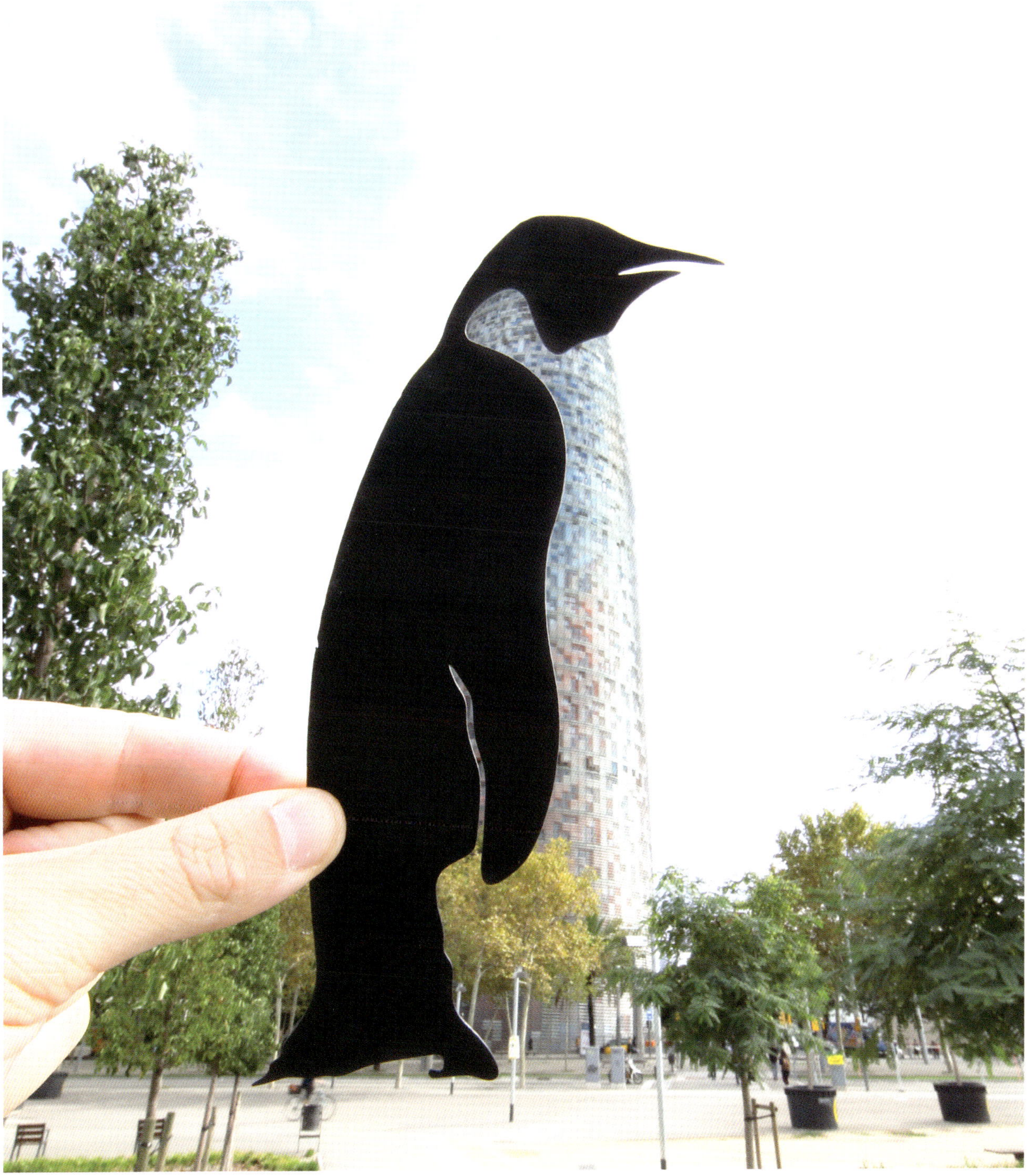

© TORRE AGBAR PENGUIN, 2016 BY @PAPERBOYO

LILY MEI

#ANIMALS

Our cover photograph with the humorous title 'Flight over zoo' belongs to Lily Mei, who comes from Montenegro. The dream-like view of a giraffe's head peeping into the window of an airplane suspended over the clouds shows the artist's imagination and wit. This surreal view is truly amusing, additionally the composition makes the viewer feel as if they were sitting on the plane and facing the long-necked animal.

Lily was raised in an artistic family and originally studied art in Monetenegro, then continued in Belgrade to graduate in painting and installation at Stavanger in Norway, where she is currently based. From the very beginning Lily was fascinated by photography and digital manipulation as well as the possibilities it gives to translate imaginative concepts into great photos. The artist finds the inspiration within herself, because as she states, 'working on oneself is the most important work we do and art becomes a medium for healing'.

FLICKR.COM/PHOTOS/ANCHIKATA

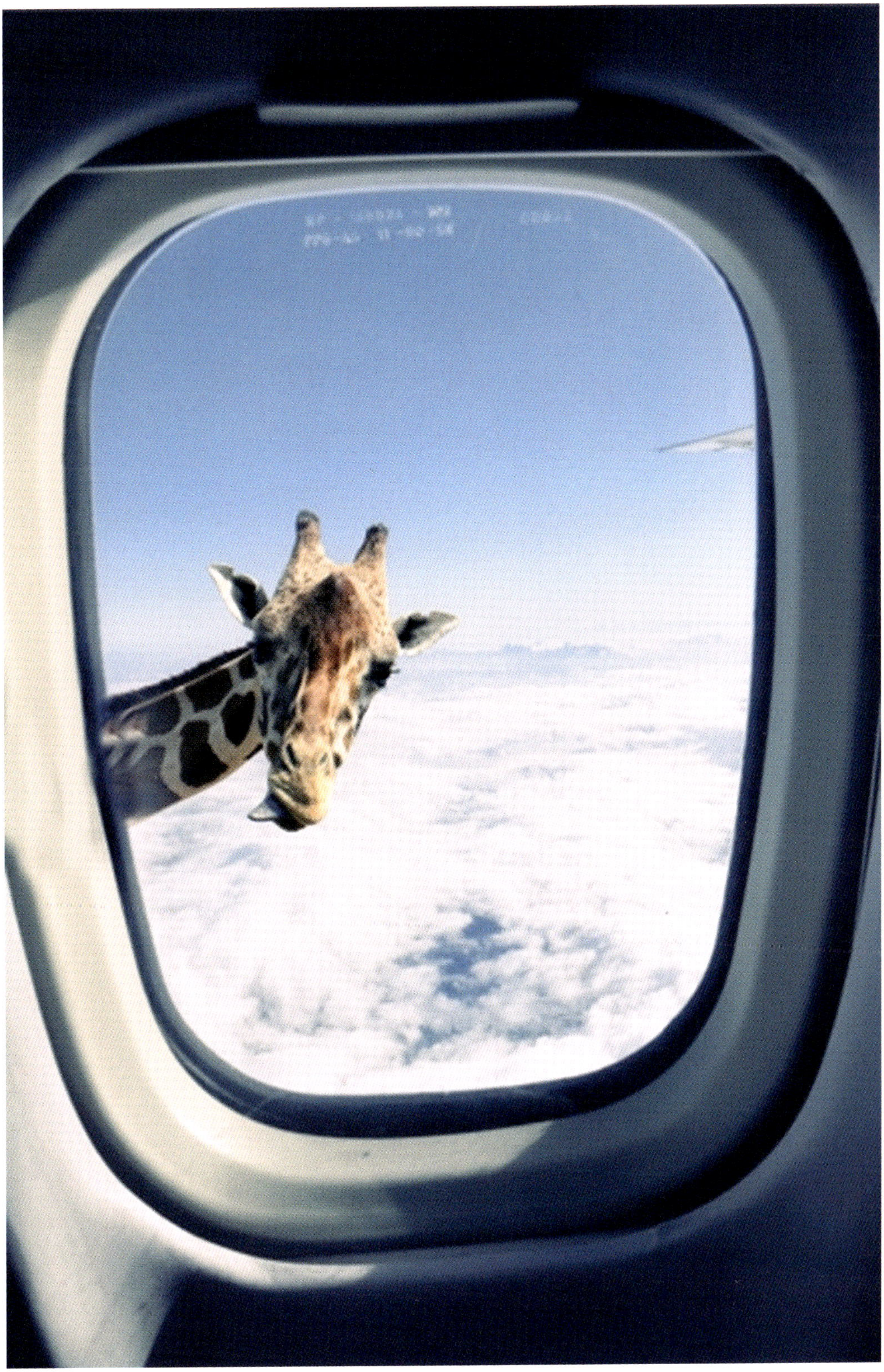

© LILY MEI, FLIGHT OVER ZOO

MINIMIAM: PIERRE JAVELLE AND AKIKO IDA

Pierre Javelle was inspired by the professional photographers he worked with at a photo lab in Paris. Akiko Ida, after photographing her culinary experiments at a young age, became a professional food photographer for magazines and cookbooks. They met at the École des Art Décoratifs in Paris and since 2002 they have been developing the Minimiam project.

What is Minimiam? A miniature world of gourmandise, which is taken over by tiny train figurines experiencing various stories with food. 'Relive your childhood emotions and smell, taste the photographic adventures that come alive on your plate' invite the photographers. Their ingenious images come as diptychs: the first photo features a close up of a figurine in action, while the second one shows a bigger picture allowing the viewer to discover the general concept. Together they create truly original compositions in a challenging scale. The Minimiam world is very sensual, full of vivid colours and visually pleasing forms.

#LITTLE PEOPLE

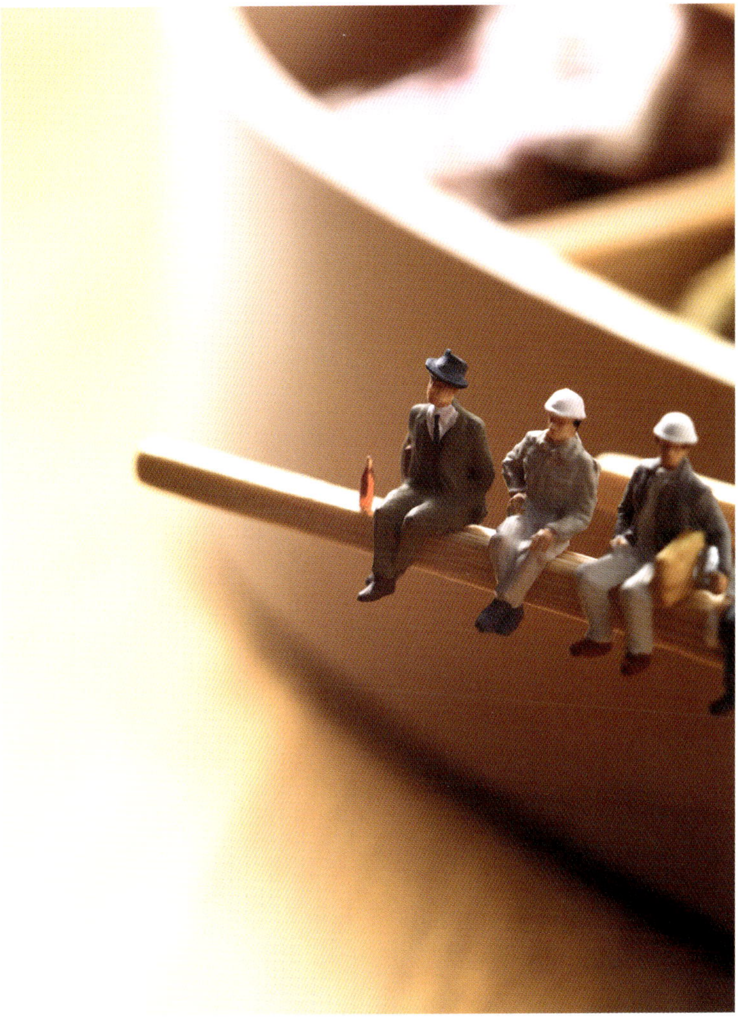

© PIERRE JAVELLE AND AKIKO IDA, BENTO

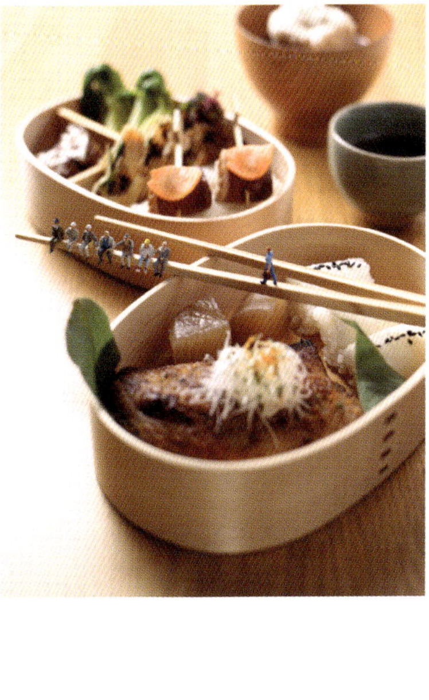

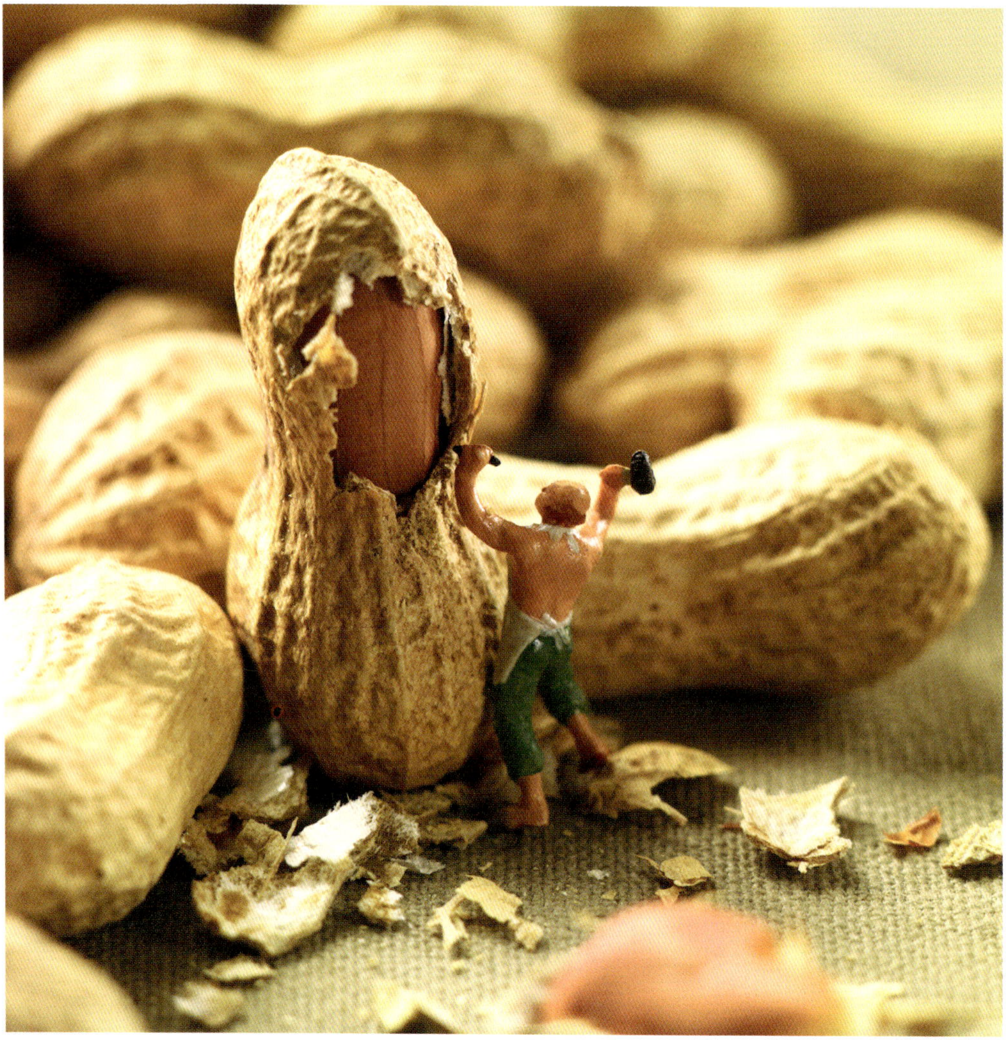

© PIERRE JAVELLE AND AKIKO IDA, CACAHUETTES

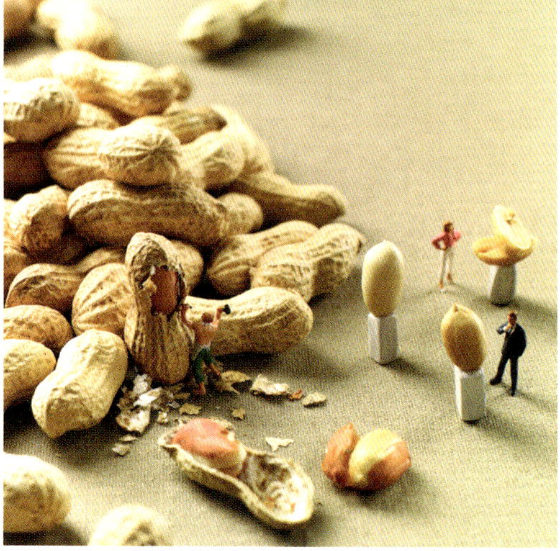

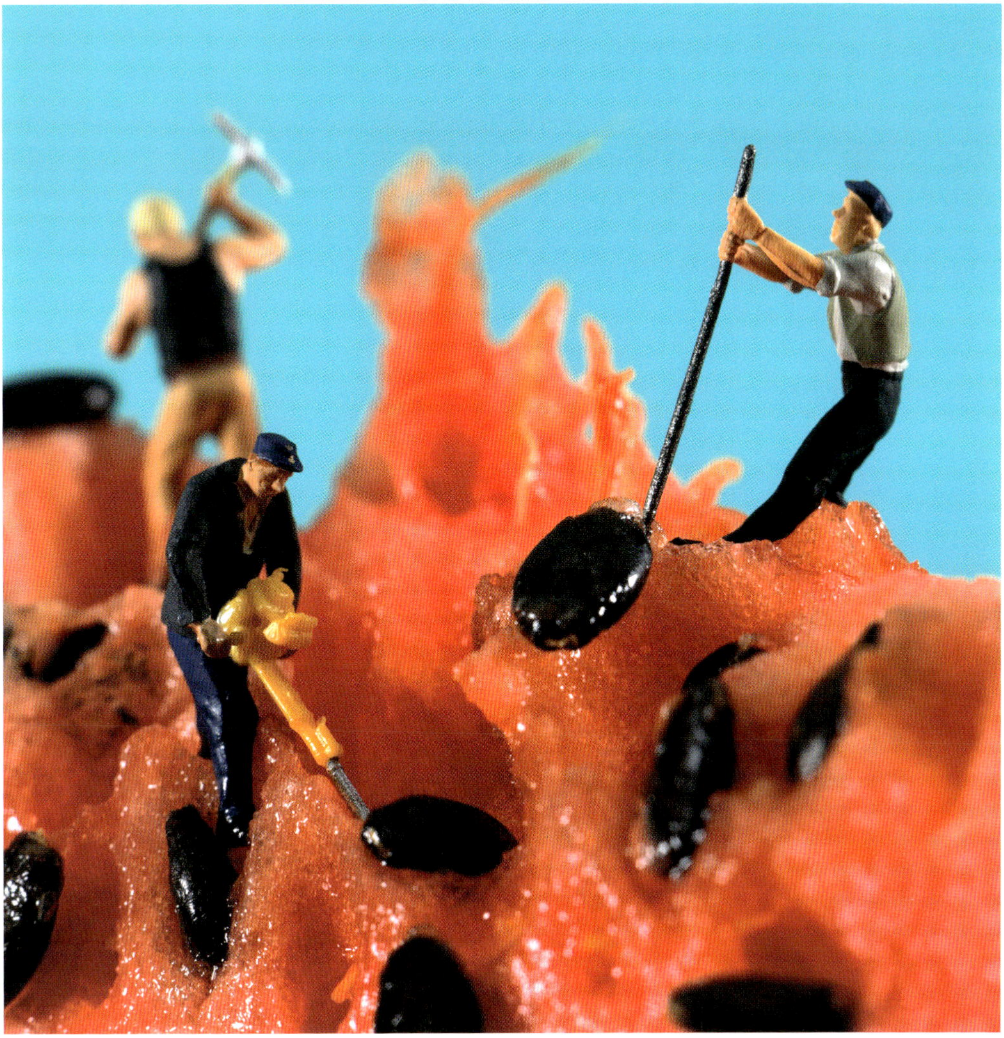

© PIERRE JAVELLE AND AKIKO IDA, LES ÉPÉPINEURS

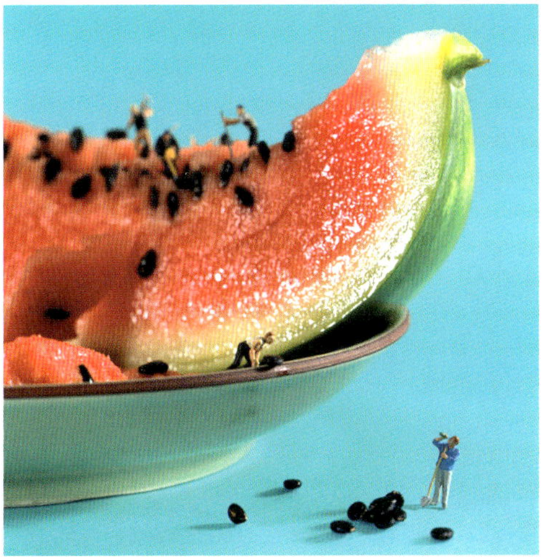

OLEG OPRISCO

Born in Lviv and based in Odessa, Oleg Oprisco started his adventure with photography by working in a photo lab in his hometown. Three years of practice allowed him to master digital photography and playing with colour. Surprisingly he decided to work with traditional film photography, which did not stop him from achieving a dream-like and surreal mood in his works. Asked what is most challenging about photography, Oleg answers that it is finding something new to surprise the viewer. When looking at his photos there is no doubt that the photographer has no problem in coming up with novel ideas.

Images of solitary women in different picturesque and atmospheric settings are what Oleg is recognized for. A toned palette, sophisticated compositions and carefully selected locations, as well as elements of scenography characterize all his works. The artist prefers working alone on each project, from concept, to selecting clothes and make-up, to finding locations.

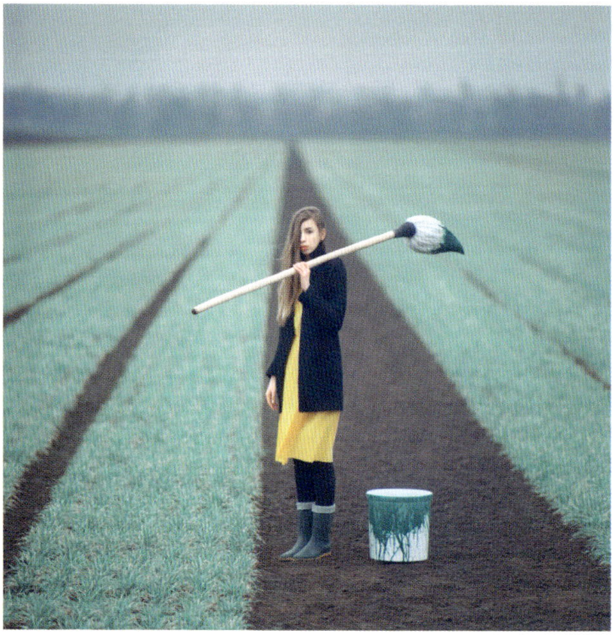

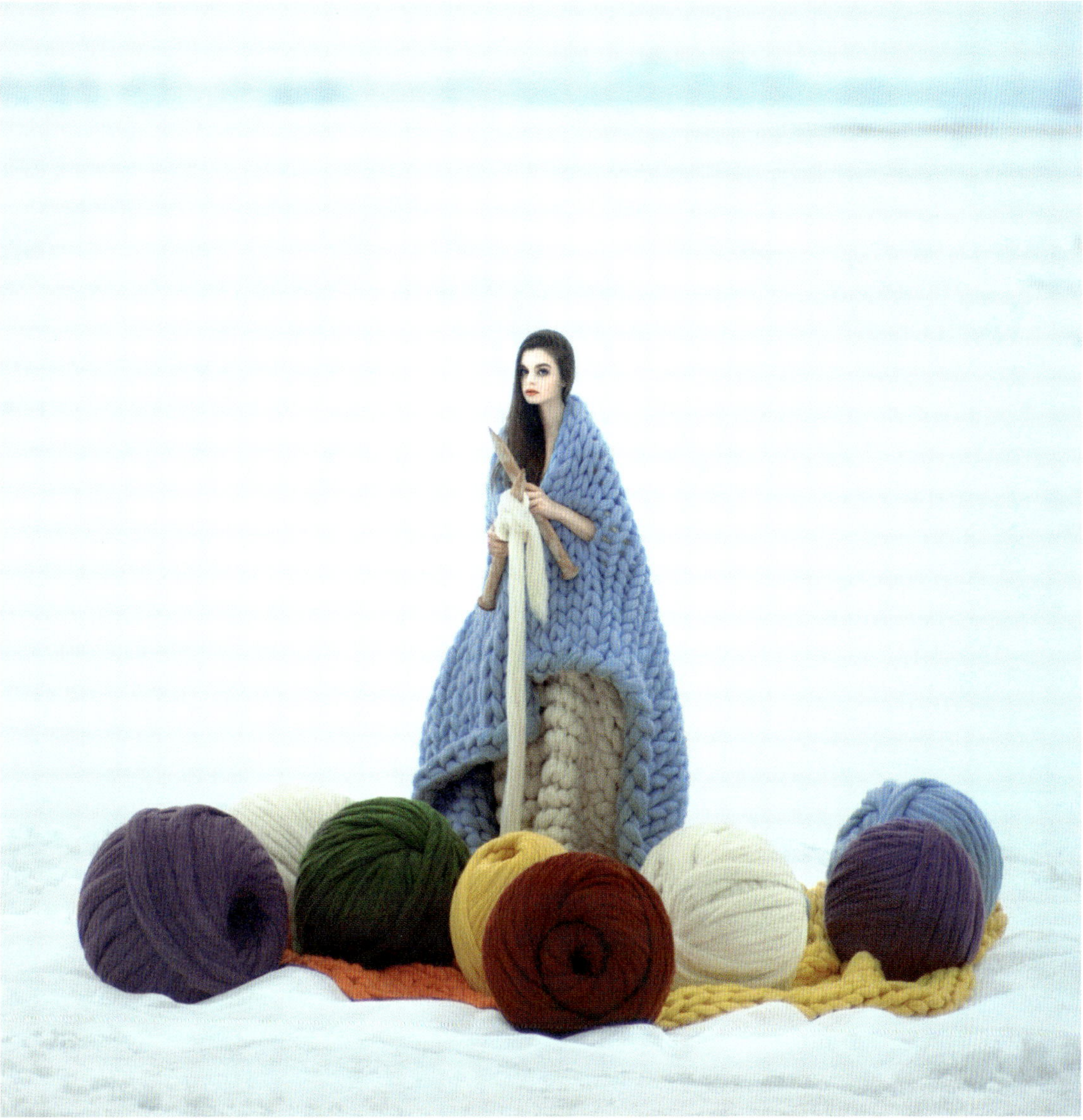

© OLEG OPRISCO

#PORTRAIT

#LAND-
SCAPE

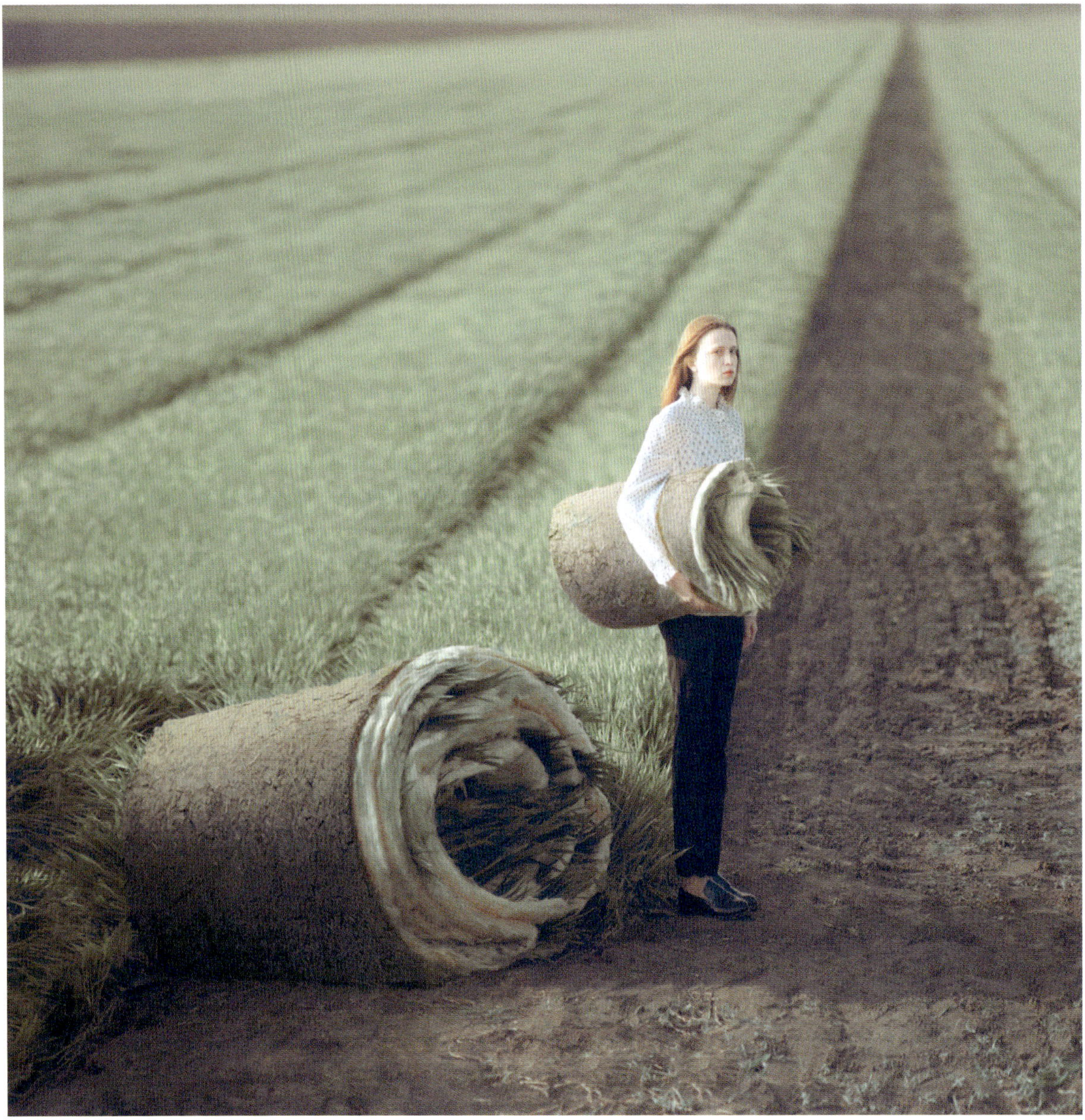

© OLEG OPRISCO

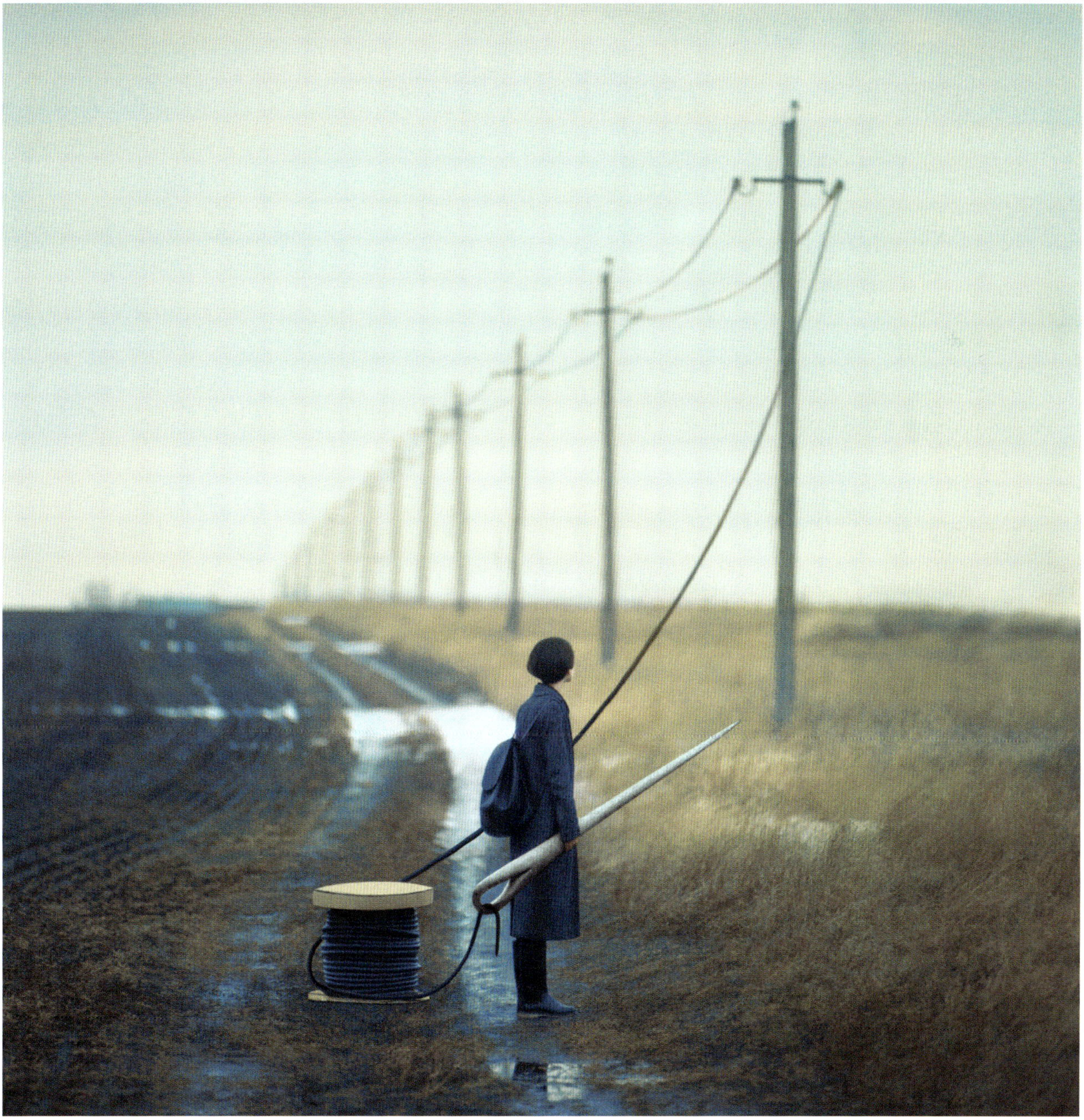

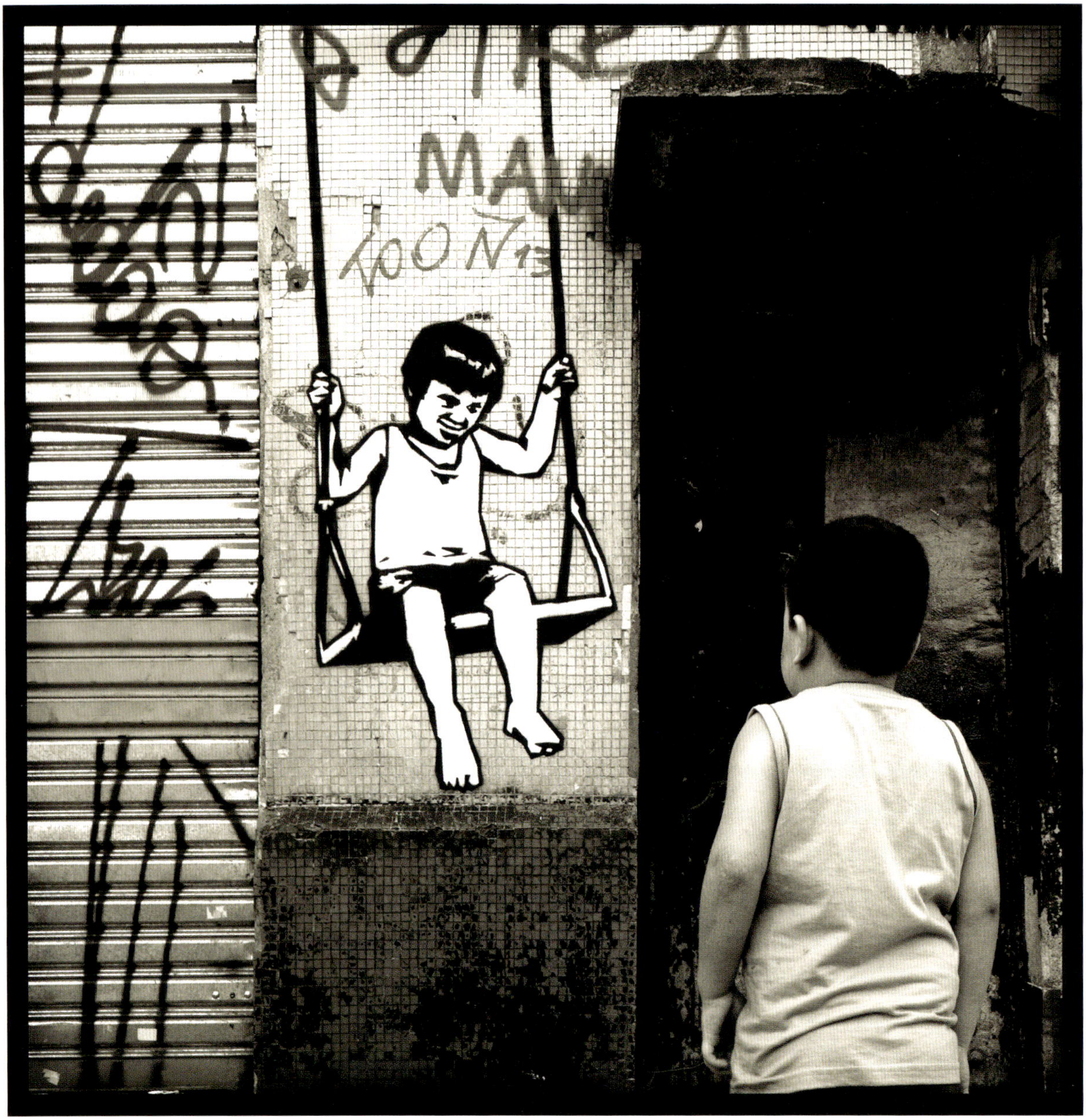

© ALEXANDRE ORION, METABIÓTICA 25. 2013

ALEXANDRE ORION

#B/W

The city is the major inspiration for Alexandre Orion (b. 1978). The multimedia artist, who is based in São Paulo, says that it's full of meanings. He likes tracking cities with his camera. The universe of streets, buildings and most of all original graffiti is what he draws on in his works. But the photographs are not complete without the city dwellers.

When exploring a city, Alexandre searches for extraordinary spots to paint stunning wall paintings that play fancifully with their surroundings. Then the artist hunts for passers-by who interact spontaneously with the graffiti to take a photo as a final work. These moments of intersection are at the core of the black and white images from the 'Metabiotica' series. The artist is brilliant at capturing stunning juxtapositions and fleeting moments when the reality of everyday life fuses with the art within the urban space. And all images of the 'Metabiotica' series are not only photographs taken by Alexandre Orion but also his graffiti.

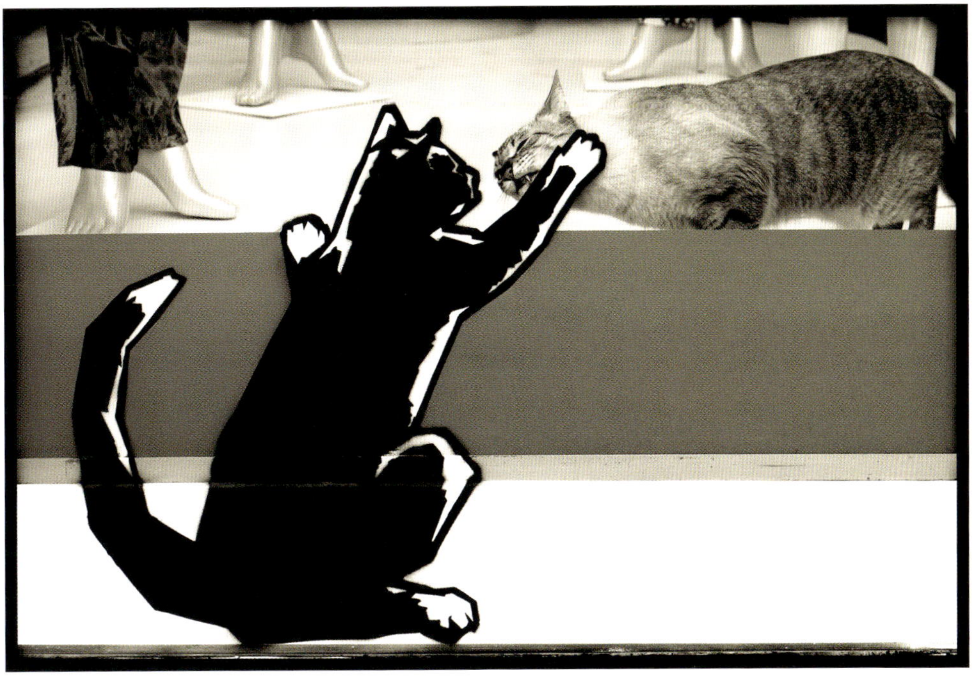

© ALEXANDRE ORION, METABIÓTICA 22 2013

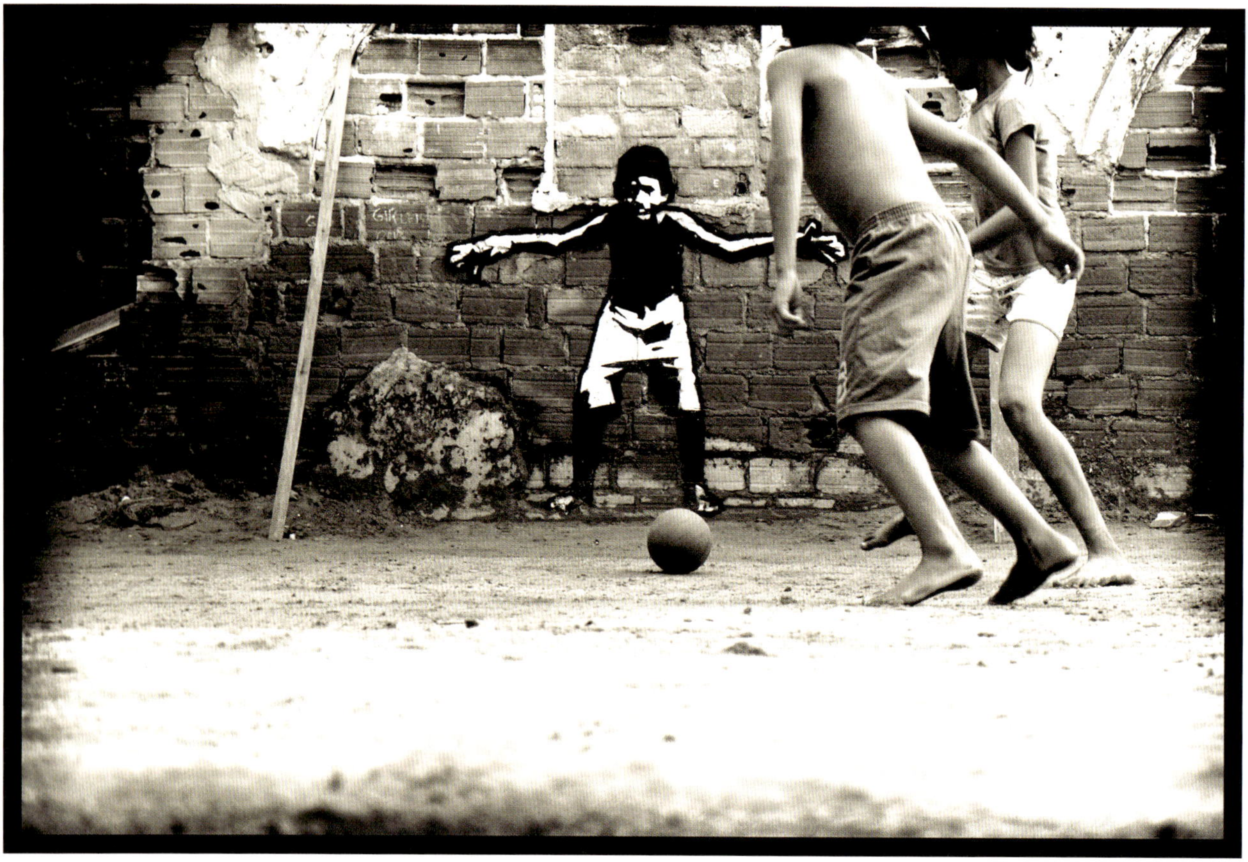

© ALEXANDRE ORION, METABIÓTICA 20, 2009

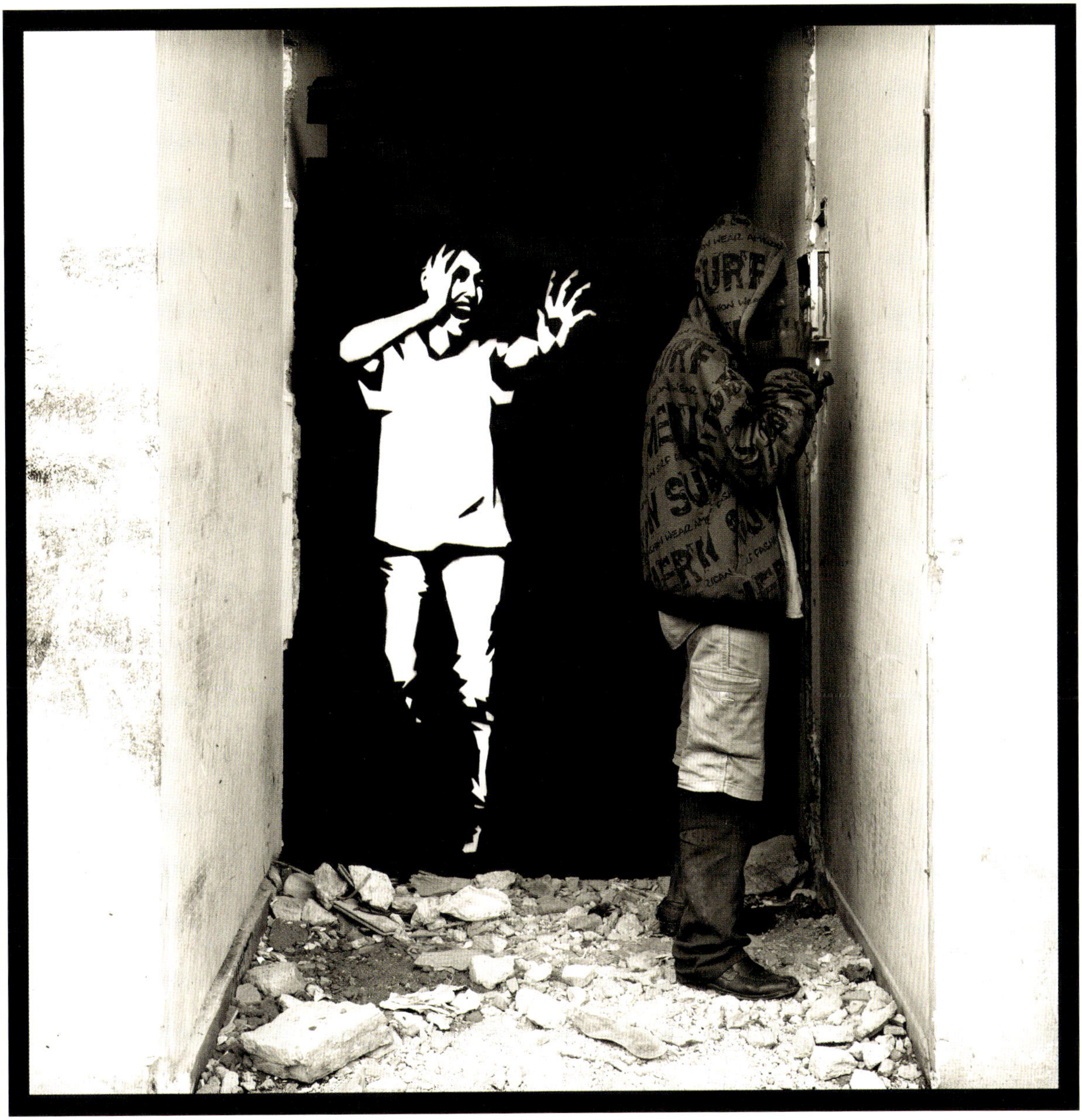

© ALEXANDRE ORION, METABIÓTICA 23, 2013

MARTÍN DE PASQUALE

Buenos Aires-based designer Martín De Pasquale (b. 1988) runs his own studio and works as an art director for various companies and advertising agencies. As a child he used to paint and draw, but after buying a camera he decided that photography would be his means of expression. Having always been interested in the surreal, he employs the digital technology to create his extraordinary photographic manipulations.

Visually strong, Martin's images are usually self-portraits teetering on the edge between satire and the macabre. The photographer is not afraid of shocking his audience with disturbing representations of his distorted body, but he can also make them smile by featuring commonplace images in quirky settings or at surprising scales. Inspired by conceptual artists, designers or other photo manipulations, he always carries something with him for noting down new ideas. 'Once I compile the information, I take the pictures, search for some elements, and go to the post-production stage', says Martin in an interview for the 'Sant' magazine.

#LAND-SCAPE

#BODY

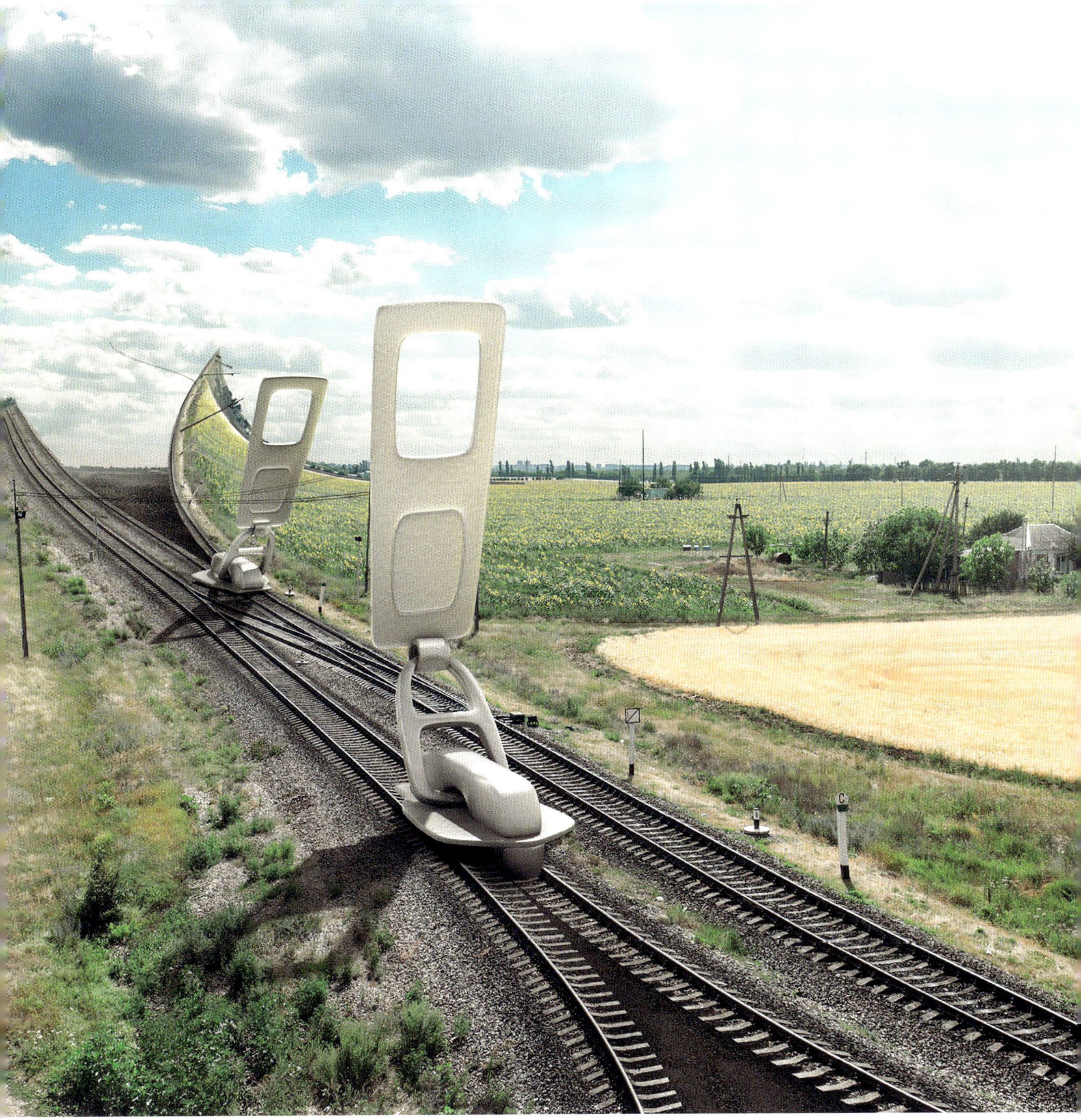

© MARTÍN DE PASQUALE, ZIPPER, 2013

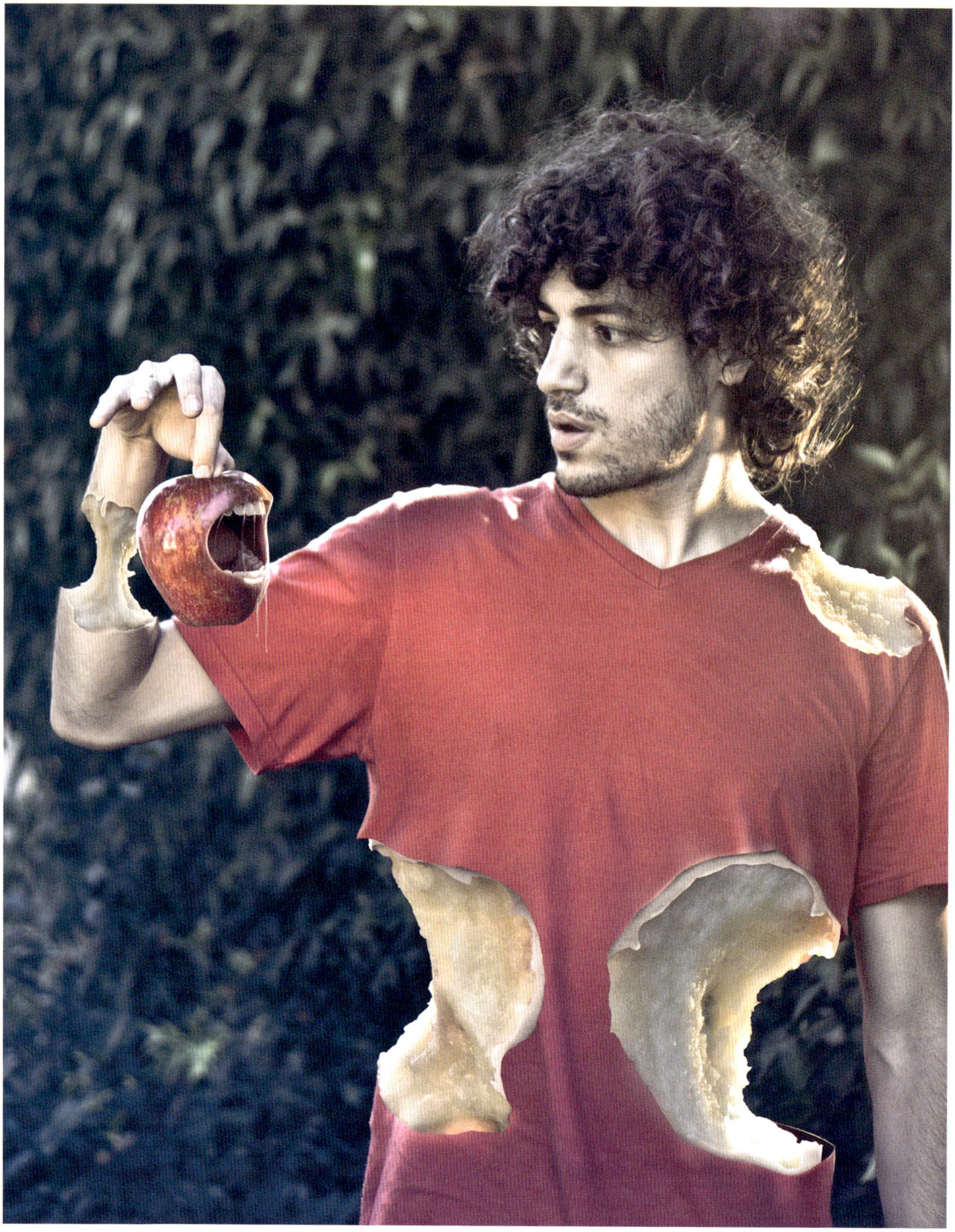

© MARTÍN DE PASQUALE, KARMA, 2013

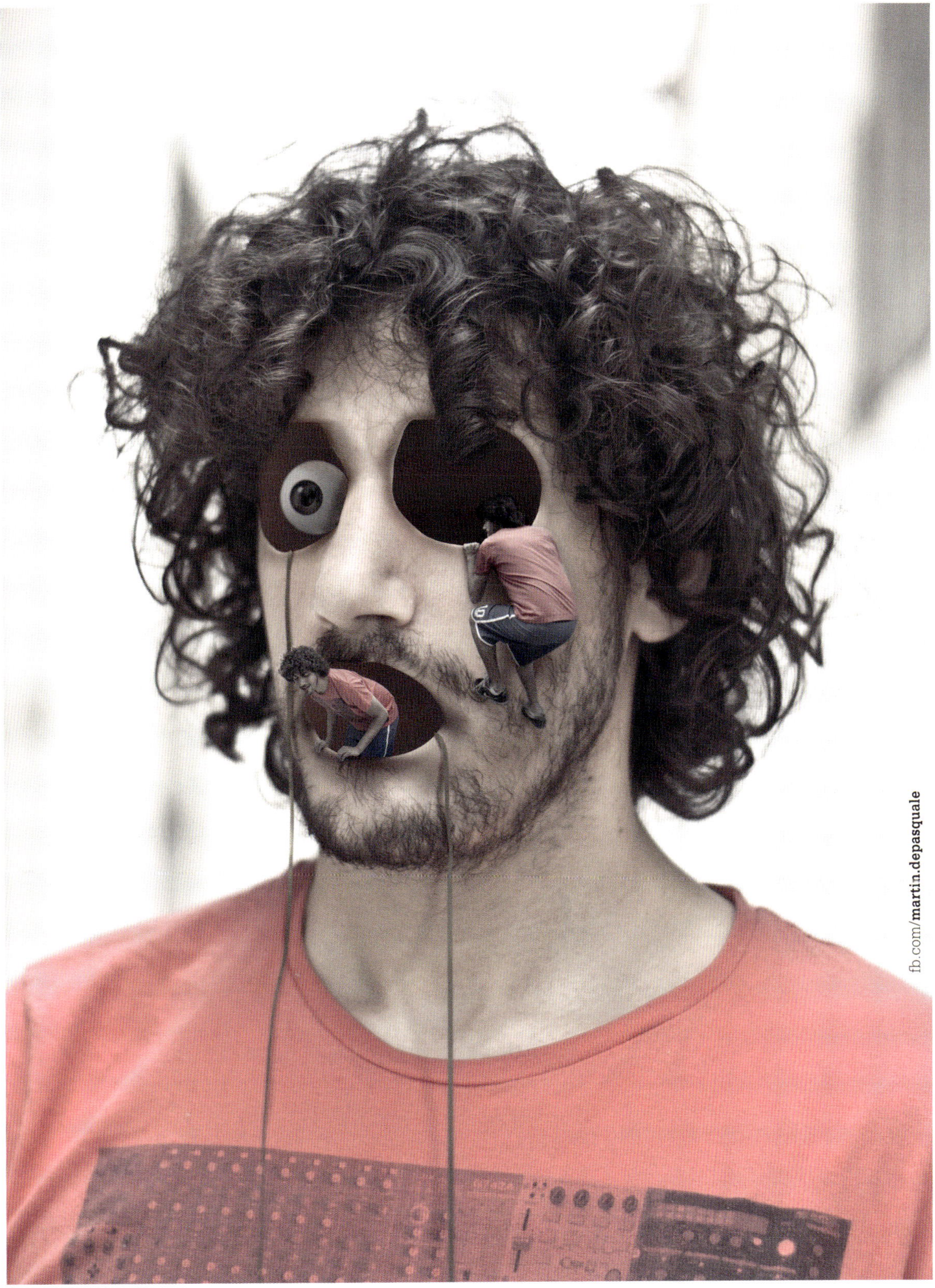

fb.com/**martin.depasquale**

© MARTÍN DE PASQUALE, HEAD, 2013

JAMES POPSYS

#LAND-SCAPE

#LITTLE PEOPLE

'Making the ridiculous images is what I love to do', states James Popsys. How does he find the best way to tell a story in an image? The photographer's ideas usually develop over a period of time, and as soon as they are ripe enough, James brings them in to life. His concepts are typically based on stark contradictions. In addition to the startling dissonance of the motifs he juxtaposes, another important feature of the artist's mischievous manipulations is playing with scale. Ordinary objects, locations or situations amaze and amuse in new settings and formats.

A large part of his oeuvre are playful portraits of London, where he comes from, but the artist also creates witty compositions relating to our everyday experience. James' surreal shots are always humorous, to the point and well-executed. He currently lives and works in Manchester.

JAMESPOPSYS.COM

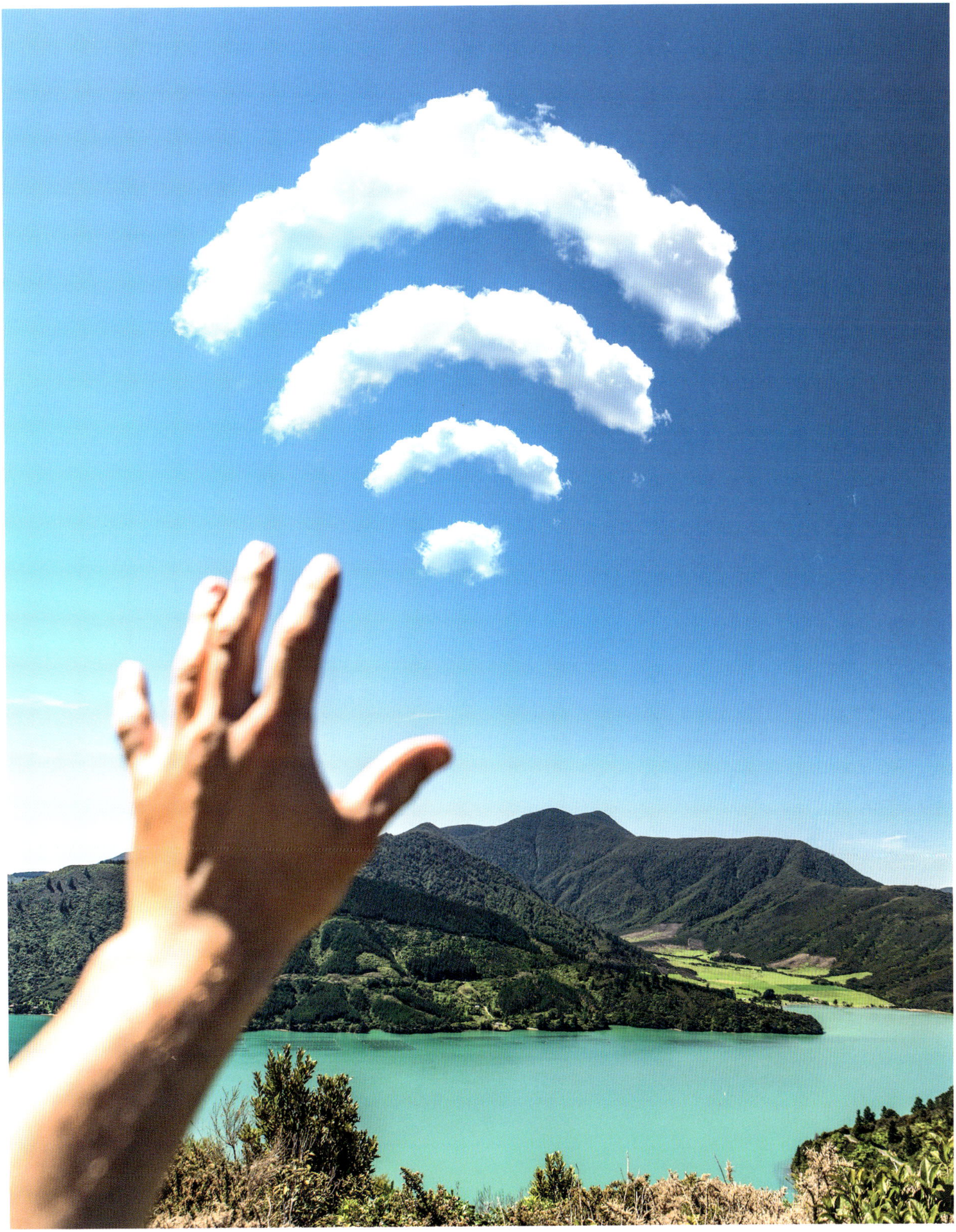

© JAMES POPSYS, NO WIFI, 2016

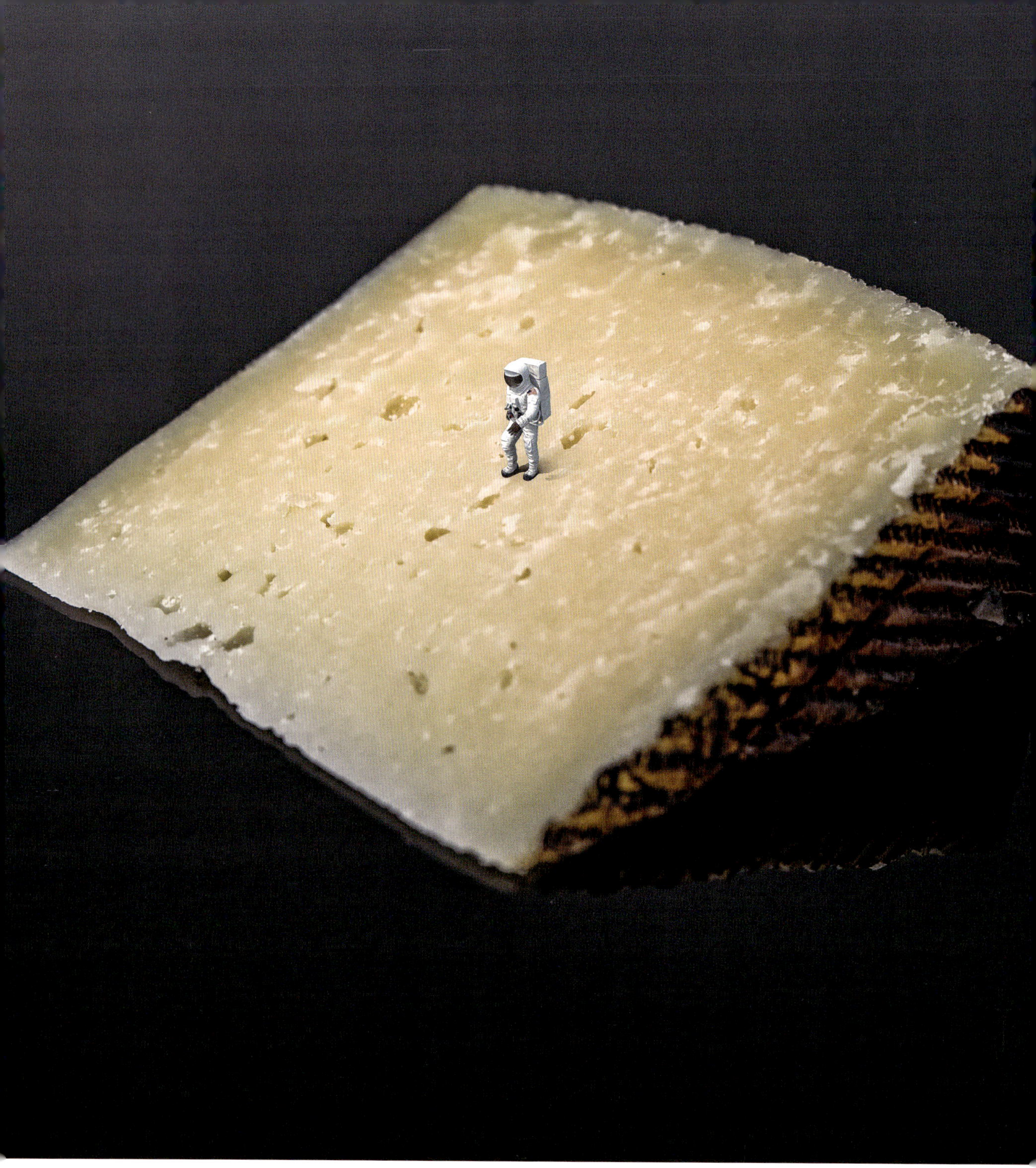

© JAMES POPSYS, MOONWALK, 2017

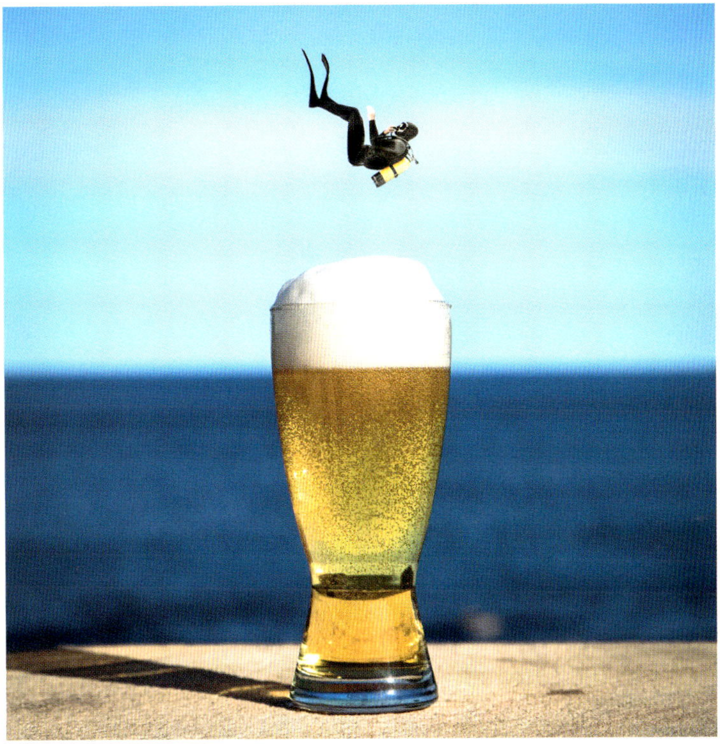

© JAMES POPSYS, FRIDAY, 2016

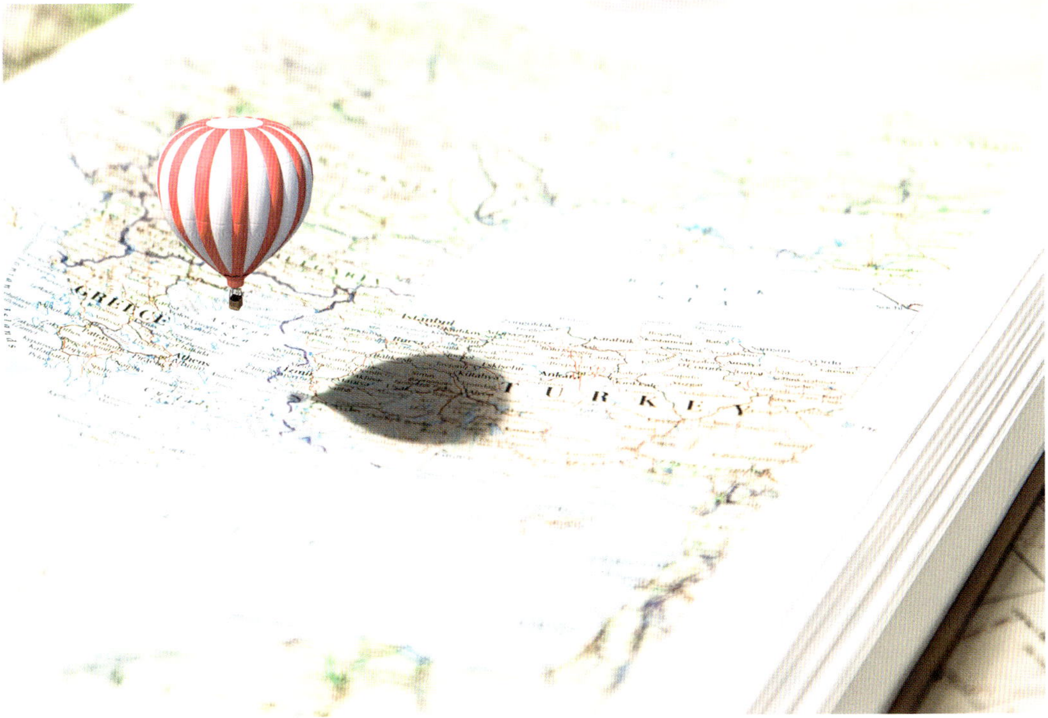

© JAMES POPSYS, HIGH LIFE, 2017

JEAN-FRANÇOIS RAUZIER

Jean-François Rauzier (b. 1952) calls himself the 'dreamweaver of reality'. The French artist has worked digitally since 2002, when he invented the concept of hyper-photo, which involves assembling hundreds and thousands of images to create a new cosmic view. The compositions are always based on existing places but the huge num-berof snaps featuring them when put together throw a new light on the well-known locations.

The artist's vedutas combine so many elements of each city, which normally could not be seen simultaneously, that the effect is quite surreal. Given this technique, the format of the digital collages are gigantic, but that allows the possibility of immersing into the fascinating multi-layered urban compositions. Visually sensational, the hyperphotos focus on some of the most famous cities around the globe. The photographer wants to question the viewer's perception of the world and reflect on the place of man in the city. Cacophonous cityscapes also draw attention to their architectural heritage.

#LAND-SCAPE

#ARCHI-TECTURE

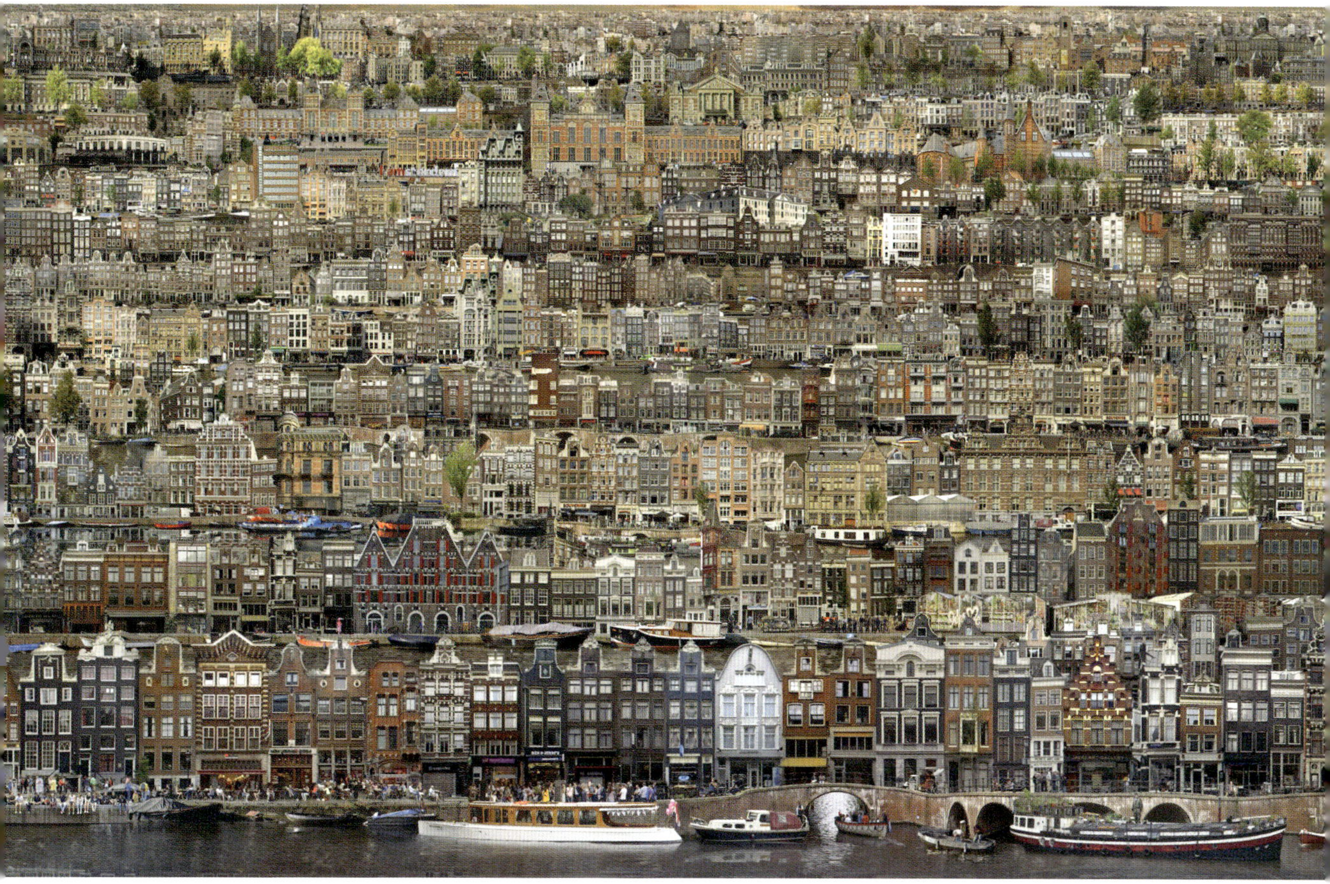

© JEAN-FRANÇOIS RAUZIER, VEDUTA AMSTERDAM I, 2015

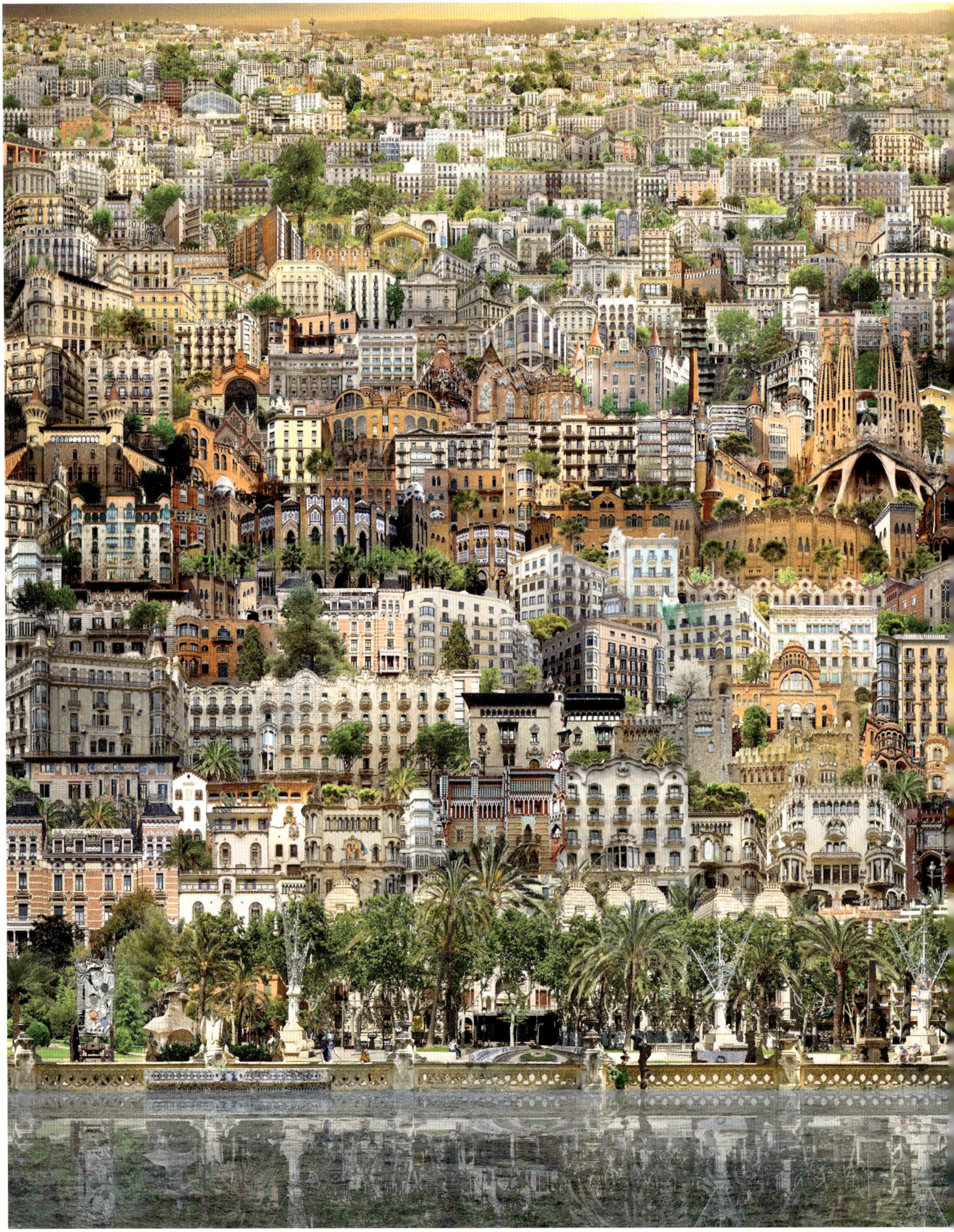

© JEAN-FRANÇOIS RAUZIER, BARCELONA VEDUTA, 2014

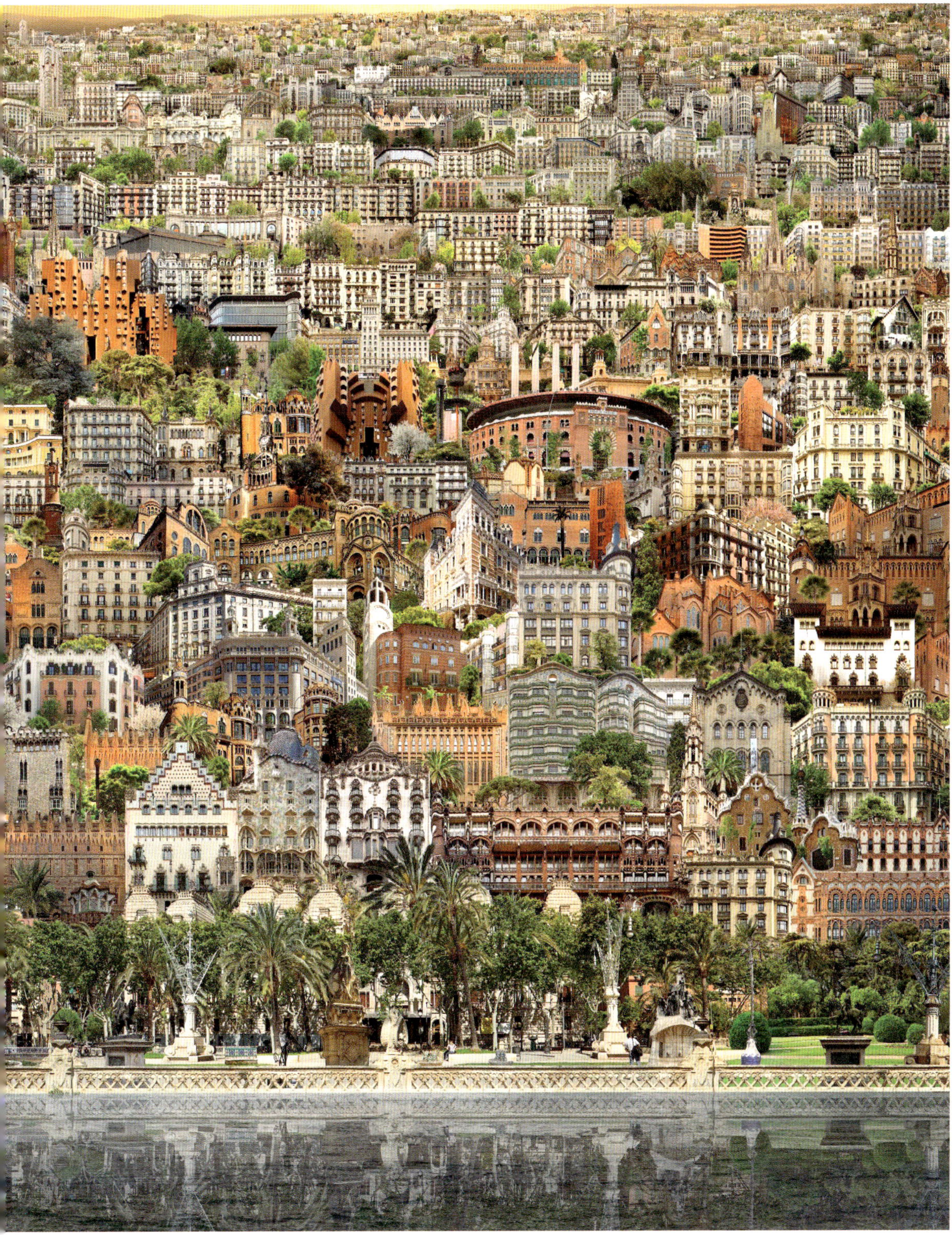

JOEL ROBISON

#PORTRAIT

The dream-like world of Joel Robison (b. 1984), a Canadian photographer currently based in the United Kingdom, is a way to share his conceptual self-portraiture. Imaginative compositions, be it the balloon stairway to heaven or mini-version of reality crafted for miniature inhabitants, are fueled by fantasies and fairy tales. As if motivated by keeping in touch with the inner child, Joel's manipulations are well-thought through in every detail and thus create a special mood. Storytelling is what interests him most in photography.

Between 2013 and 2014 Joel worked exclusively with Coca-Cola and FIFA as the lead photographer and as the voice of social media on the FIFA World Cup Trophy Tour by Coca-Cola. Over 9 months he visited more than 80 countries. His photographic adventures during this amazing trip deserved more attention, so Joel runs a very inspirational blog (Find Joel), where one can admire these pictures resulting from his wanderlust.

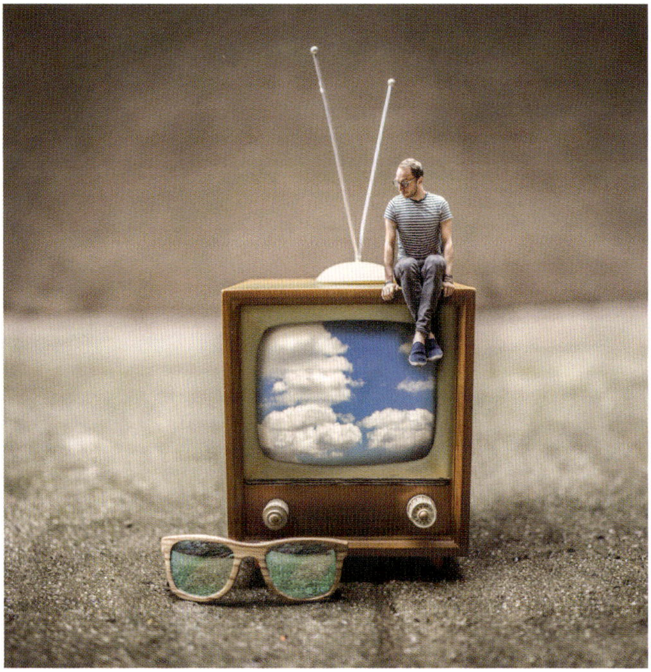

© JOEL ROBISON, TV, 2017

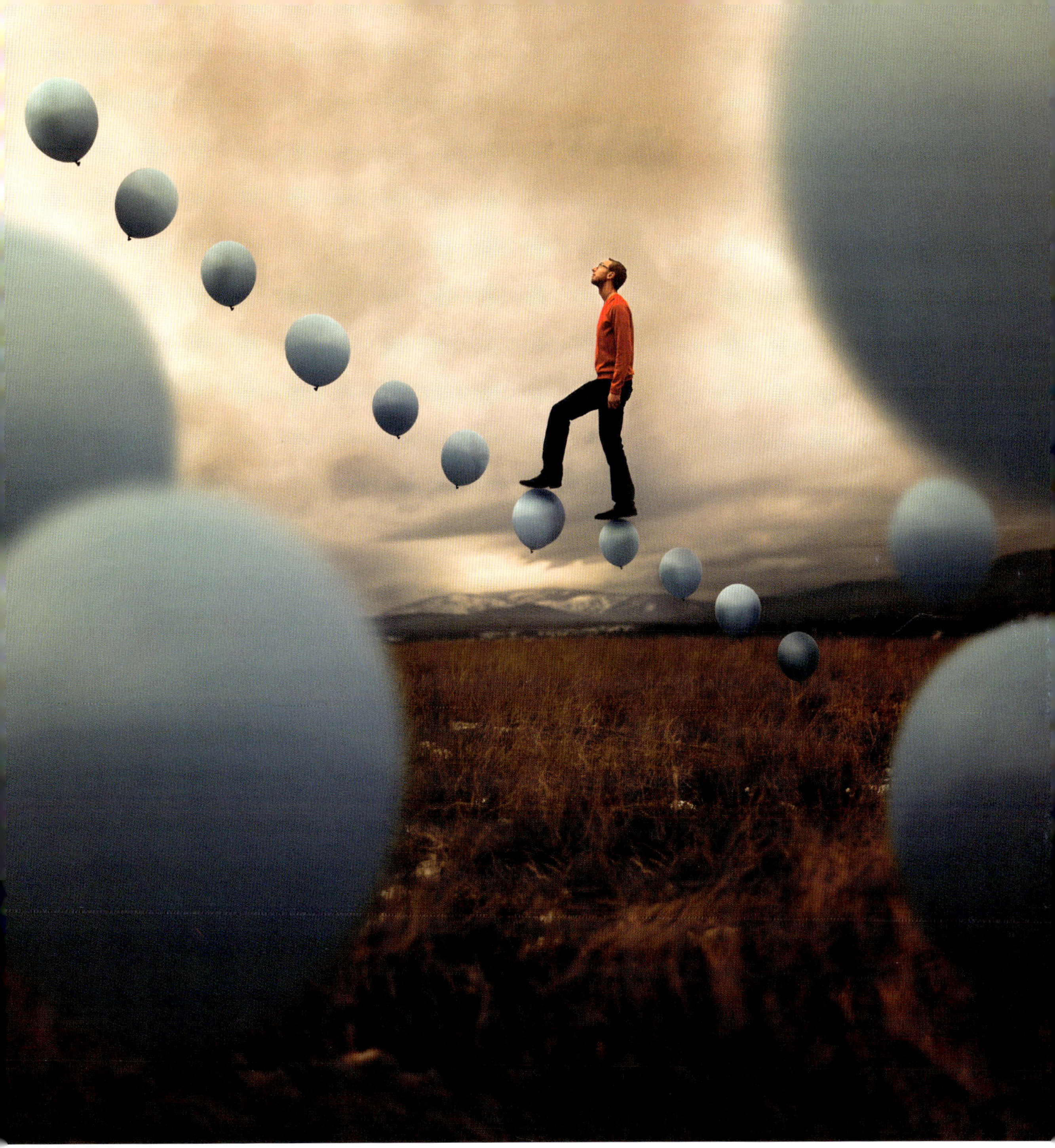

© JOEL ROBISON, STEPPING UP, 2012

JORGE SAENZ

#TOYS

#LAND-SCAPE

Jorge Saenz (b. 1958) calls himself a 'concerned dinosaurs photographer' in summarizing his artistic practice on his Instagram account. Born in Argentina, he lives in Paraguay. In parallel with his work as a photojournalist for newspapers and magazines, Jorge also develops numerous long-term personal works. His favourite theme for exploring is dinosaurs. It all began from one shot published on Instagram. As it became a hit, Jorge obtained more dinosaur toys and now he takes photos of them while travelling across Latin America. His account has more than 40,000 followers and the many dinos (each plays a different character in this surreal collection) are photographed in both natural and urban environments.

Jorge is currently working on a children's book with stories about dinosaurs travelling around the globe to understand human nature. To manipulate the compositions of his images (mainly the perspective to make the toys look real), the photographer uses only his iPhone.

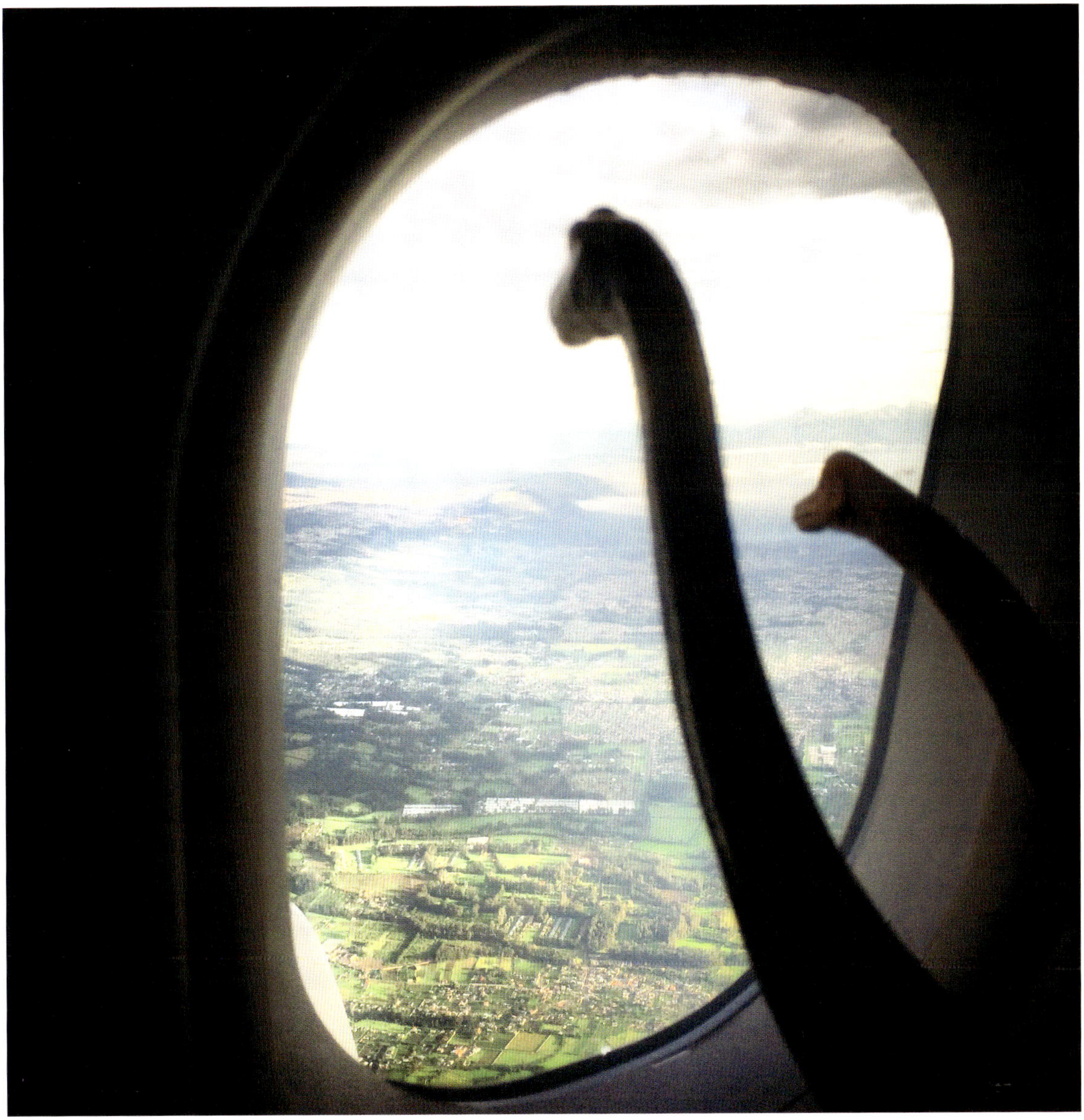

© JORGE SAENZ, 1 DE DICIEMBRE DE 2015

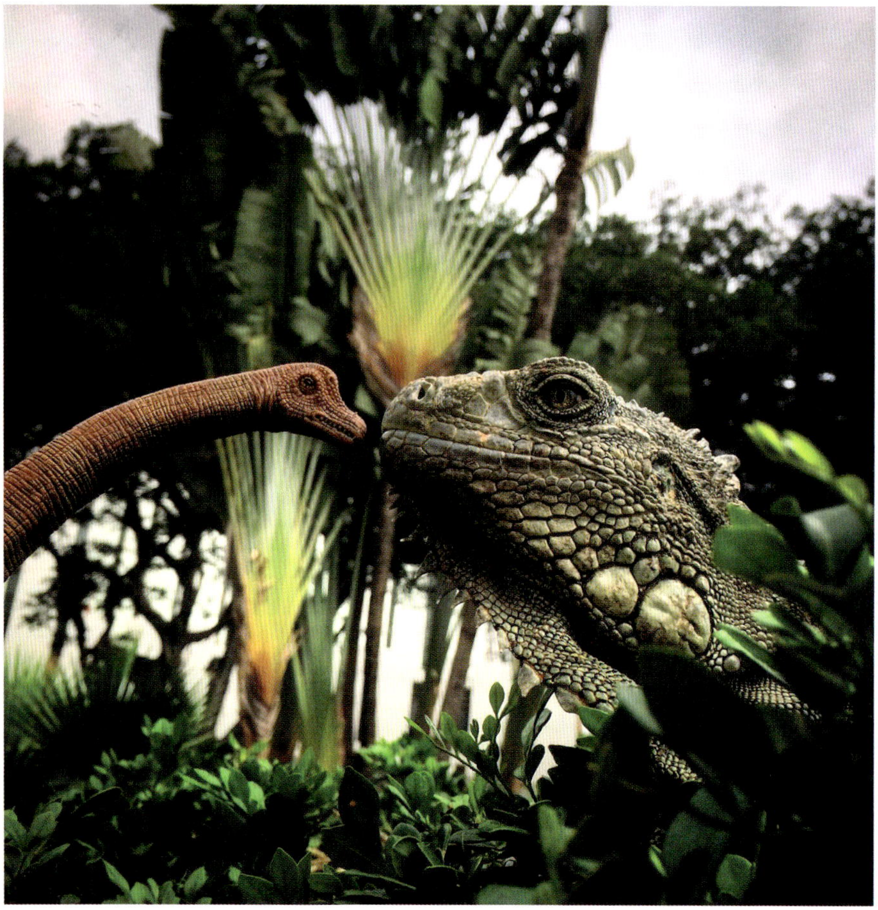

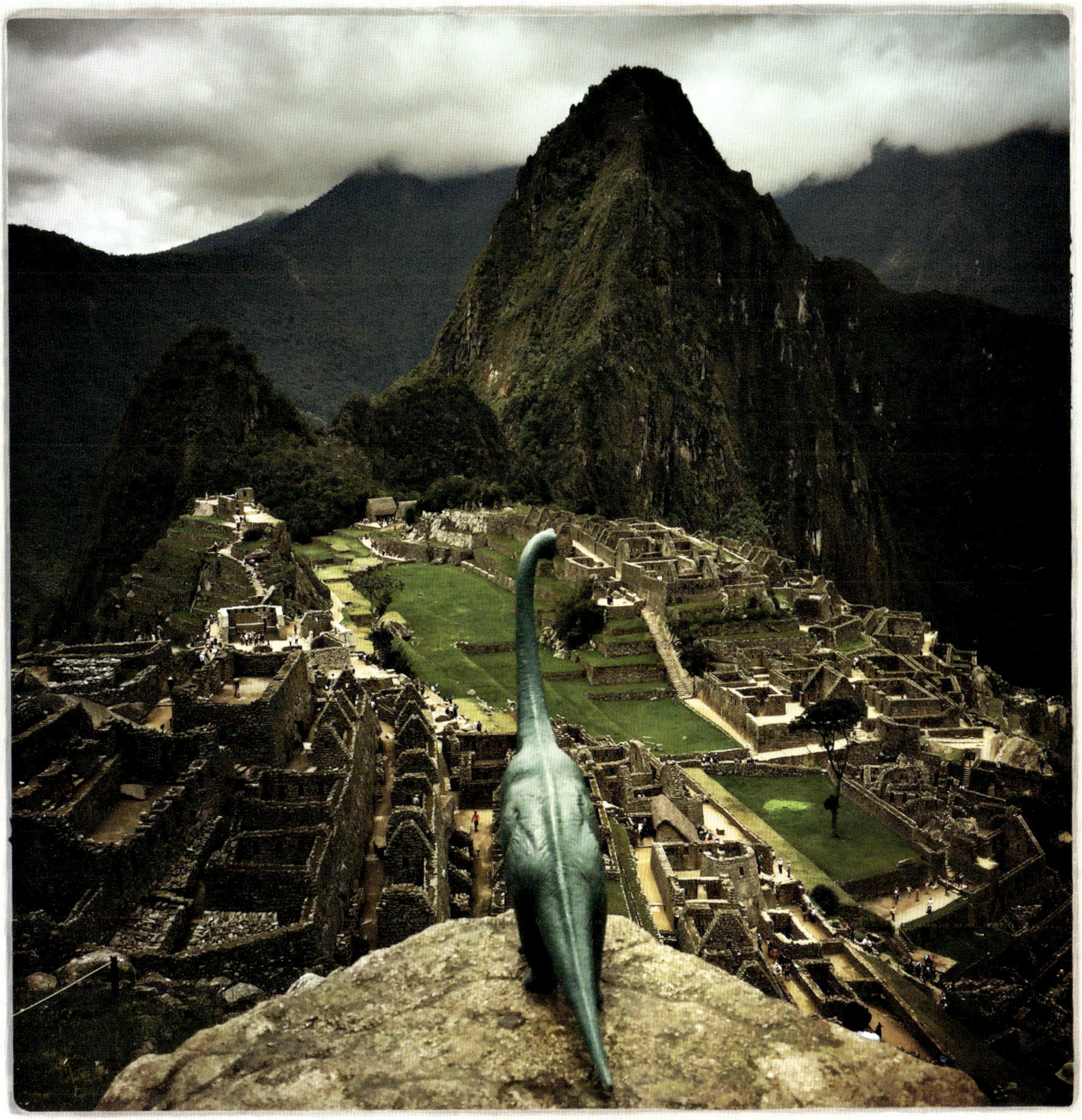

© JORGE SAENZ, 28 DE ABRLI DE 2016

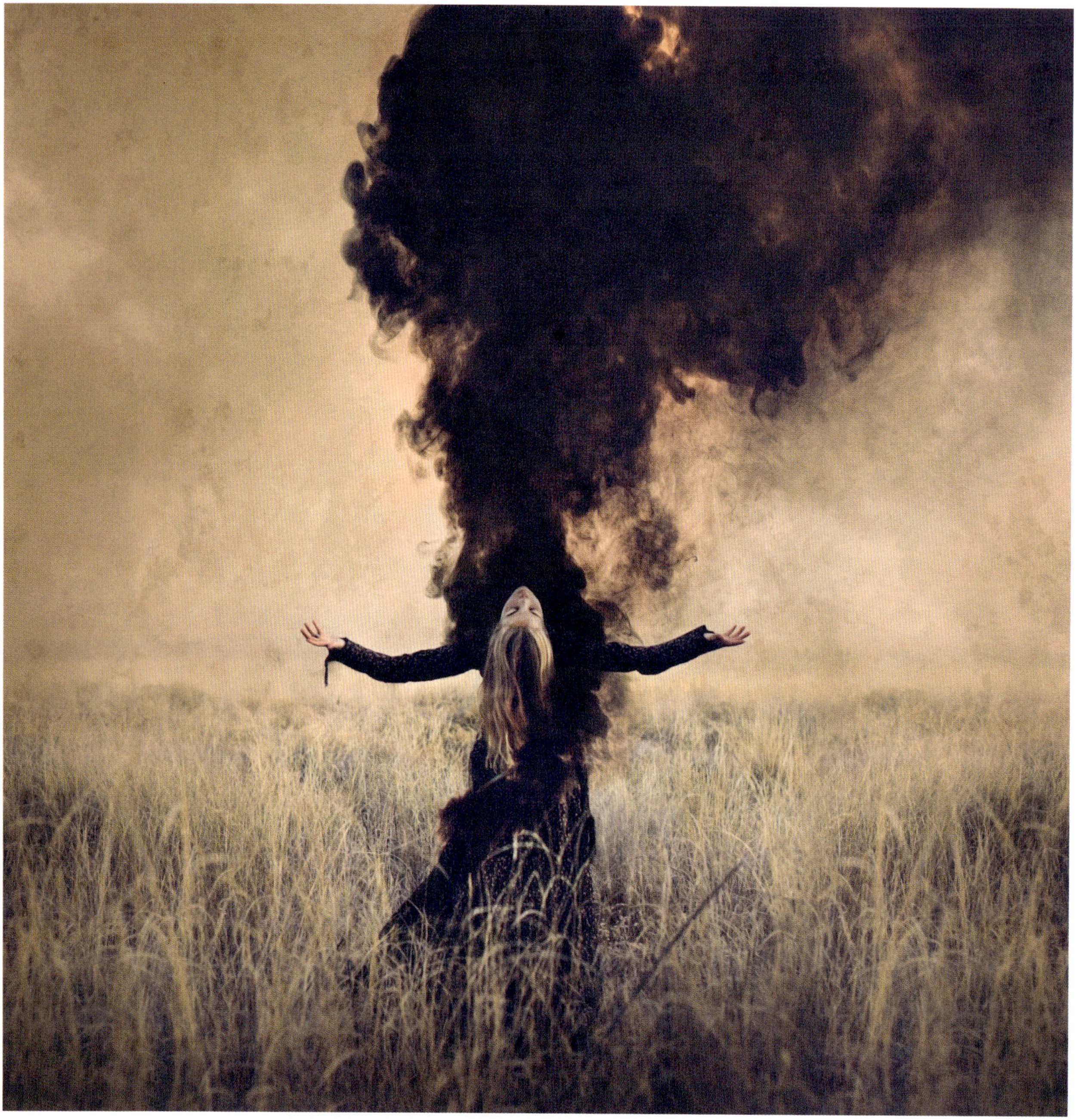

© BROOKE SHADEN, CATHARSIS, 2016

BROOKE SHADEN

#BODY

Although Brooke Shaden (b. 1987) studied filmmaking, it's photography to which she has devoted her artistic practice. Her two main goals – to create visually and to be a storyteller are realised in her signature series of mysterious, extremely atmospheric and uncanny self-portraits. Surreal in style, they explore the most complex aspects of human condition.

Asked about her inspirations, Brooke remarks: 'For as long as I can remember, I have had dark daydreams or nightmares. When I picked up a camera for the first time, I felt like photography and Photoshop would help me confront my fears and help others get a glimpse of the surrealistic visions in my head.' Thanks to her skillful use of manipulation techniques, the artist can transform her otherworldly imagination into stunning visions. While 'Catharsis' is a dark self-portrait of the body in a state close to collapse, 'Rapt' was created with rebirth and strength in mind.

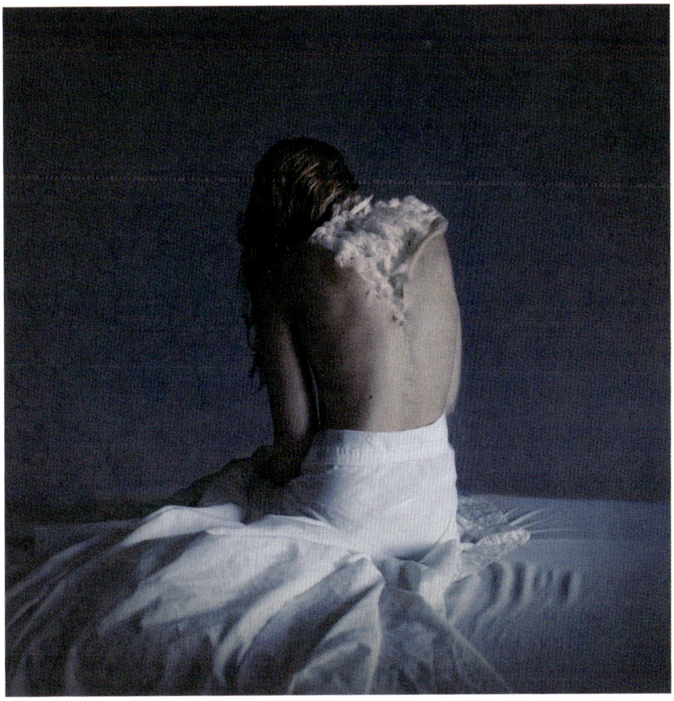

© BROOKE SHADEN, RAPT, 2016

DUDI BEN SIMON

Dudi Ben Simon is a top creative executive at an ad agency in Tel Aviv. 'Working in advertising by day', he says, 'my ideas are driven toward a goal and my work is done within marketing formats, through this creation I find that there are no limits to the world'. The channel for sharing his personal work is Instagram, which the photographer appreciates for being a democratic platform and widely available visual art gallery.

Fascinated by the history of art and inspired by ready-made art, Dudi creates his photos using common objects. By showing them in a different context or playing with their shapes and meanings, the photographer creates some crazy compositions that are visually simple yet telling. All aim to challenge the conventional way of thinking and ways of looking at everyday life from a different angle, with a certain twist that also brings humour.

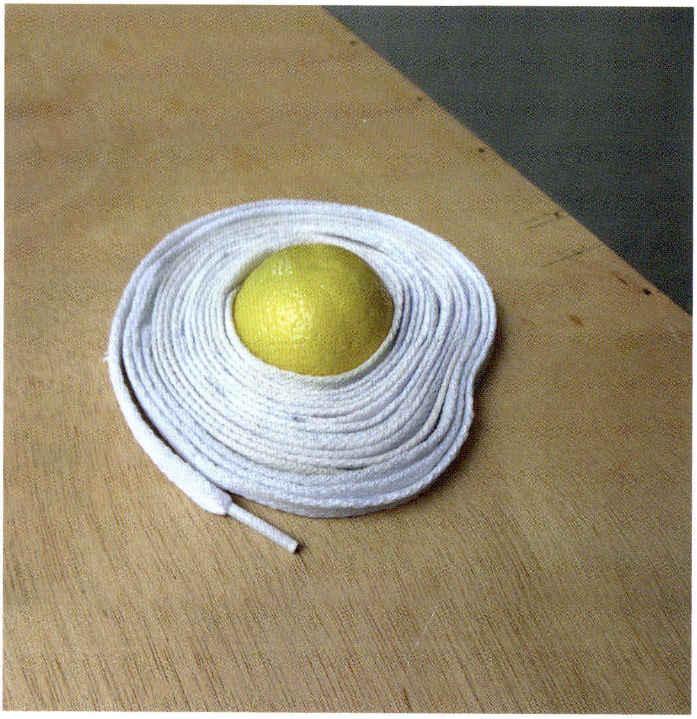

© DUDI BEN SIMON, SUNSHINE, 2015

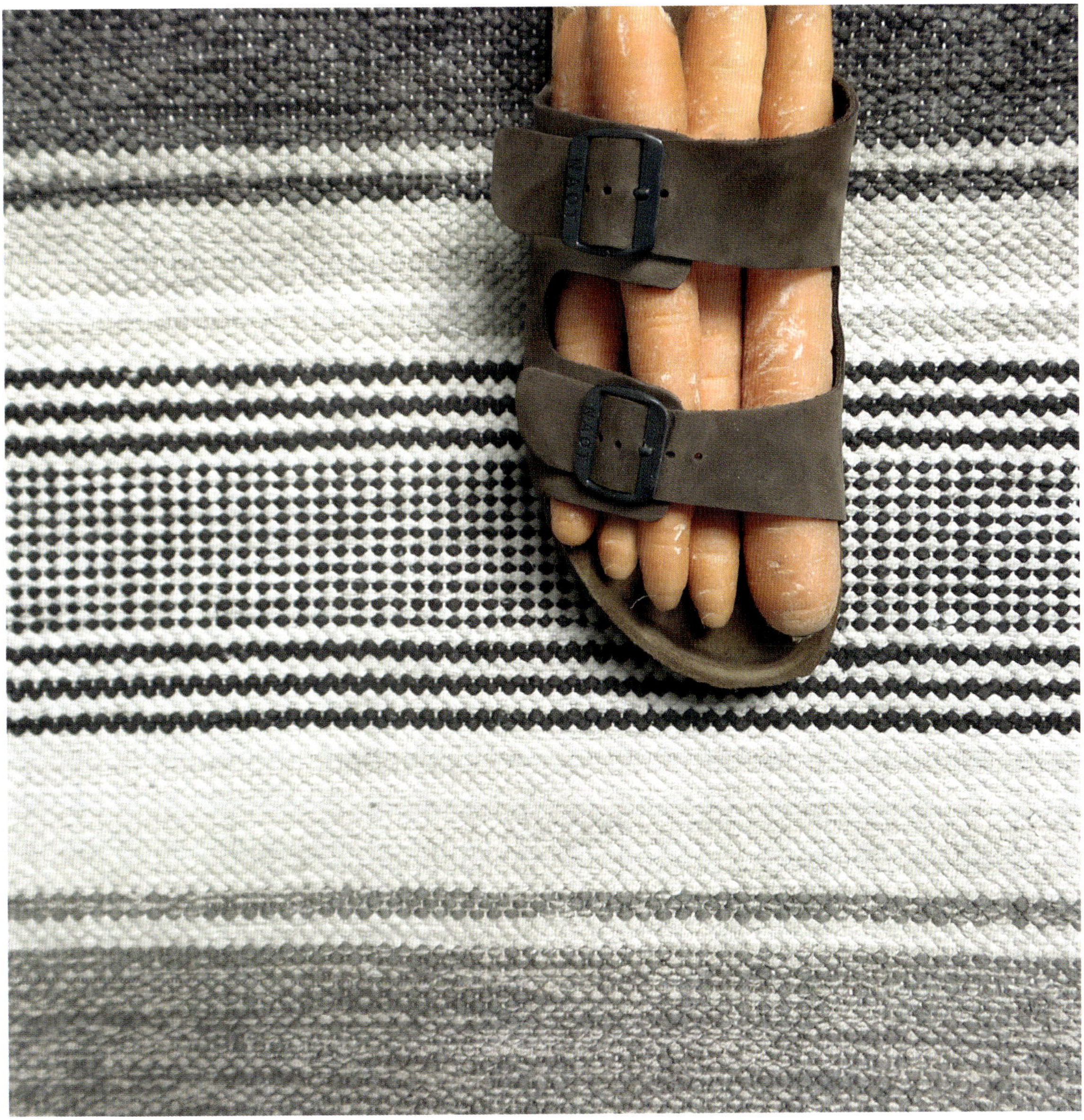

© DUDI BEN SIMON, LOCALLY PRODUCED GOODS, 2016

RANDY SCOTT SLAVIN

Randy Scott Slavin is a film director and photographer. As a drone expert, he founded the New York City Drone Film Festival and is renowned for his mind-bending 'Alternate Perspective' series of panoramas. Surreal as it may sound, Randy makes it possible to include a full 360-degree view on a flat image. Interested in both natural landscapes and urban spaces, when he photographs a scene, he shoots around one hundred single pictures and then puts them together into digitally mapped stereographic projections. Interestingly, the final effect is unpredictable until the very last stage of post-production.

Randy takes the manipulation to a different level in his whirlpool-like compositions. In these distorted panoramas, the world spins psychedelically in all directions. City skylines bend into perplexing vortexes that pull the viewer into the very heart of the vista. Be it iconic cities or natural spots, the spherical panoramas are amazing.

#LAND-SCAPE

#ARCHI-TECTURE

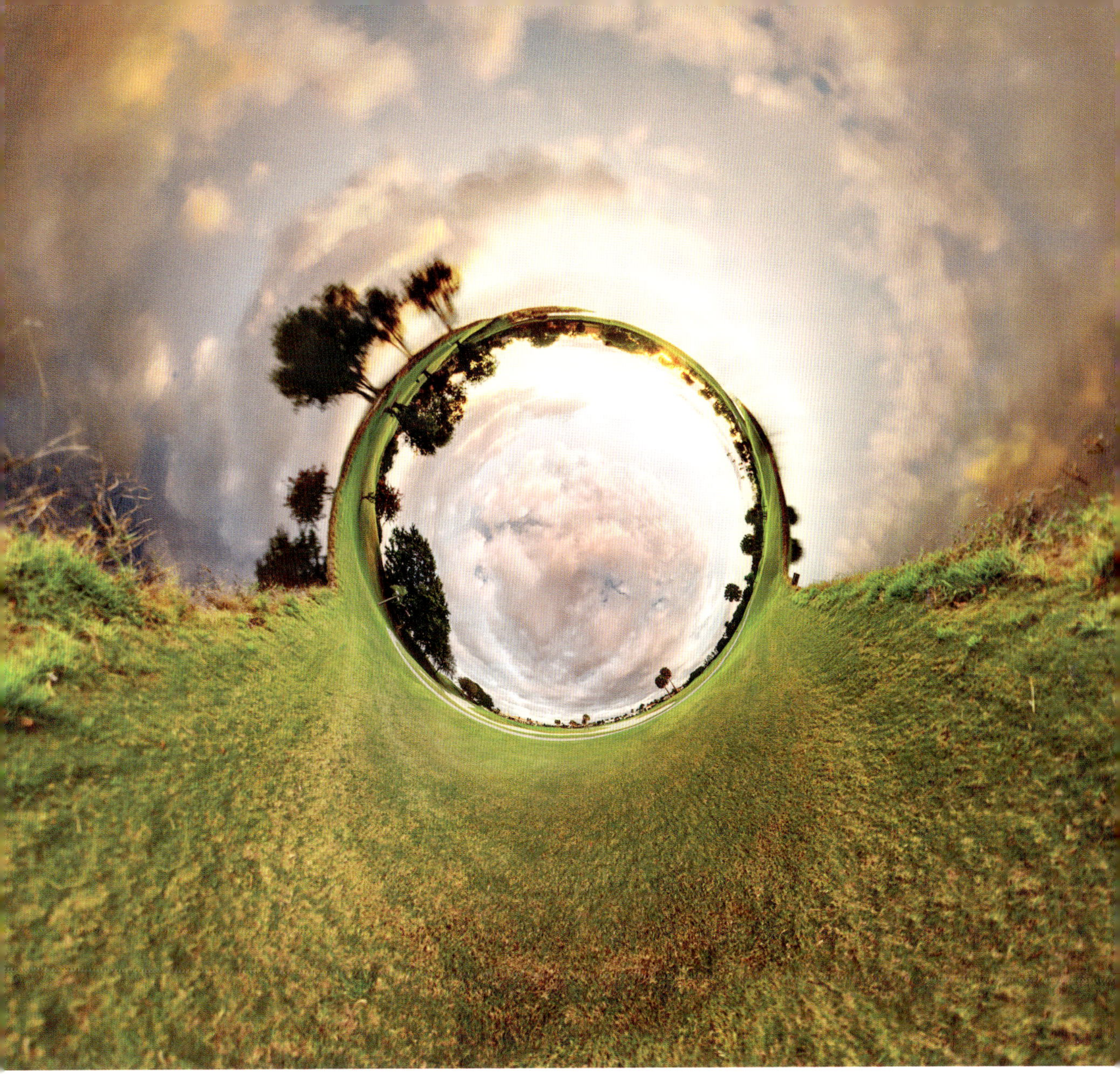

© RANDY SCOTT SLAVIN, IN DREAMS

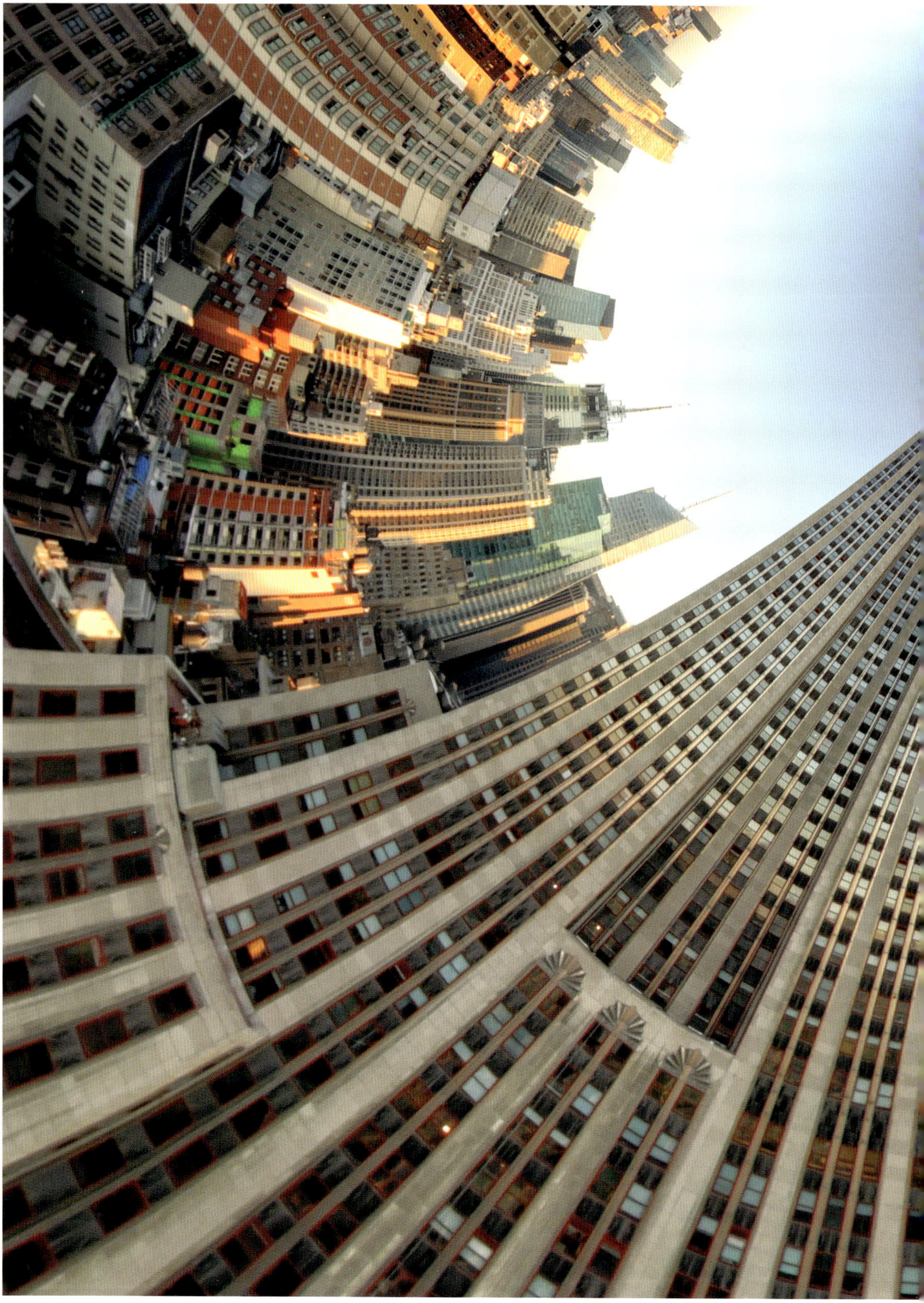

© RANDY SCOTT SLAVIN, EMPIRE STATE

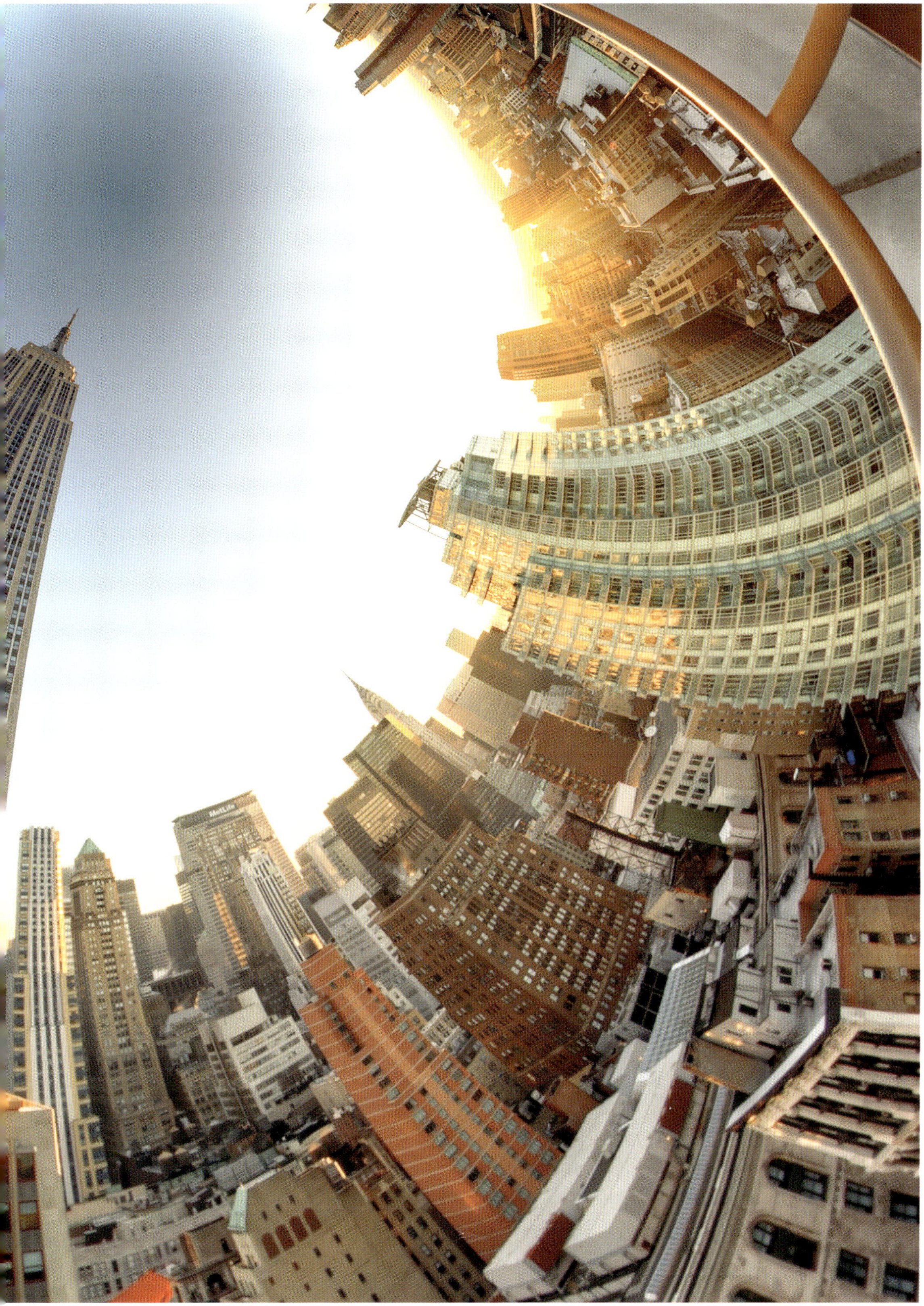
MetLife

STAUDINGER+FRANKE

Staudinger+Franke is an award-winning, Vienna-based photo-studio with inhouse retouching and CGI Division established by Andreas Franke and Robert Staudinger. Among the best ad photographers in the world, they see photography and retouching as inseparable resulting in the most daring visual concepts possible ('Every conceivable idea is doable', states the studio).

Staudinger+Franke seduce by creating very realistic scenes with a twist. The results are often hilarious. The whimsical portrait of a cat is part of a campaign for animal rights in Switzerland. The handsome squirrel comes from a poster promoting a trimmer. The 'world's smallest bakery' introduced a new product for an Austrian bakery; a dough pocket with a filling that you bake by placing it in your toaster. Ad photography can be successfully surreal! What's more, the advertising world needs more original craziness.

#LITTLE PEOPLE

#ANIMALS

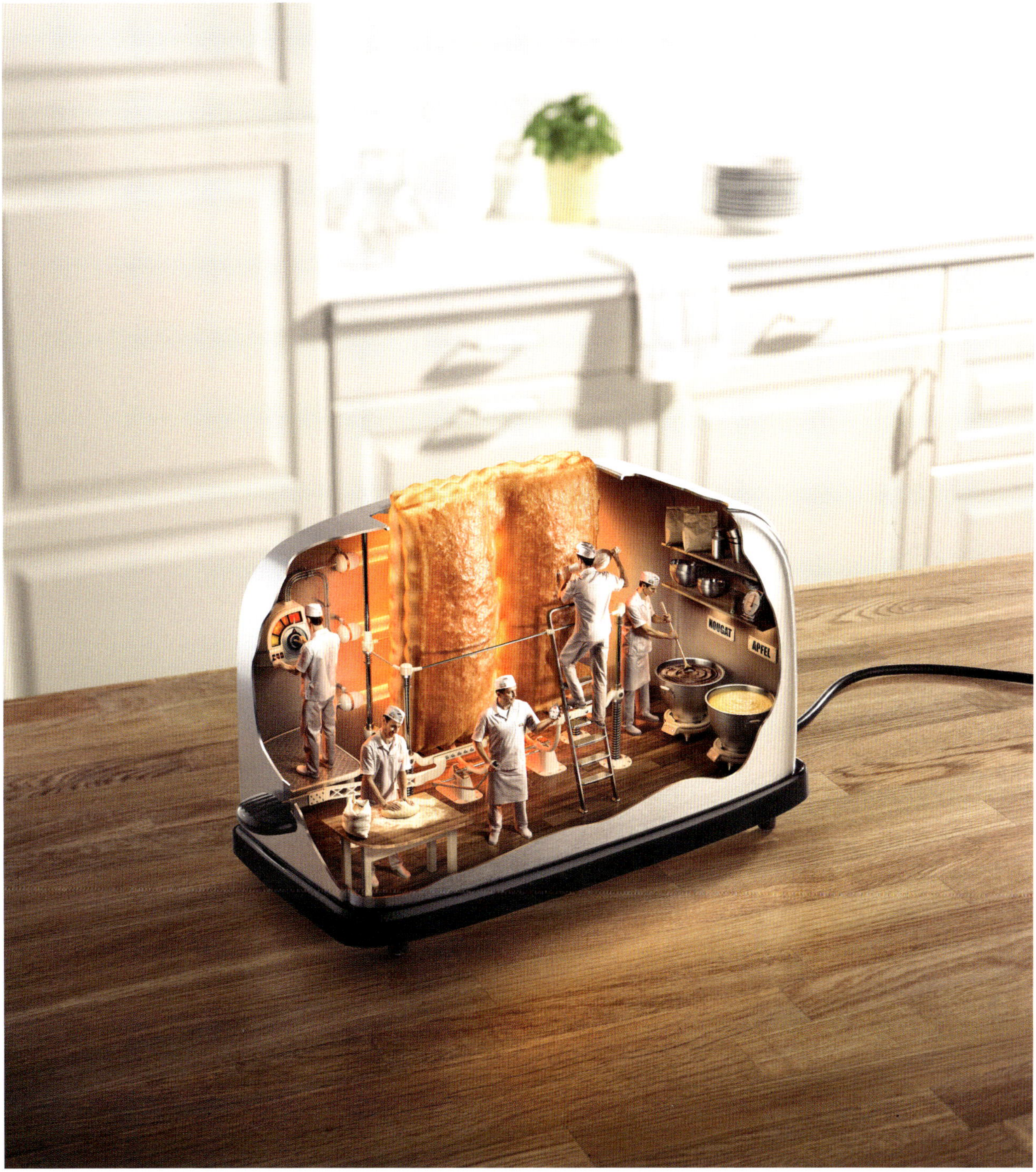

© STAUDINGER+FRANKE, WORLD SMALLEST BAKERY, 2014

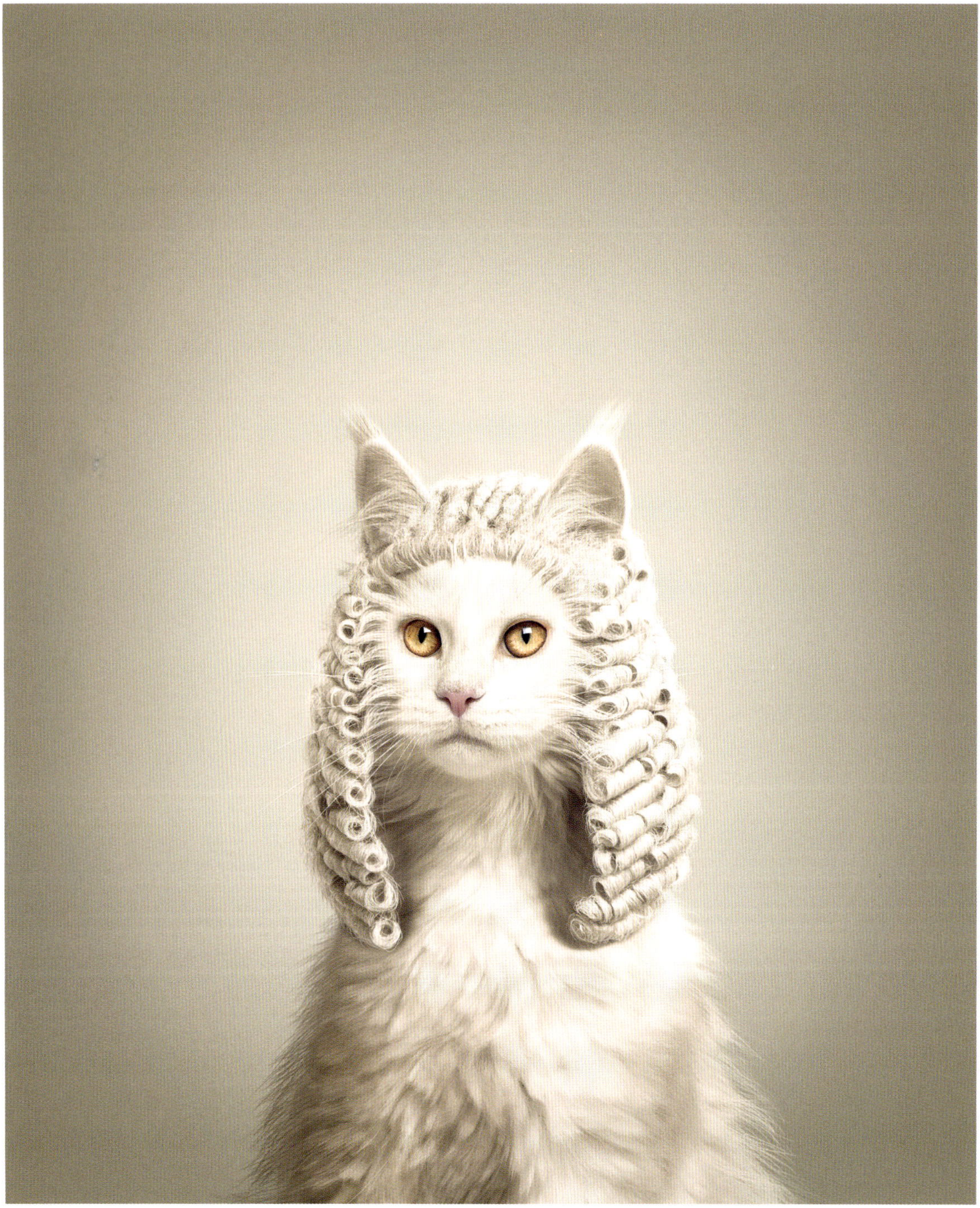

© STAUDINGER+FRANKE, IF ANIMALS COULD JUDGE, 2013

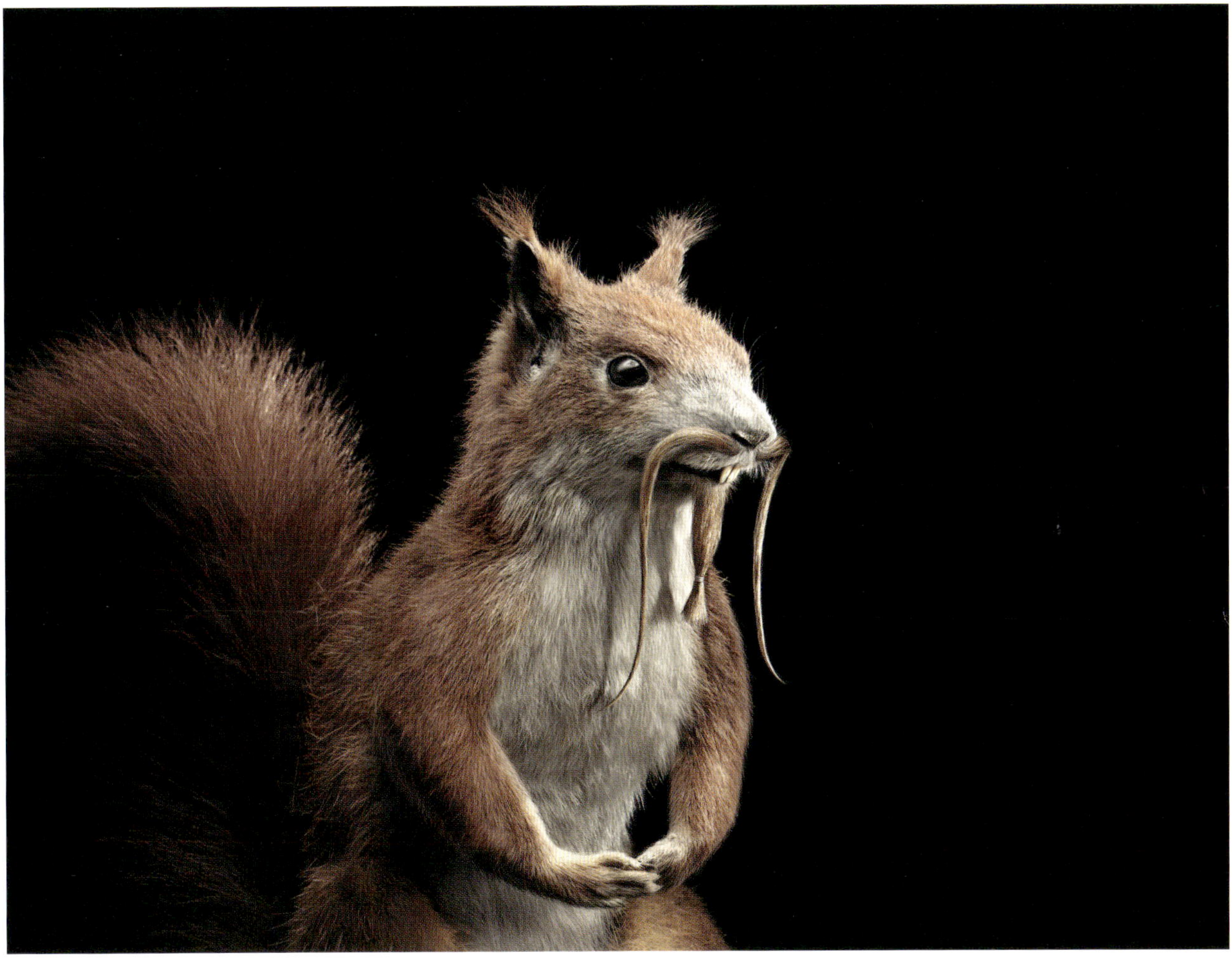

TATSUYA TANAKA

#LITTLE PEOPLE

At the core of 'Miniature Calendar' by Japanese photographer and art director Tatsuya Tanaka (b. 1981) are amazing, teeny tiny scenes which he has been updating online daily since 2011. 'Everyone must have had similar thoughts at least once' he says. 'Broccoli and parsley might sometimes look like a forest, or the tree leaves floating on the surface of the water might sometimes look like little boats. Everyday occurrences seen from a pygmy's perspective can bring us lots of fun thoughts.'

In creating miniature dioramas every day, the artist lets his imagination play with the ordinary in a most imaginative way. Just like a magician, he turns common objects and everyday activities into miniaturized realities mimicking our human world with a great sense of humour. While he makes us see the quotidian in a new and creative way, Tatsuya's ideas for portraying life in miniature are funny, colourful and playful.

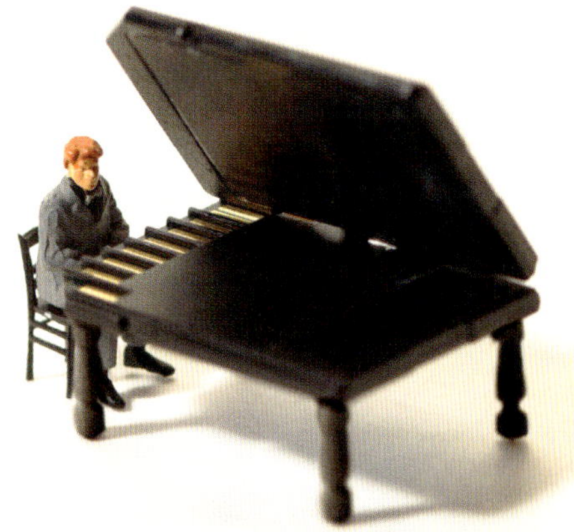

© TATSUYA TANAKA, MEMORY (MINIATURE CALENDAR)

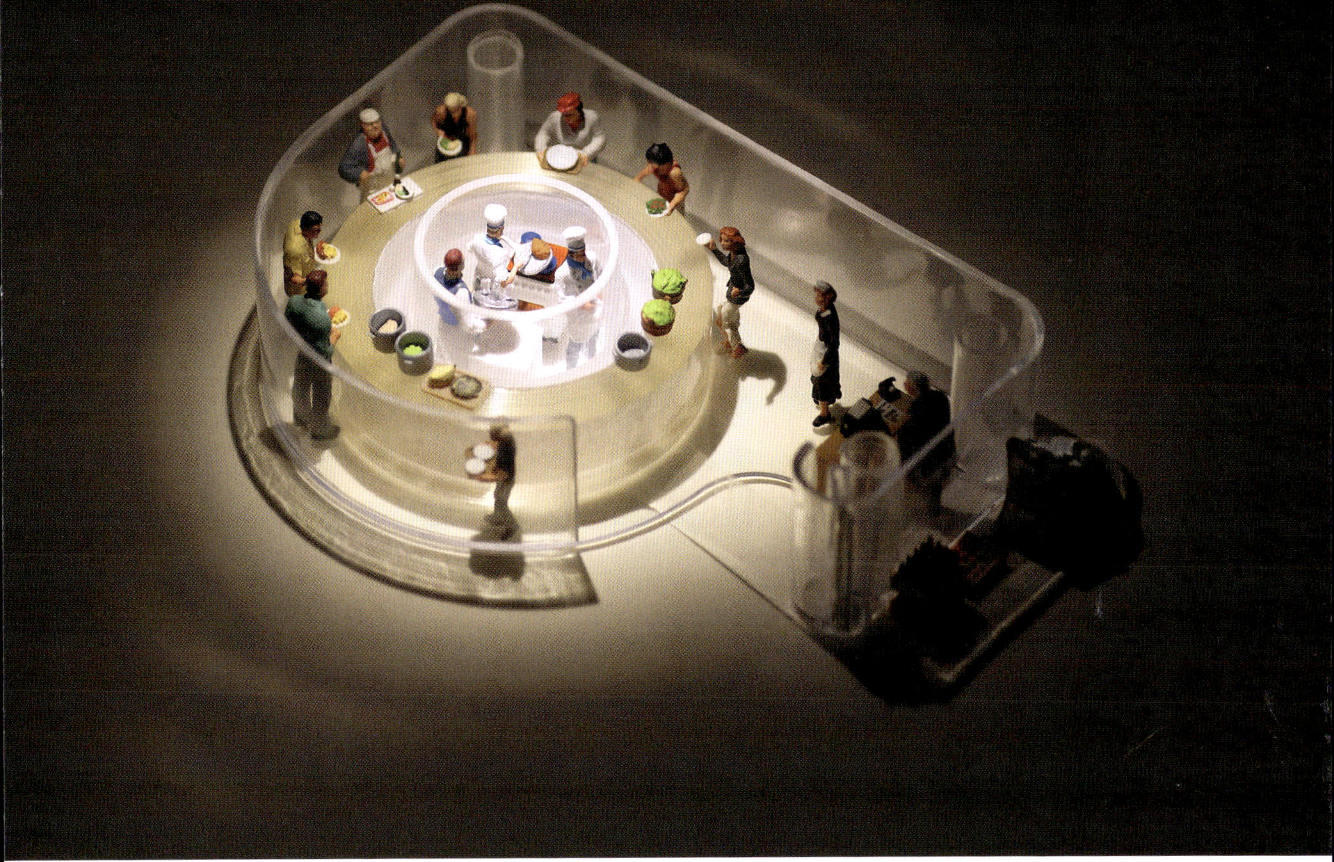

© TATSUYA TANAKA, COUNTER TAPE (MINIATURE CALENDAR)

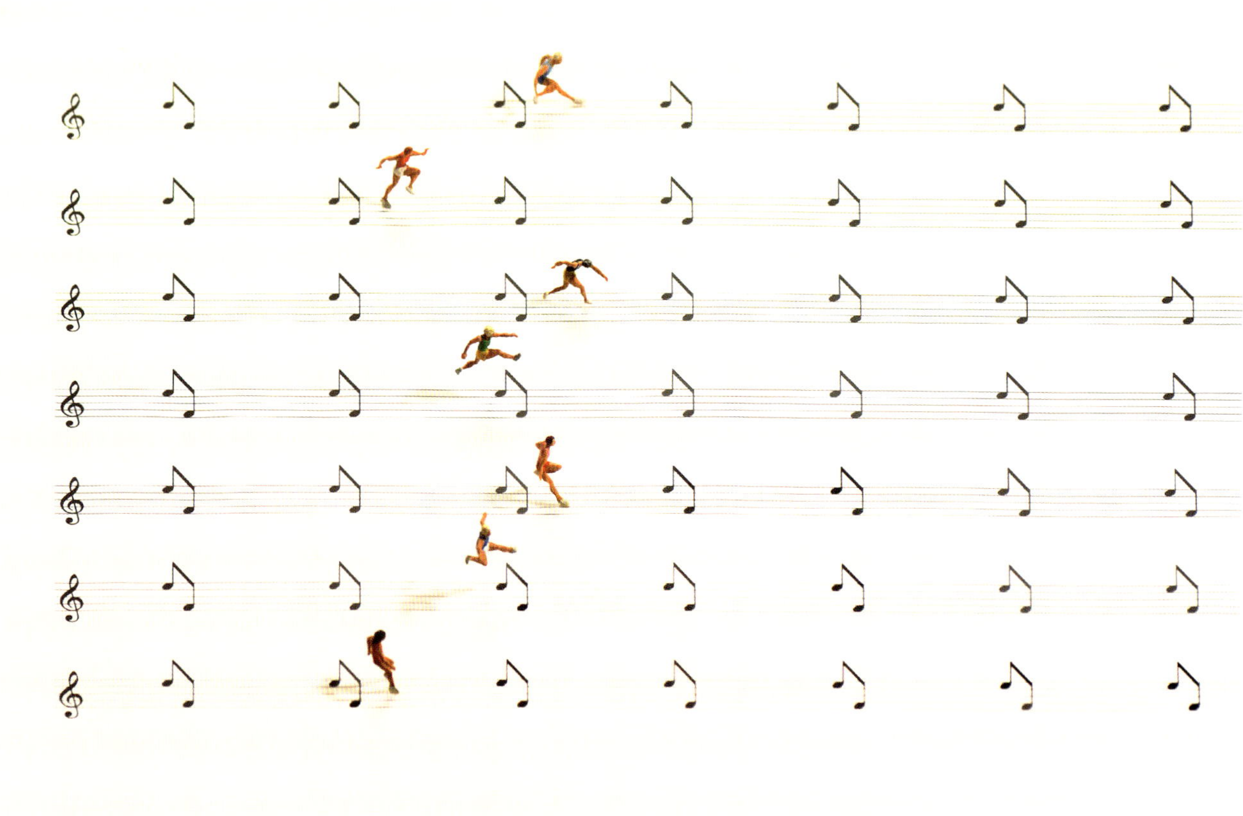

© TATSUYA TANAKA, PACE (MINIATURE CALENDAR)

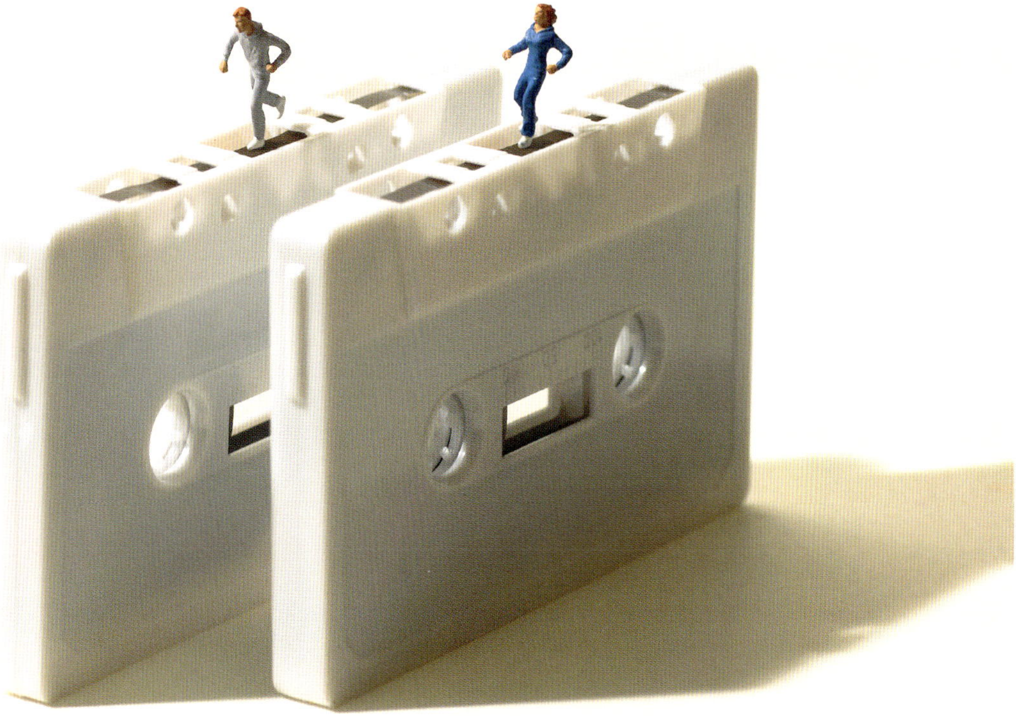

© TATSUYA TANAKA, ENDLESS RUNNING (MINIATURE CALENDAR)

ROY TYSON

#LITTLE PEOPLE

A bottle cap as an umbrella for a couple? A snail as a gigantic monster? Pieces of cigarettes as biohazard material? Humorous scenes that intrigue our senses lie at the core of 'Roy's People', a project by urban artist Roy Tyson fusing miniature figurines, photography and the streets of London, to create unique artworks. The works, inspired in large part by the contemporary urban art scene, are also often witty reflections on our emotions, activities and environments.

Roy's miniature world is artful and even if the artist uses just a couple of elements, the compositions are effective and fun. The surreal scenes, in which the figurines playfully interact with the surrounding, are arranged with a great eye for detail. 'All of the miniature figures are hand painted to give them personality and charm" Roy's original imagery drew the attention of many companies and charities as well as other artists, which resulted in many interesting collaborations.

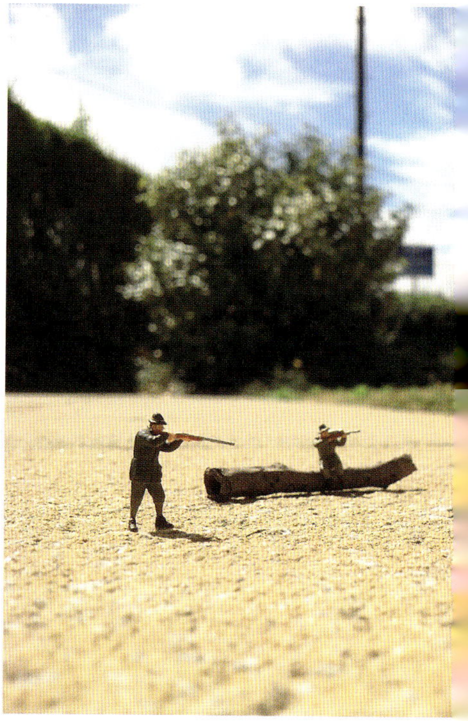

© ROY'S PEOPLE, I COME IN PEACE

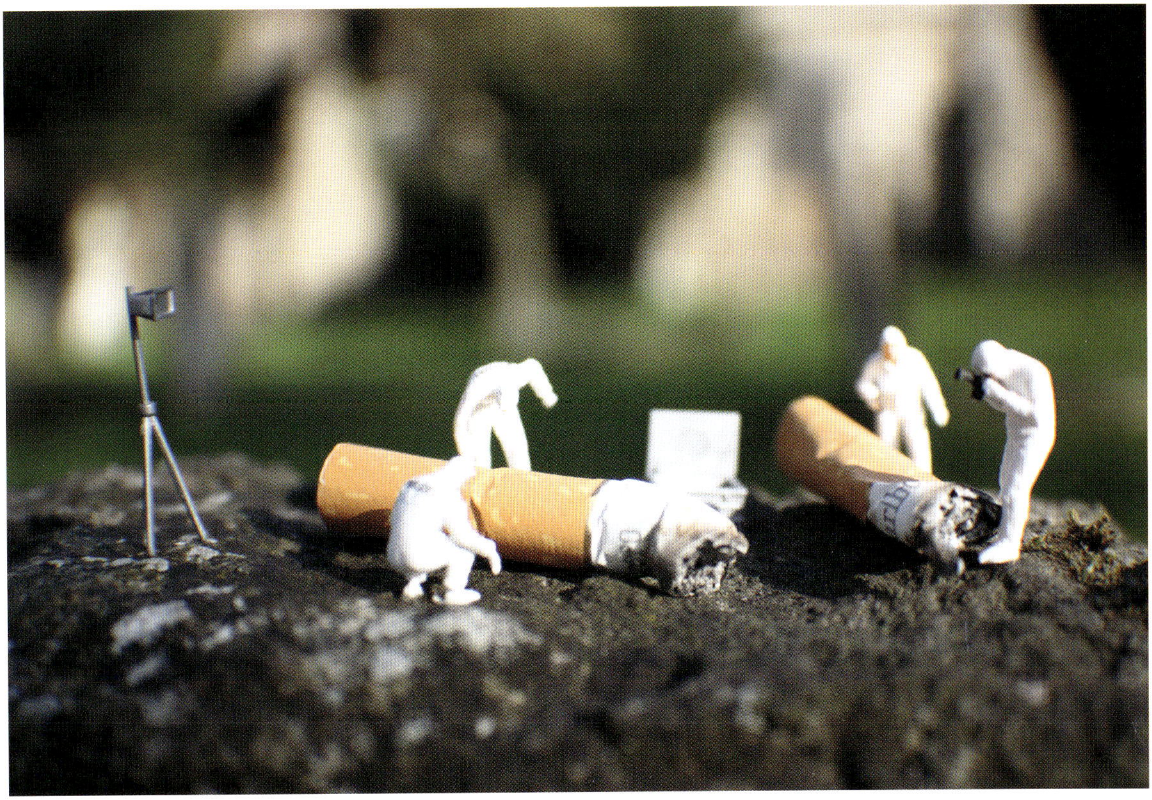

© ROY'S PEOPLE, CSI ESSEX

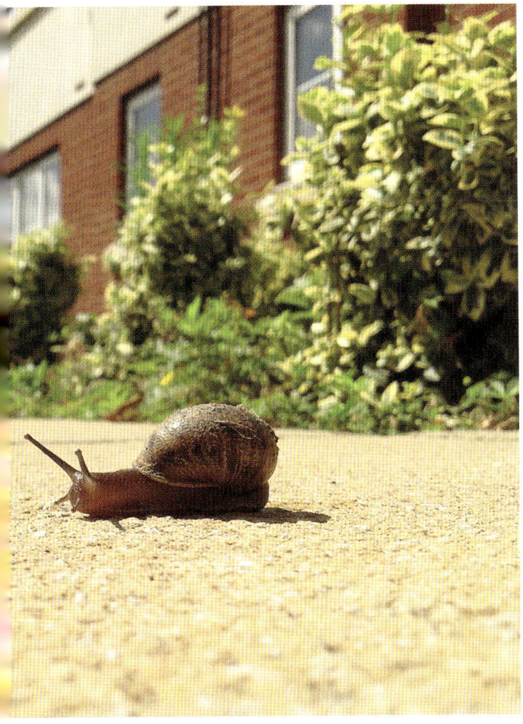

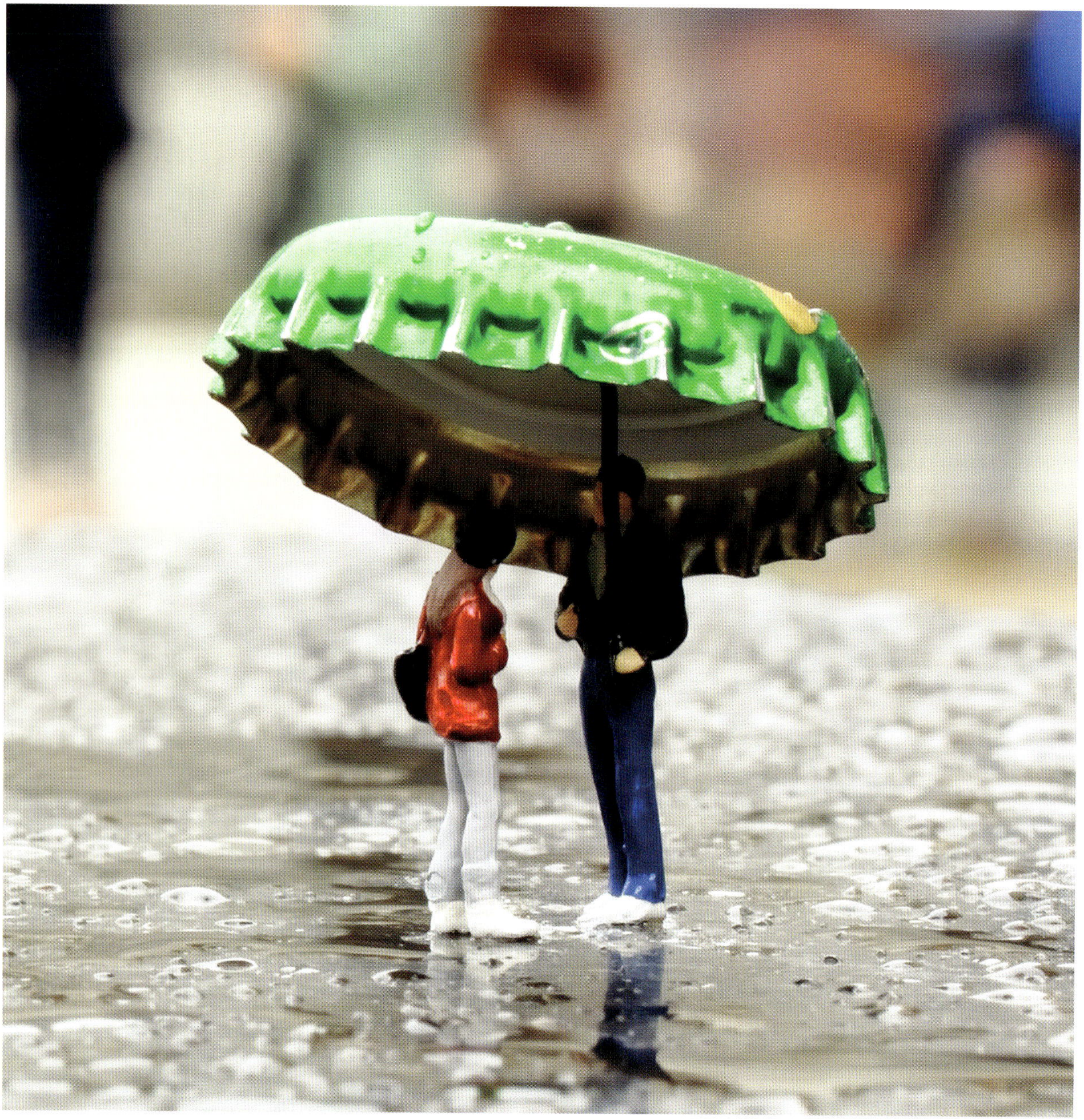

© ROY'S PEOPLE, ROOM FOR TWO

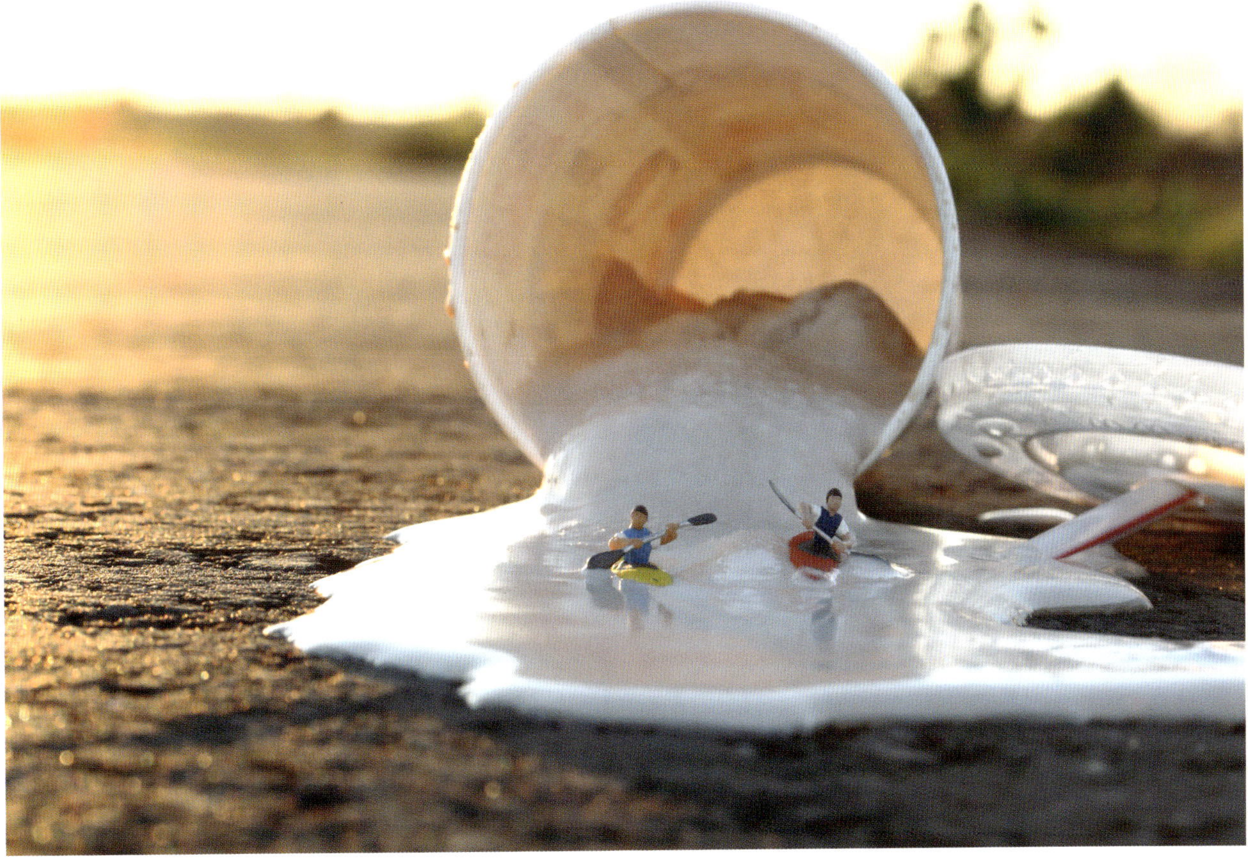

© ROY'S PEOPLE, THE RACE

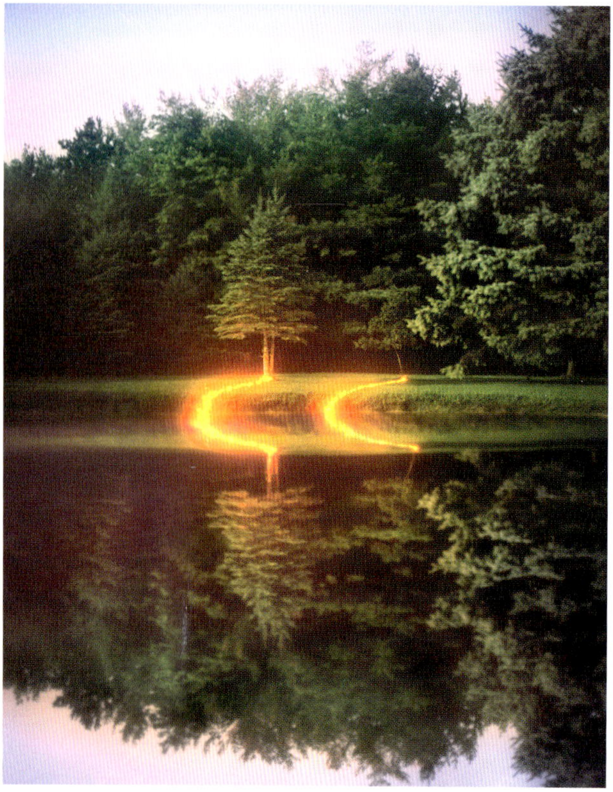

© BARRY UNDERWOOD, WAKESHIGAN RIVER, 2016

© BARRY UNDERWOOD, STRING LAKE, GRAND TETON NATIONAL PARK, 2015

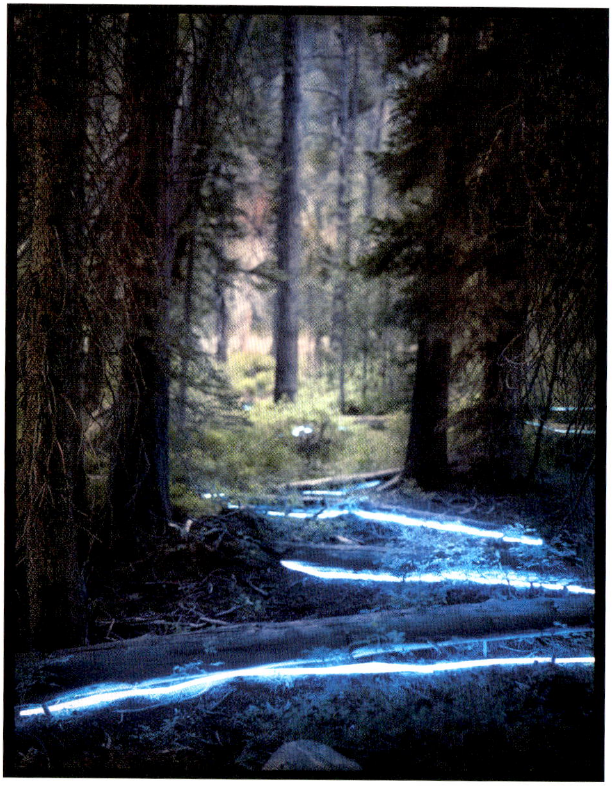

BARRY UNDERWOOD

#LAND-SCAPE

Barry Underwood (b. 1963) is a specialist in surreal landscape photography. His 'Scenes' series comprises long-exposure images that document temporary sculpture structures built on-site in specific landscapes. 'I construct these tableaus by immersing myself in a given place, researching and instinctively reading the landscape', explains the photographer, 'and then marking the site through using foreign materials (LED lights, luminescent substances, and other physical processes) to emphasize and to call attention to environmental blight'.

Abstract intrusions, colour in particular but also shapes, lines and light reflect upon the impact of human abuse on nature. The dream-like atmosphere is deceptive, as playful interactions with the landscape comment on how altering a landscape to our use changes it. Barry's practice is driven by the ecological as well as social history of places. The way a specific location is used, lies at the heart of the photographer's work.

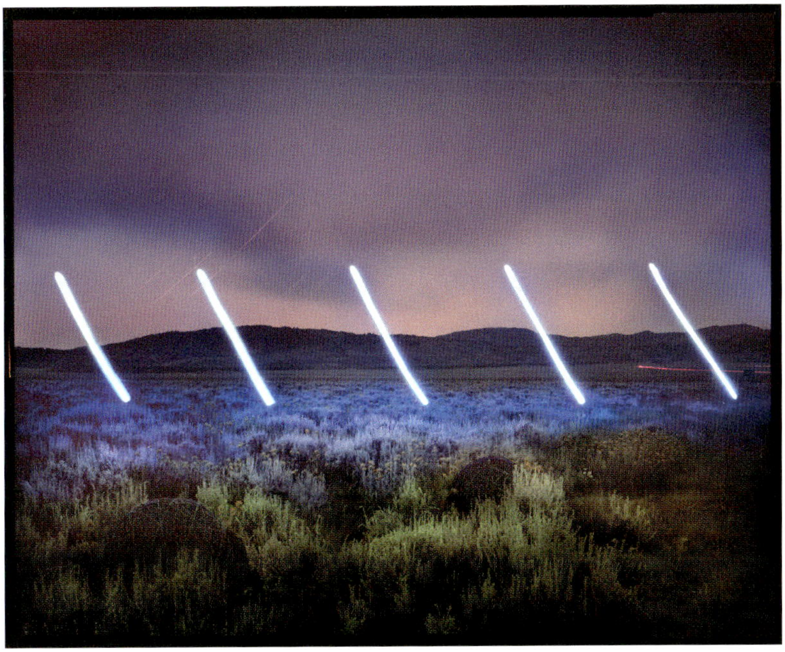

© BARRY UNDERWOOD, JACKSON, WYOMING (FOR RAINER), 2016

DIGGIE VITT

Diggie Vitt started photographing as a result of a broken heart and we should be grateful to the girl. Initially it was, as he calls it, an outlet for communicating feelings back to her, but it soon became a medium exploring human condition. Diggie comes from Jacksonville, Florida which he decided to leave some time ago to travel across the United States (his next destinations are Iceland and Europe). Throughout the trip the photographer captured a series of self-portraits envisioning the feeling of longing and misplacement.

A surreal approach seems to be the only way to translate the most complex and often complicated states of mind into the conceptual and, at times, eerie shots. We're featuring two works that are just as otherworldly, but less gloomy. Both confront the human body with the power of nature in most surprising ways. Basically, playing with visual improbabilities is the main feature of Diggie's oeuvre.

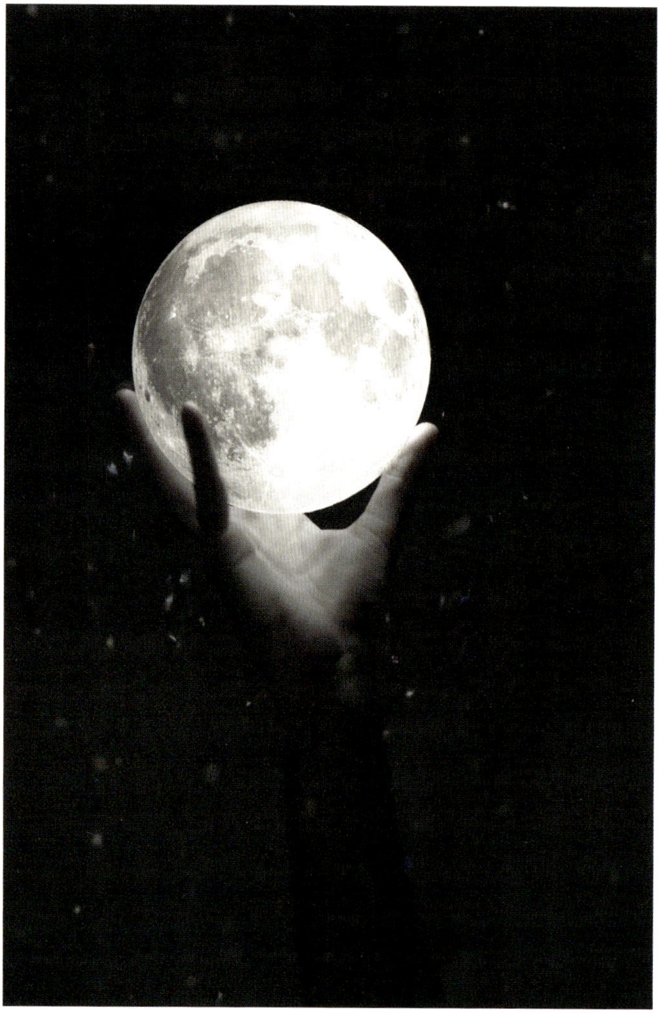

© DIGGIE VITT, UNTITLED

#BODY

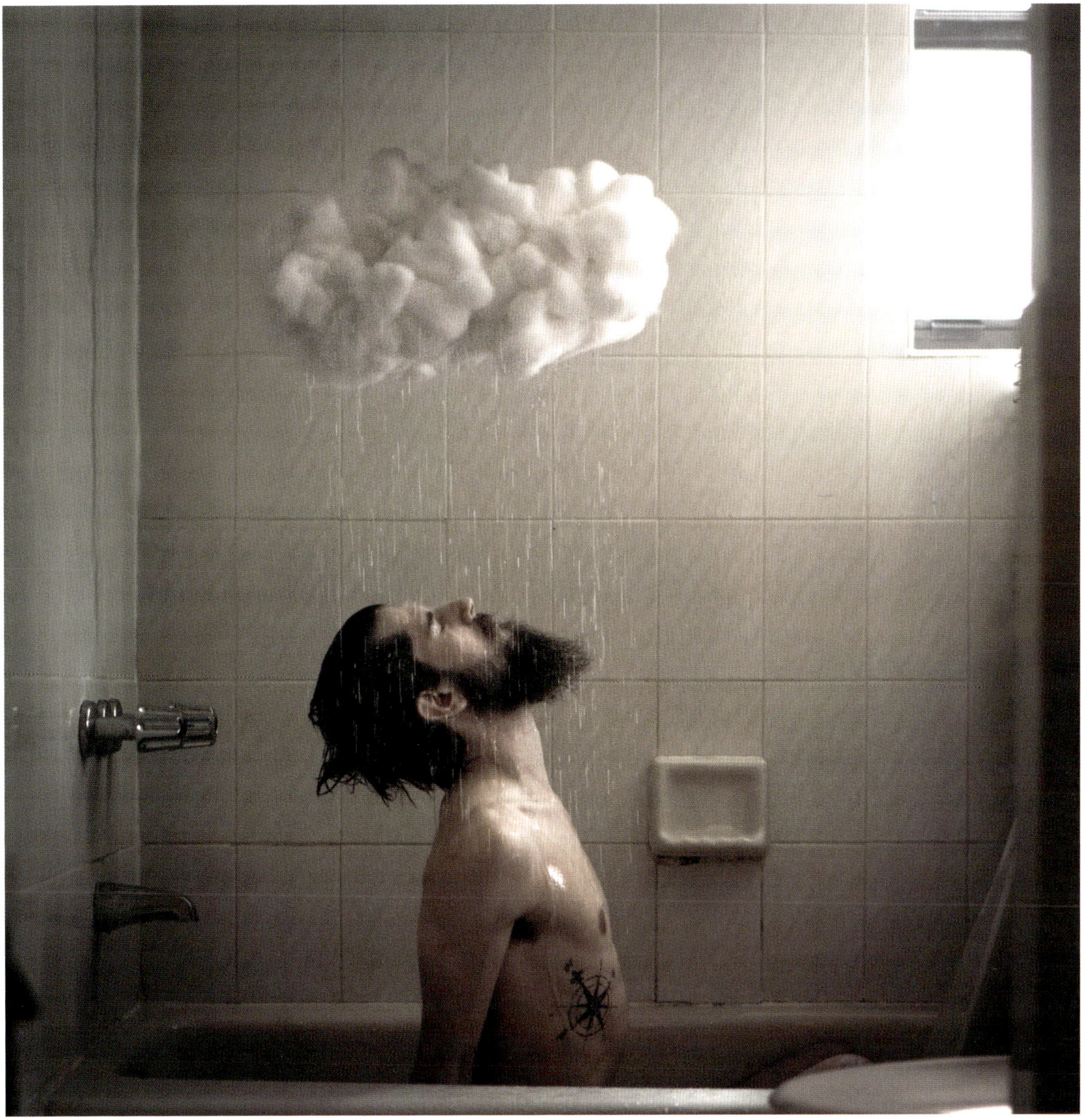

© DIGGIE VITT, 246/365

LI WEI

#BODY

If you happen to see a human figure flying high in the sky (be it dressed up, alone or with a female companion), there is strong possibility that it is Li Wei (b. 1970). The Beijing-based artist, fuses photography and performance art to deceive the viewer. In his shots, he likes to defy gravity and create a dramatic atmosphere. The artist stresses that his visual tricks are not a result of digital manipulations but rather through using mirrors, wires or acrobatics.

As Li states, his main goal is to make everything impossible possible and through his photos, he keeps encouraging the viewer to see things from a different perspective. The borderline between reality and fantasy is easily moved and the idea of truth is challenged. While Li's photographic adventures may bring a smile, the artist reflects upon topics ranging from gender relations, the rapid changes in China, to politics.

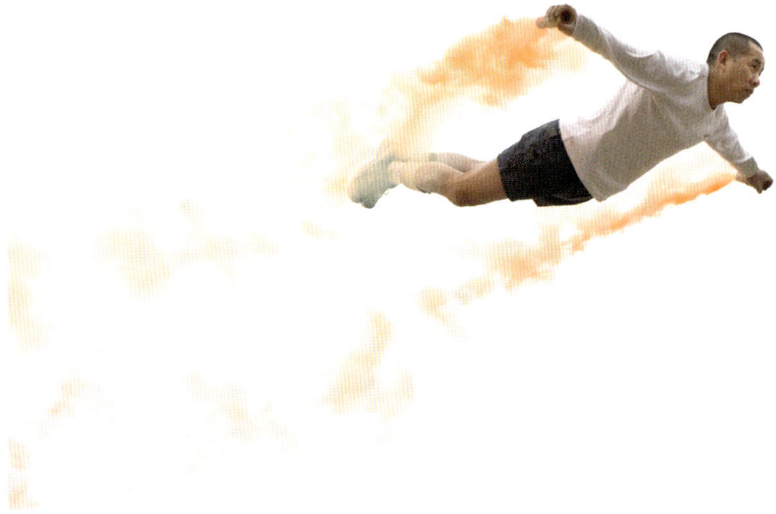

© LI WEI, BEYOND GRAVITY 2, 2010

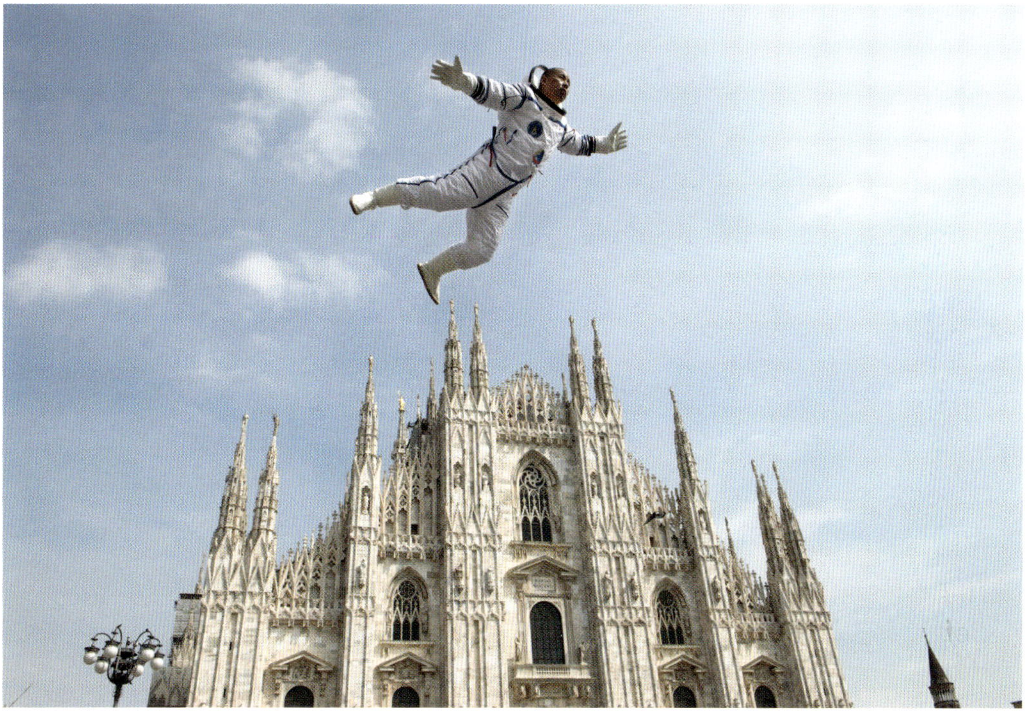

© LI WEI, FLY OVER MILAN, 2014

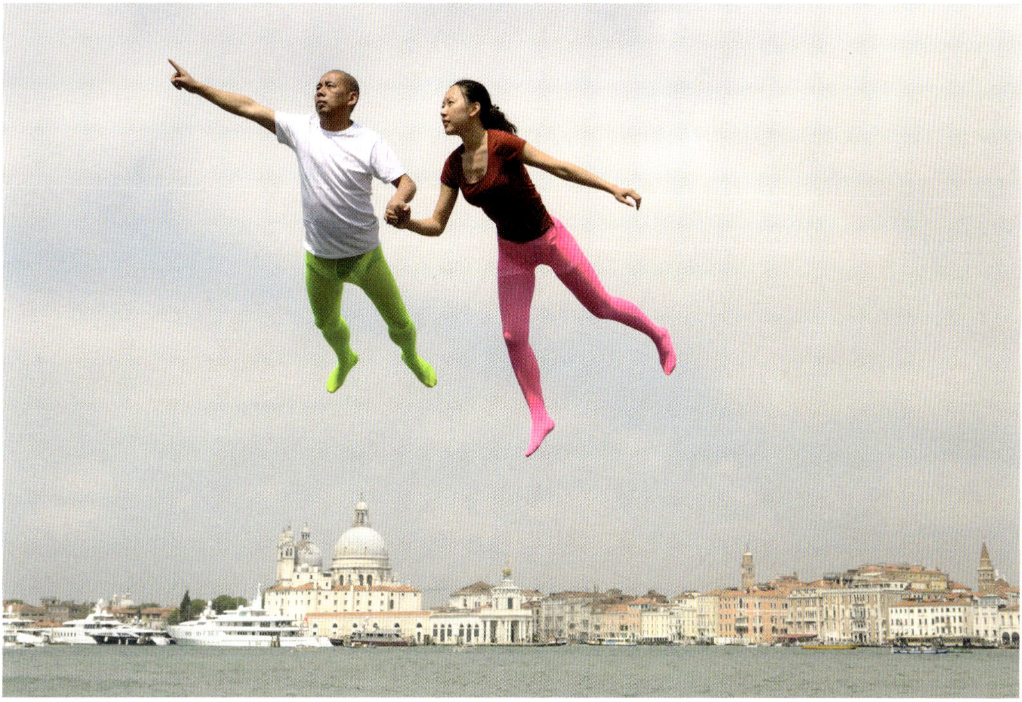

© LI WEI, FLYING OVER VENICE, 2013

LAURA ZALENGA

Laura Zalenga (b. 1990) studied architecture, but found her vocation in photography. She treats the medium as a liberating kind of personal therapy that has the power to heal herself and others. 'I think you can rework many issues with photography', she remarks. 'When I am fine, I usually take little photos. When I am not very well, I simply take the camera and then it gets better'. Many of her pictures are self-portraits, which she says make her happy and able to handle emotions.

One of Laura's main inspirations are the fairy tales of the Brothers Grimm but Laura's limitless imagination is surreal on its own. She tells stories that normally could not happen or mixes fantasy and realism to picture the weirdest visions from inside her head. Some of her self-portraits are truly haunting, like the one featuring the twisted body or the even creepier half-lamb/ half-human face image.

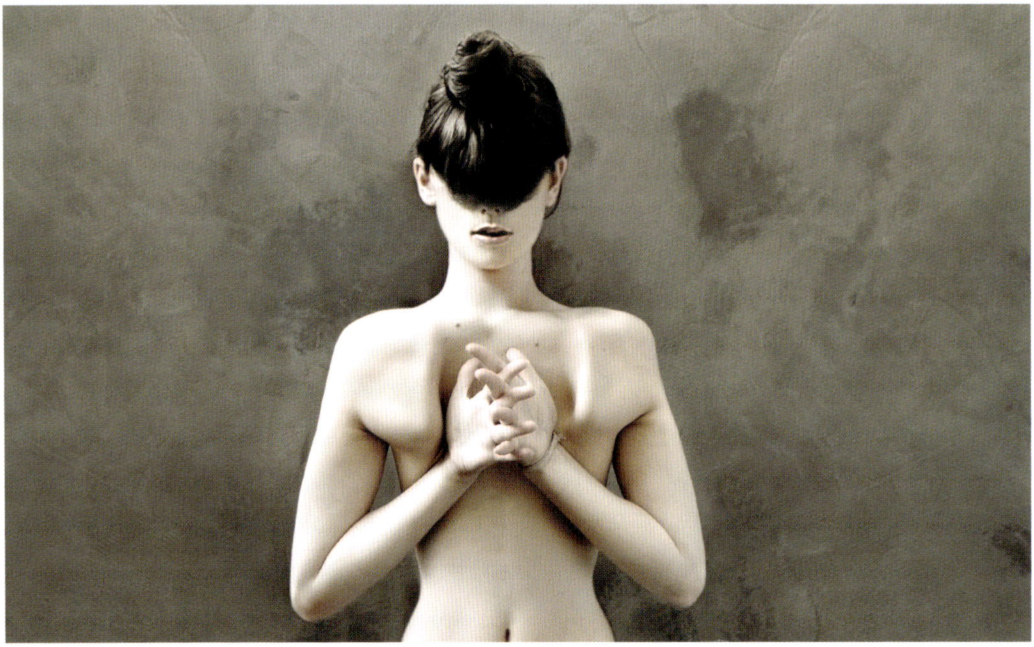

© LAURA ZALENGA, NORMAL

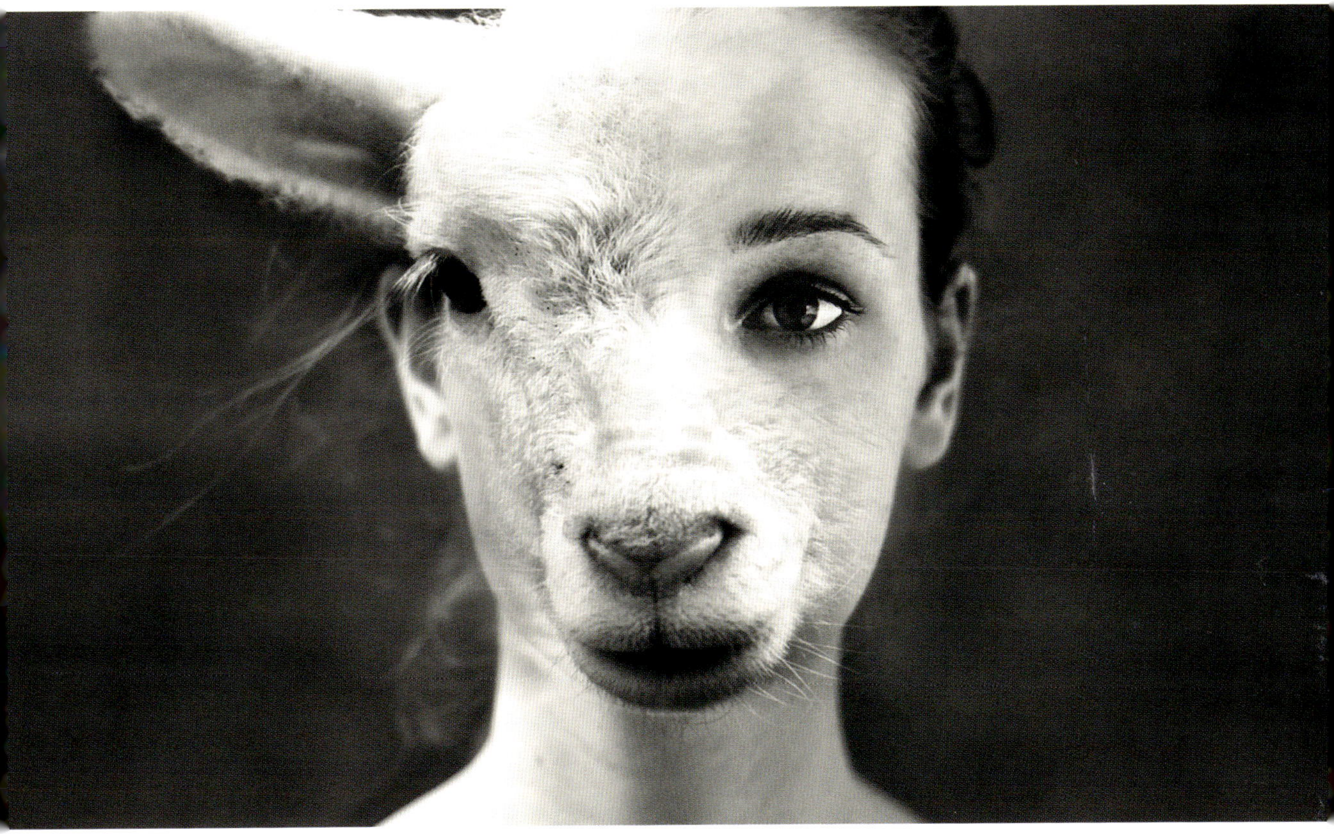

© LAURA ZALENGA, LAMB ME

#BODY

#PORTRAIT

BEN ZANK

#BODY

The phrase 'thinking outside of the box' comes to mind when one looks at Ben Zank's (b. 1991) photography. The settings where he decides to place human figure are truly surreal and often hilarious. The body appears in the most unexpected places and forms. It is probably the surprising contexts that are so striking. Ben studied journalism, but chose taking photos instead as he always preferred to tell his side of the story rather than being objective. Visually intriguing, essentially ironic, the scenes he creates fascinate through their simplicity with a clever hook.

'My real secret is the ability to find a small scene and make it look much larger than it really is', he claims. A large part of his creative process is editing the images, yet given the quirky final result, the conception stage is also important. Asked about his inspirations he points to Tumblr, where he finds many inspiring artists.

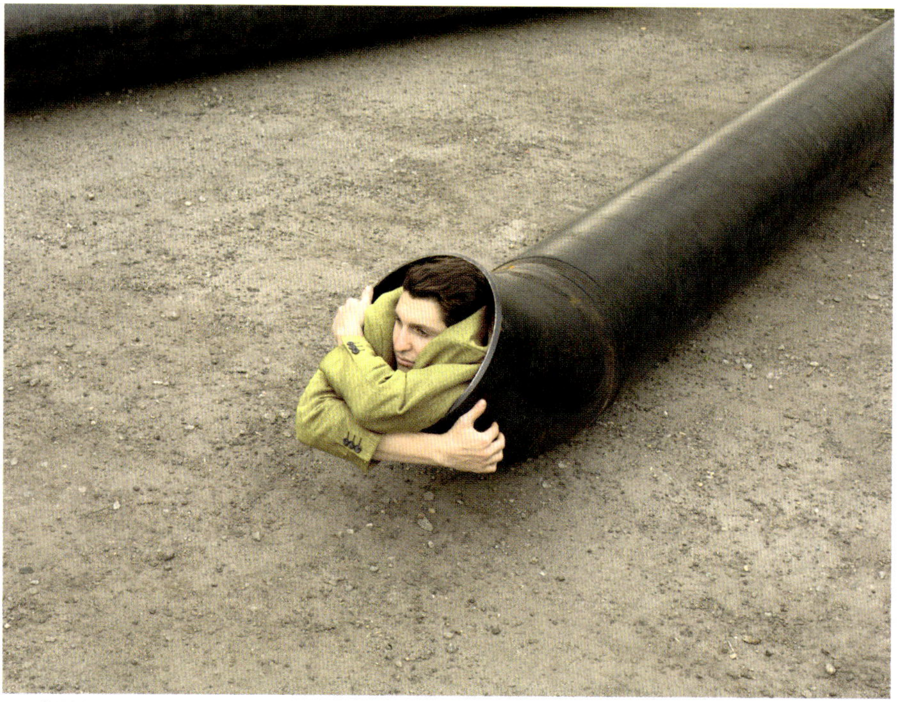

© BEN ZANK, UNTITLED, 2017

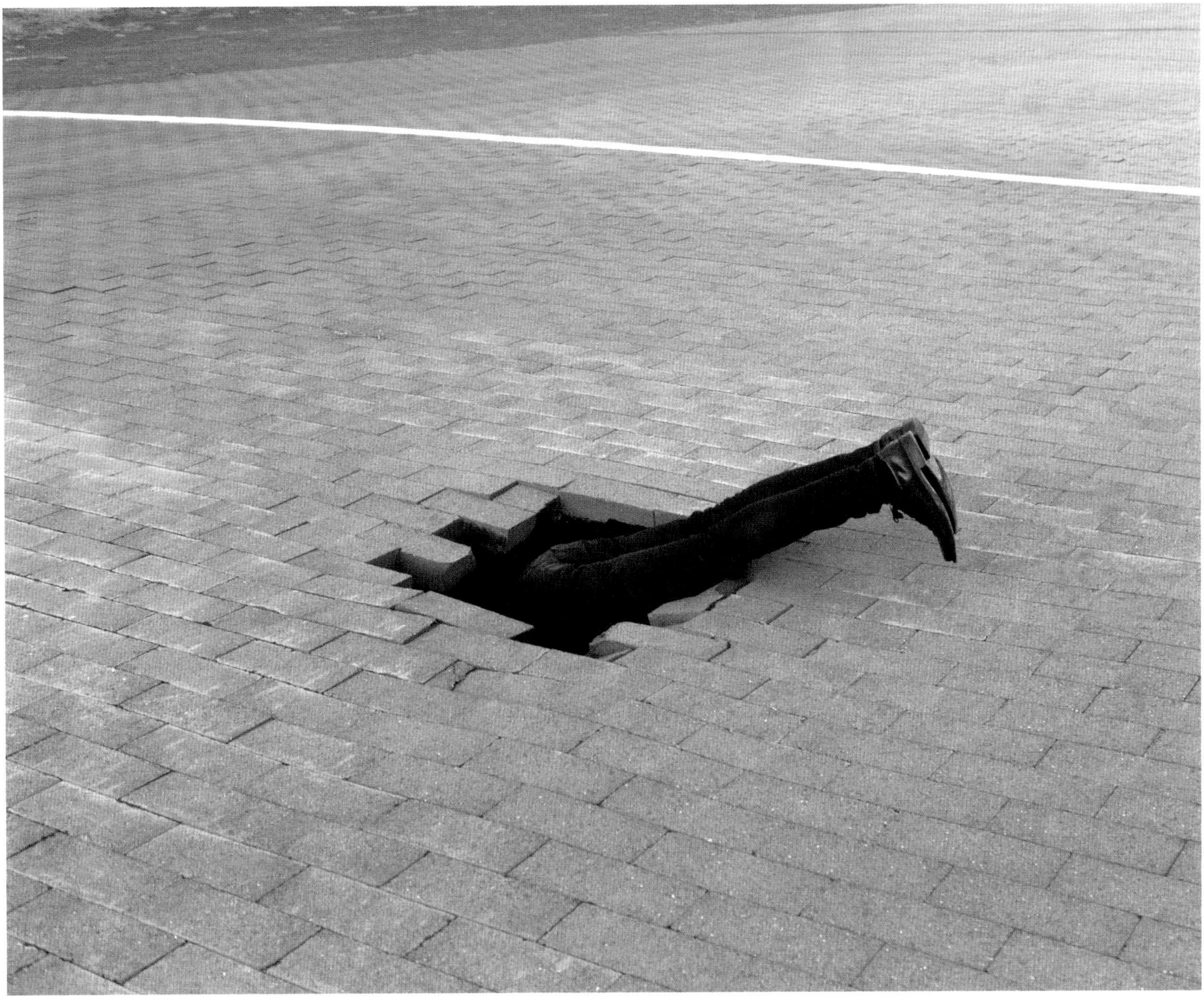

© BEN ZANK, ETRM, 2017

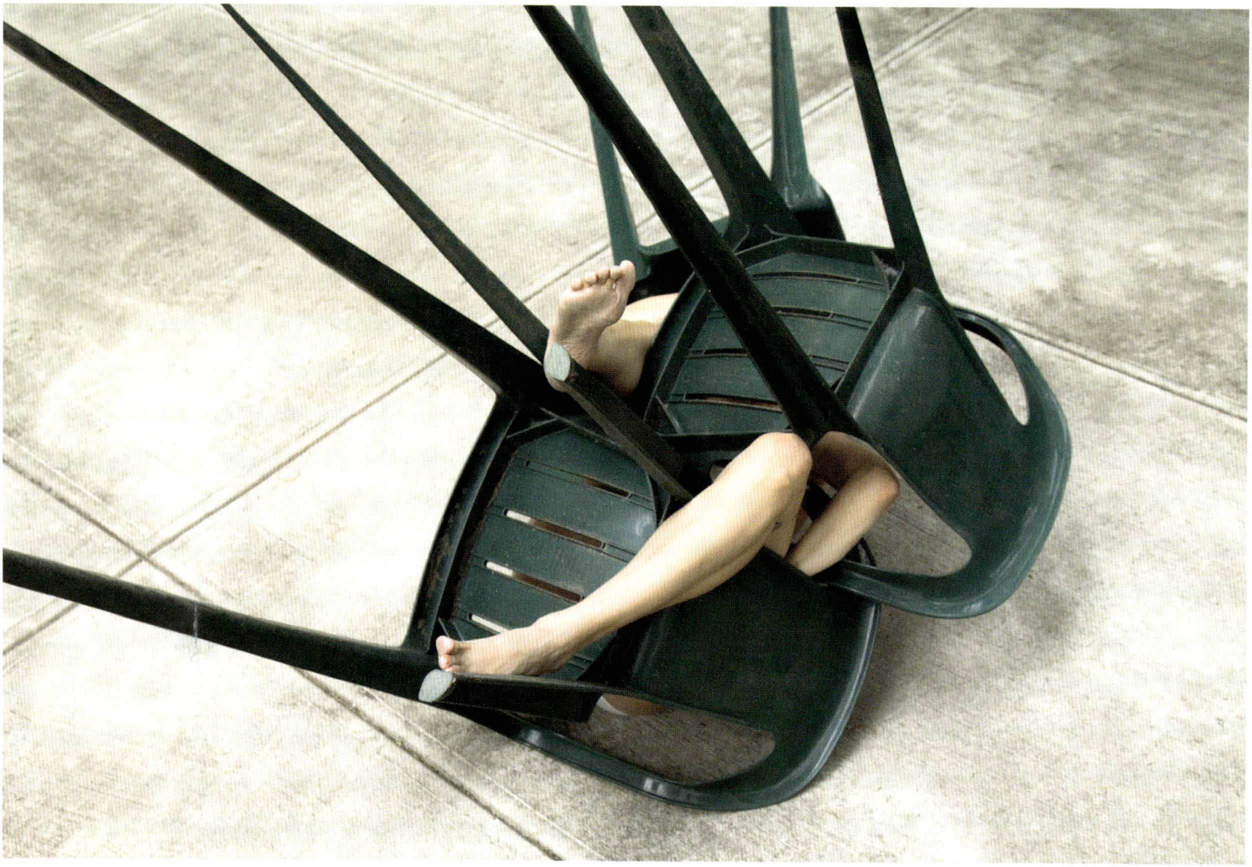
© BEN ZANK, UNTITLED, 2017

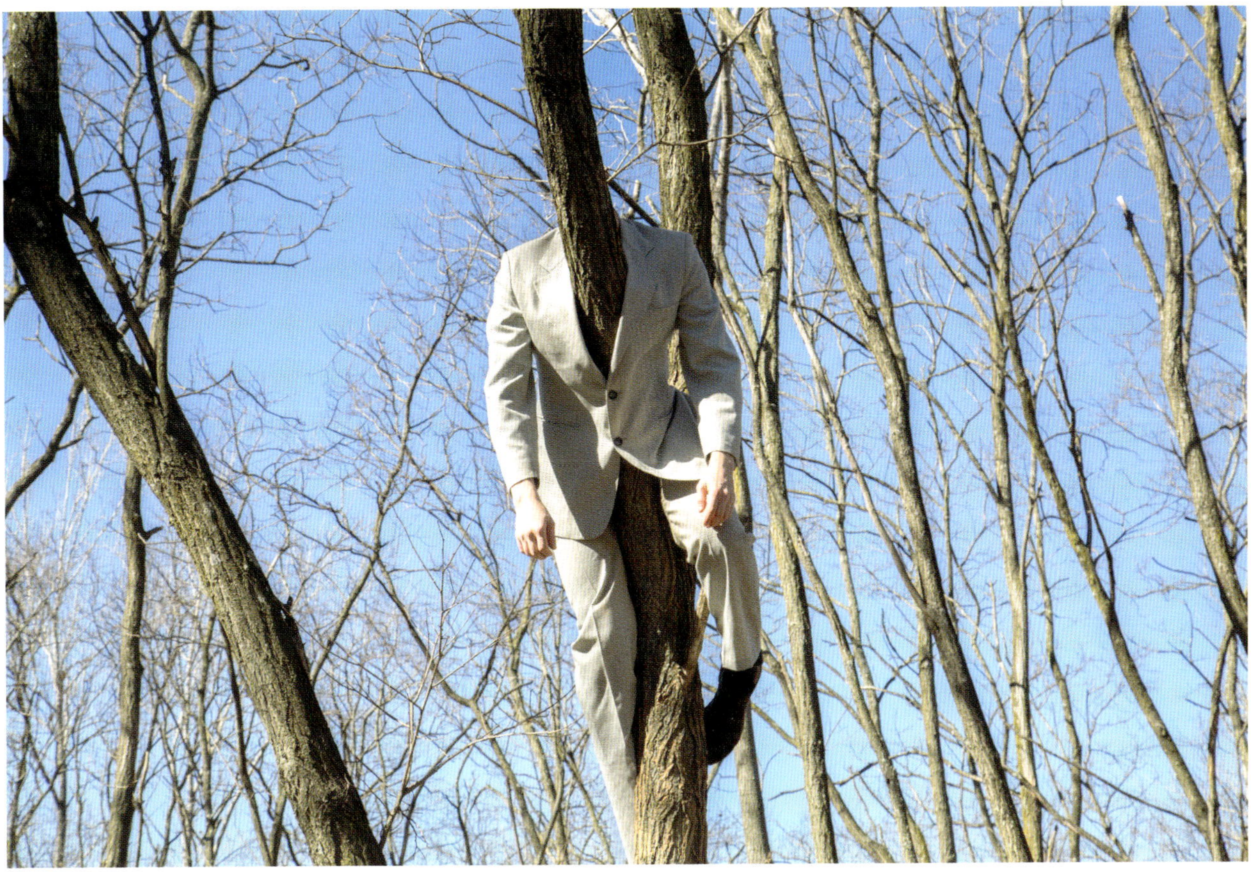

© BEN ZANK, THE POLITICIAN, 2017

LARA ZANKOUL

You surely know that feeling when stories in your dreams include real people and places but all seem totally wrong. People turn into animals, behave in the most unusual way, interiors look rather surreal, everything has very specific and strange colours. The works of Beirut-based Lara Zankoul (b. 1987), a self-taught photographer and interdisciplinary artist, balance the probable and the out-of-this-world in the same way. Especially in 'The Unseen' series from 2013, Lara places strangely dressed people in rooms half-filled with water and gives them enigmatic tasks to perform.

The photographer creates a bizarre atmosphere by using a palette of blues and greens, the scenes are lit in a very particular way. As Lara stresses, she wants to create and craft moments rather than just document them. 'Her work captures everyday human behaviour and issues that occur within society through photographic media' according to the artist's statement.

#ANIMALS

#PORTRAIT

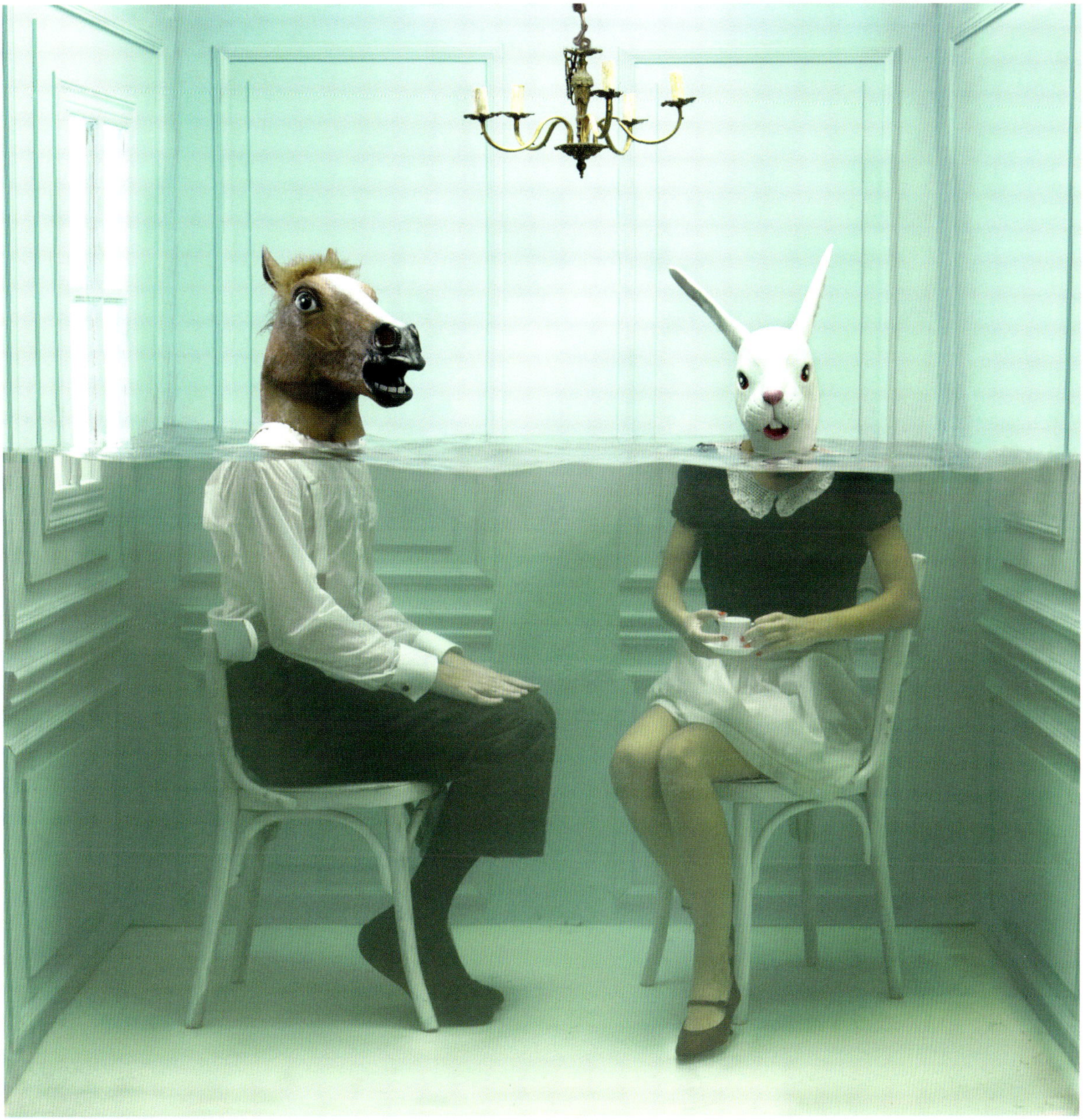

© LAURA ZANKOUL, THE ZOO, 2013

ANKA ZHURAVLEVA

Anka Zhuravleva's (b. 1980) childhood was filled with art books. In her youth, after the death of her parents caused her life to change, she explored alternative lifestyles as a tattoo artist, a rock-band member and a model. In her creative path, after experimenting with drawing, oil painting, post-production and graphic works, Anka noticed that her inspirations often came from photographs. She decided to take up photography to explore this more and the results are stunning.

Her photos have a sophisticated color palette, well-thought out compositions and dream-like scenery. One of Anka's series features women's bodies gracefully suspended in the air. 'Every human being sometimes has a feeling of distorted gravity. When falling in love, when sleeping, dreaming, reading, doing favorite things...' she muses. Anka originally visualizes these emotions. Her works appear in magazine publications and are often used as book and CD covers. Anka also takes part in numerous exhibitions. Born in Moscow, Anka is currently based in Porto, Portugal.

#PORTRAIT

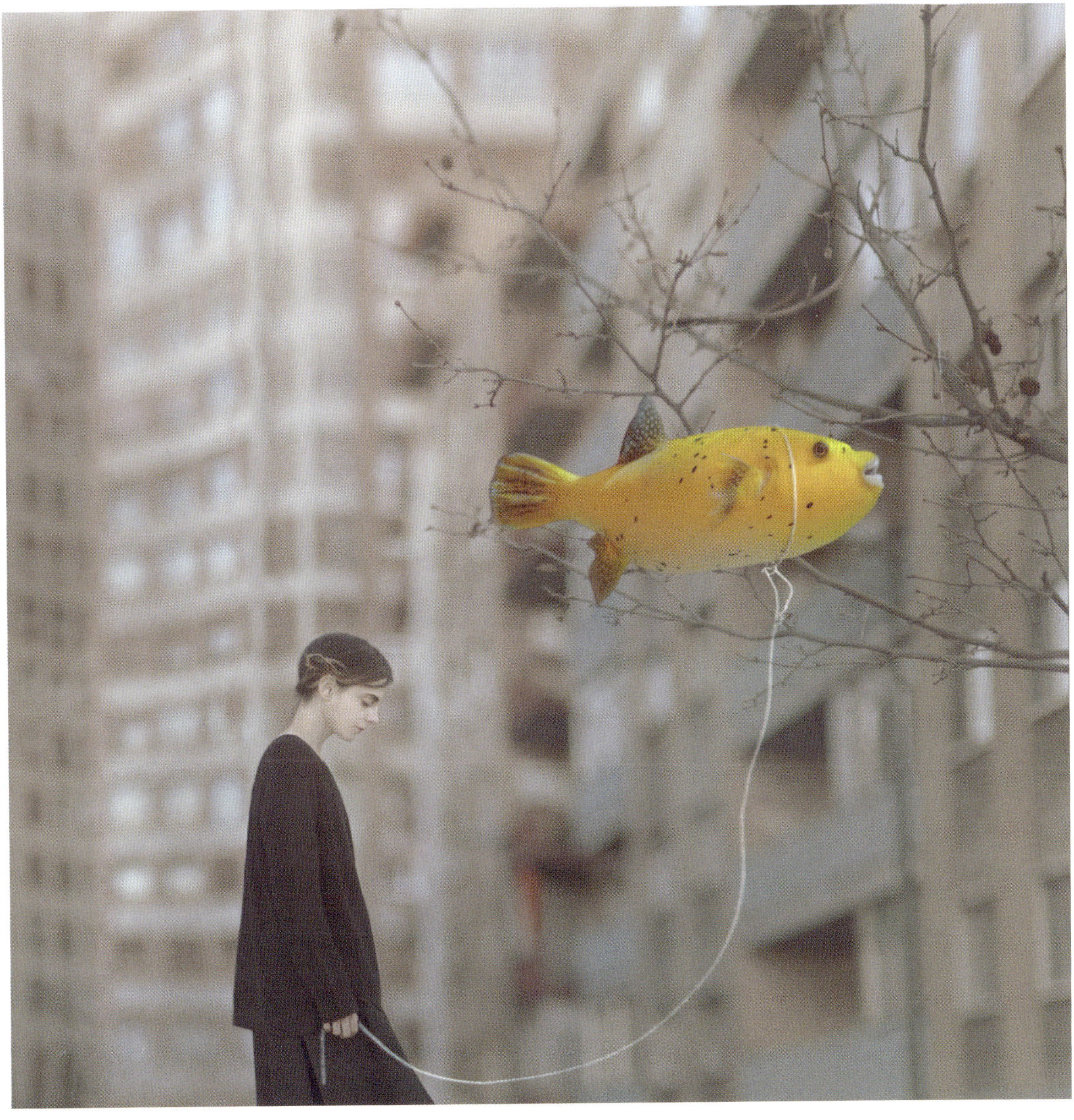

© ANKA ZHURAVLEVA, WALKING, THE FISH, 2016

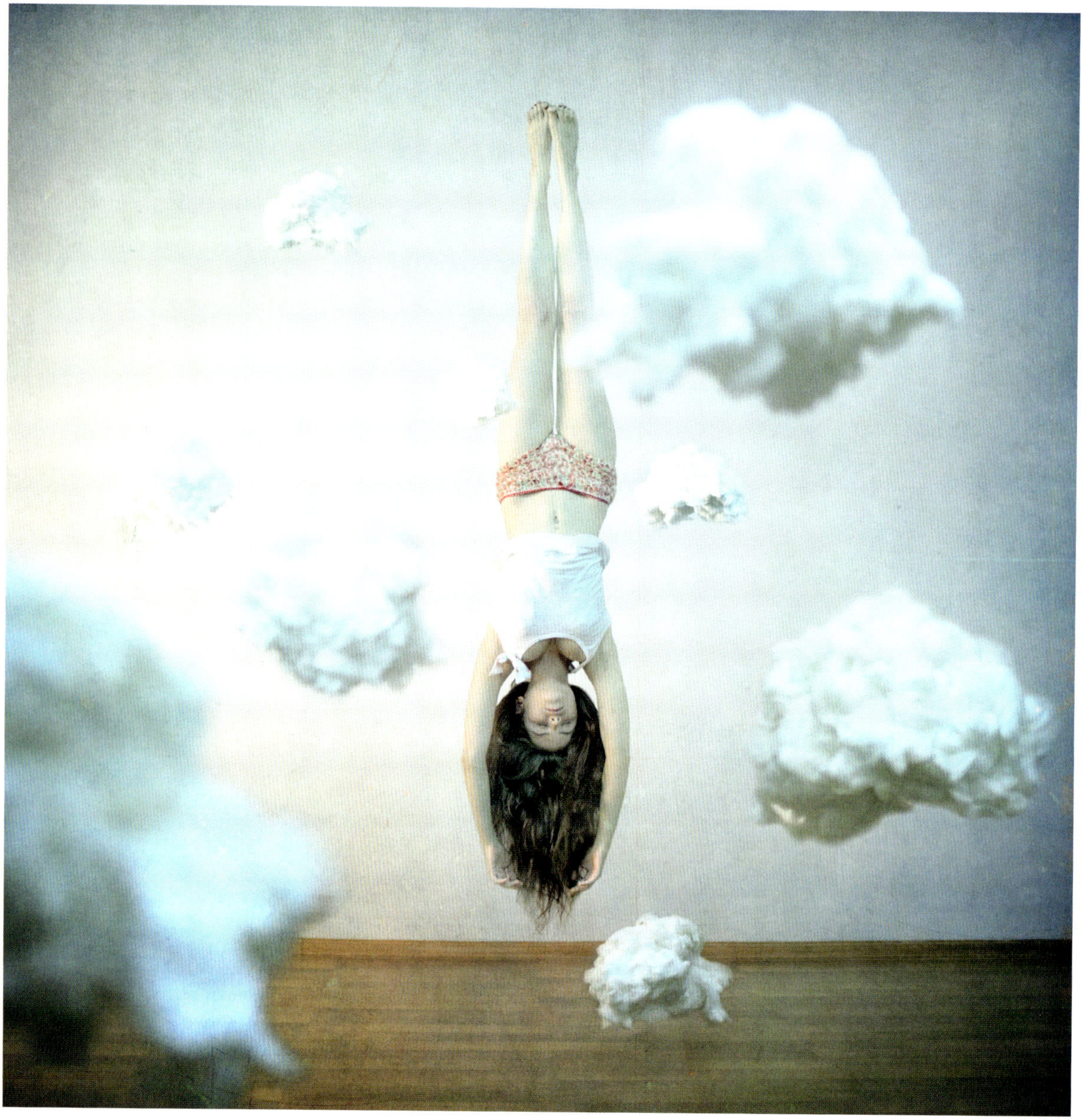

© ANKA ZHURAVLEVA, HEAD IN THE CLOUDS, 2011

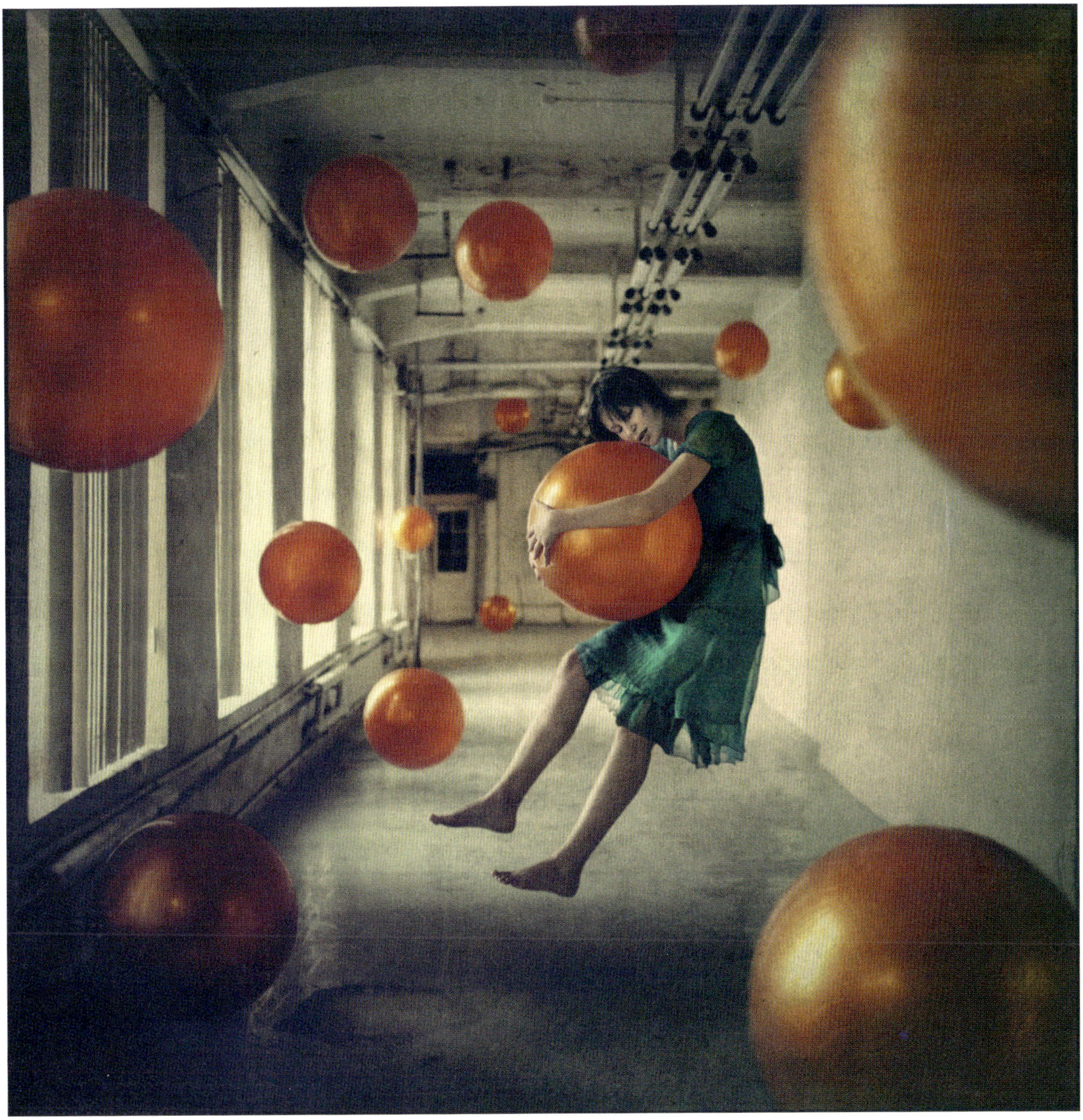

© ANKA ZHURAVLEVA, SPHERES, 2010

THANK YOU

Special thanks to all photographers who contributed their amazing works to this selection. Many thanks to Stefan Lindström who made the publication of this book possible. And last but not least, to Pierre for the inspiration and support.

Created by:

FANCY
BOOKS

www.fancy-books-packaging.com

Copyediting: Lee Ripley
Layout & Cover Design: Fancy Books Packaging

Printed in Estonia, 2017

ISBN 978-1-908233-11-0

Eken Press Ltd. is a company registered in England and Wales under the number 7454591.
Follow us on ekenpress.com.